FOSSIL COVE PRESS

Winnipeg, Manitoba

A Pirate's History
of Doctor Who

by

D. G. Valdron

A Pirate's History of Doctor Who

Fossil Cove Publishing Suite 1301, at 90 Garry Street, Winnipeg, Manitoba, Canada, R3C 4J4

Cover: A group of youths out to make their own version of Doctor Who, dressing up as classic or new Doctors, and busily painting a traditional red British phone booth blue. Art and Design by Roberto Gonzales Lara

www.robertogonzalezlara.com/

Issued in print and electronic formats: ISBN: 978-1-990860-93-5 (IngramSpark paperback); 978-1-990860-24-9 (ebook); 978-1-990860-25-6 (audiobook)

Please feel free to visit our website at:

www.denvaldron.com

A PIRATE'S HISTORY OF DOCTOR WHO
TABLE OF CONTENTS

INTRODUCTION

What on Earth is a Pirates History?

Well, there's the official history. The approved history, where all the rough edges are sanded off, the conflicts and disasters erased, the approved information and products are put forward, and the rest is erased.

A Pirates History is the unauthorized and unapproved stuff. It's the events and the productions that don't make it into the official history, whether it's the high and mighty doing dirt to each other, or gatekeepers erasing or sanitising. A Pirates History is about the things they want to leave out of the official record.

For example, right now, Jody Whittaker is the first woman to play the Doctor, in October, 2018. Except she's not. Barbara Benedetti played the Doctor in September, 1984, thirty-four years earlier.

Barbara Benedetti played the Doctor through four stories, when the BBC series was being cancelled, uncancelled, put on hiatus, floundered through the Trial of a Time Lord, saw the official Doctor fired and McCoy's awkward first year. And you know what? She was brilliant. She hit it out of the park. And she's erased, excluded from history. But you can watch her stories right now.

And after her, other women would play the Doctor. Particularly, Sharon Crookes, Lily Daniels and Krystal Moore would each play the Doctor for multiple episodes, all before Whittaker. They're all erased.

Jevocas Green was the first black man to play the Doctor, years before Ncuti Gatwa will take the role.

On the other side of the coin, Jon Pertwee, Sylvester McCoy and Colin Baker have all played the Doctor in unofficial videos not approved by the BBC.

How about the season of the Rupert Booth Doctor, twelve episodes and five adventures, when the show was officially cancelled?? Did you know that the BBC licensed Nick Scovell to play the Doctor through five consecutive stage productions? There are whole worlds of unrecognized, unofficial Doctors in great stories on video. There are stage plays, and audio adventures, licensed and unlicensed.

Did you know that Doctor Who was cancelled in 1984? That fans brought it back? Only to have the BBC sabotage the show until they could finally cancel it five years later? That it was all about backstabbing and pettiness?

While the official historians were writing their sanitized histories of designated people doing approved things, there's an undercurrent, where people take control, where technology and fandom intersect and evolve. There's a whole history that we're supposed to ignore. And there are wonderful productions, amazing stories that we're not supposed to acknowledge.

Well, that's what these books are about. These are works of Doctor Who unauthorized and unapproved by the BBC. But these are the very, very best and most important. These are the ones you would enjoy watching, the ones worth seeking

A Pirate's History, Page 2

out, that give you new perspectives on the Doctors and their monsters.

They are worth it. And I'll make you a promise, just about everything I write about, you can find. Some of it might take a little work. But it's out there to be found, and it's worth tracking down.

A Helpful Reading Tip

This book, and the others in the series, are not necessarily meant to be read in order. You can if you want to, but going back and forth and reading what seems most interesting first is perfectly okay.

They consist of chapters and reviews which are by and large stand-alone, so it's perfectly fine, and I completely encourage just wandering back and forth, reading the bits that strike your fancy in whatever order you want.

The world of Doctor Who is a timey-wimey, wibbly-wobbly place and often things overlap, so I've built a degree of redundancy and repetition into the various chapters and articles, touching on the same information in different places to make your reading experience easier and more satisfying.

The downside is that after a while, you may be afflicted with flashes of déjà vu the more you read. Don't sweat it, just relax and keep on going.

CHAPTER 1: A GENERAL HISTORY OF FAN FILMS

What is a fan film? I think that the narrow technical definition is a film or video of a popular production made by fans and for fans, usually without commercial intent, and often without rights or permission.

Fan films have historically been pretty marginal. Film and television are incredibly expensive. Even back in the old days, film and television production cost upwards of a thousand dollars a minute and required an army of technicians and labs to pull off. The cameras were 16 or 35 mm and required a fair bit of technical sophistication to operate. That was out of reach for most people.

Still, fan films were around. As early as 1926, there was an Our Gang/Little Rascals pastiche shot in Anderson, South Carolina, although it was less a fan film and more a peculiar sort of swindle in the early days of film.

Back then, it was theoretically possible for precocious children with very rich parents, or for adult enthusiasts, to make their 16 millimeter films. Some of these might technically have been fan films, although mostly it wasn't really driven by fan culture.

For my money, some of the earliest genuine fan films were made between 1953 and 1969's, by Don Glut, a young man from Los Angele. His family was actually rich enough to own a 16mm camera, and to indulge a young Don if he wanted to shoot his own three minute version of Beast From 20,000 Fathoms in the back yard. His mom would operate the dinosaur for him.

During this time, he created an astonishing forty-one short fan films, starting with the Universal Monsters, Frankenstein, Dracula, etc., but eventually moving onto Marvel and DC Superheroes.

Glut wasn't just a strange kid with indulgent parents though. Glut was a fan, so he wrote in to Famous Monsters of Filmland, run by Forest J. Ackerman, and touched base with the fan culture, becoming semi-famous for his films in the process.

He eventually broke into the lower ranges of the entertainment industry and is best known for his connections to the Star Wars and He Man franchises. Among Glut's claims to fame is the earliest known live action Spiderman film, a twelve minute short from 1969, featuring crude miniatures and stop motion effects.

But, as noted, even 16 millimeter was a professional format, which required considerable technical skill and expensive processing. It was expensive and difficult to make these films. The potential Don Gluts were few and far between out there. And mostly, they had nowhere to show them and no community to connect to.

In 1965 the landscape changed when Kodak released Super 8 millimeter. Regular film stock came in 35 millimeter and 16 millimeter, which required big bulky reels, cost a lot to process, and had to be painstakingly loaded by hand. As I said, it required a lot of technical skill, and was often a pain in the ass.

Super 8, on the other hand, could be shot in a small handheld camera. The film came in cartridges no larger than an audio cassette and you could get them processed at the local drugstore, along with your regular film. For the first time the average person could literally make home movies. For the small additional price of a projector, you could show your home movies to your friends.

A few years later, in 1973, Kodak added sound to its film strip so that you could make talkies.

The Super 8 cameras and projectors became the staple of home movies. Even commercial film producers got into the market, releasing Super 8 versions of theatrical movies for home enjoyment. You could buy cut down versions of Planet of the Apes, Seventh Voyage of Sinbad, or Three Stooges shorts, cartoons, old westerns. Typically Super 8 came in 200 or 400 foot reels, for ten or fifteen minute showings.

Mostly, Super 8 was just home movies: Children's birthday parties, family reunions, excursions to the beach. That was all it was really meant for.

For the small additional price of a projector, which itself was somewhat relatively easy to use and small enough to be portable (in the sense that sticking a handle on a 15 kilogram box of gears and wires was portable), you could show your home movies to your friends and family. In fact, the ease and portability of Super-8 projectors made them popular at schools, at community centres, in small organizations, with charities, business and even government.

There started to be a demand for educational and training films in Super-8. These already existed in 16 and 35 mm formats, so it was easy enough to just re-issue them in the new, cheaper format. Commercial film producers got into the market, releasing 8 mm versions of theatrical movies for home enjoyment.

My grandparents had a Super 8 projector back in those days. I can remember being a little kid, me and my cousins being brought over to Grandmother's house on Sunday afternoon, to watch cartoons, old westerns and newsreel footage of astronauts. Or being a little older and reliving birthday parties and vacations, on screen, with our parents. When I got a little older, I tried to do stop motion and special effects on the Super 8 camera, I didn't even have a tripod, so the results are best buried in a radioactive landfill.

Success breeds success. Super-8 caught on big, and when that happens, you want to follow up on it with accessories. A few years later, in 1973, Kodak added sound to its film strip, and a microphone to its Super-8 camera, so that you could record voices and music with your film. Kodak started selling tripods for the cameras, so it didn't have to be handheld and shaky. They started selling lights, editing equipment, external microphones. They improved their cameras, adding a frame by frame feature, so you could literally do stop motion animation, or try for special effects. Cameras became cheaper, more diverse, more durable, and so very user friendly.

But a Super 8 camera was a tempting toy. You could make your own narrative stories. If you wanted to go a little further, you could actually edit bits of film together to cut scenes, just like a real movie. Special effects were a kind of camera magic, and people, particularly children and teenagers were fascinated with the possibilities.

Amateur film making became a hobby. A whole subculture of Super8 film makers emerged in the 1970s, making movies for their own pleasure, or showing them to each other at gatherings or at Super 8 film festivals. There were even magazines devoted to the Super 8 enthusiast with articles on everything from cinematography to special effects and animation.

This ease of use made it such a tempting toy for teenagers and young people. Dedicated amateurs began experimenting with actually telling stories or incorporating special effects, doing stop motion, or cartoon animation. Mostly, it was home movies. But you could make your own narrative stories. If you wanted to go a little further, you could actually edit bits of film together to cut scenes, just like a real movie, and use a couple of cartridges. Special effects were a kind of camera magic, and people, particularly teenagers were fascinated with the possibilities.

Of course, Super 8 filmmakers were hamstrung in a lot of ways. Let's be honest; it didn't look terribly good. Super 8 cameras were by no means professional or semi-professional instruments. The image wasn't great to start with, the film quality was grainy and the machines were often quirky.

Sound, after 1973, consisted of a microphone mounted in the camera itself, so the sound quality was generally poor - full of camera noises, pops, glitches, ambient omnidirectional noise, you name it. Sound recording was on a different part of the film strip than the image, about so that complicated editing. Later cameras had a plug in, so you could use a microphone or a boom. But it still wasn't great.

Processing was done by local photo labs without a lot of attention to detail, you didn't get to see rushes, and you got what you got. If you were shooting several cartridges over a period of time, you couldn't guarantee the colour and brightness would match from one cartridge to another.

In 1967, a three minute 8mm film was shot of a group of teens playing Star Trek in their living room. So far as I know, that's the earliest Super 8 fan film. This is literally only two years after the technology is on the market. Doubtless there were others around this time or earlier, cowboy films, monster films. But this is the earliest we know of, and it shows how quickly this aspect got taken up.

Super 8 was simply a very tempting toy.

But mostly the fan based social networks that gave these films an audience didn't exist yet. Yes, in the 60s and 70s there were fans and conventions, fanzines and pen pals. But typically it was confined to and focused on the printed word as the most accessible and portable medium. These conventions tended to be snobbish about movies and television, and looked down their noses at the breed of media fan. Media fandom in its modern form didn't exist. It would take a while for media fandom to emerge and fan films to find their place.

One of the biggest handicaps for fan films back then was exhibition and distribution.

Supposing that you actually made yourself a little Star Trek or Doctor Who fan film? Well, what do you do with it?

In 1974, John Cosentino, a carpet installer in Michigan made his own Star Trek film: Paragon's Paragon. Loosely based on James Blish's original Star Trek novel, Spock Must Die, Cosentino's film ran over sixty minutes. Cosentino built himself an optical printer for effects; he used stop motion, glass mattes, miniatures and superimpositions. He created the costumes and props, even re-created the bridge of the

Enterprise. It was an epic. It was an astonishing. It was legendary.

Cosentino's film ended up being well known, like Glut, because he got magazine coverage. In this case, Cinefantastique – a special effects magazine devoted to amateur film makers. But if even a thousand people actually saw it, I would be surprised. You can see fragments of it on YouTube. But the original full length film, on Super8 is now mostly lost. It was ahead of its time, a masterpiece without an audience.

You see, if John Cosentino wanted to share his Star Trek epic with a group of fans, he basically only had one physical copy. Before VCRs came along and got cheap you couldn't really make or distribute copies.

Cosentino might have been able to take it to the photo lab, have them run off a second or third print from the negative, at the cost of a couple of hundred dollars, if he had a negative. If he'd edited on the actual film and had to copy that, it would have been a lot more difficult and expensive to make a copy.

So mostly, there would only be one copy of these sorts of things. Cosentino wasn't going to hand that over to a complete stranger, or a fan club, and hope they sent it back to him, intact, eventually. So he'd have to physically travel with that one copy. And if there wasn't a Super 8 projector and screen there, he'd have to bring his own. Then he'd have to laboriously thread the film through the projector and run it.

Most Super 8 fan films existed as single copies, shown mostly to friends or small, usually local audiences and fan clubs. That's pretty limiting. Good, bad, they just didn't have legs.

Super 8 was the format of the earliest Who fan films that we have any sort of record of today. Son of Doctor Who a twenty minute film dating somewhere between 1970 and 1975 was the remarkable work of a pair of precocious teens. But they had no audience or community for it, beyond their circle of friends.

A notable exception was Mark Sinclair, who in 1976, who literally took his Doctor Who fan film, Threat of the Leviathans, on the road showing it at community centers, schools and youth centers in London. But that was the exception, mostly, these films would be limited to the creators and their families, or if they were lucky, to a local fan club.

The most well-known early fan film was a three minute animated short called Doctor Hoo. It came down to us because it played at the first ever Doctor Who convention, held in Battersea, England, back in 1977. It managed to take on a small life of its own. But even there, it was the exception that proved the rule. It only succeeded and survived because it was made for and played at a convention, one of those rare occasions back in those days when a fan audience was possible.

Then in 1977, two very important things happened.

First, Star Wars hit the movie screens, and in its wake, fan culture changed. Before that, Science Fiction fans were mostly literary. There were television shows and movies, popularized by people like Forrest J. Ackerman, but this was a rather marginal part of the fan community. Fans had tended to see themselves as fans of the overall genre, and not necessarily any specific part; with the possible exception of Star Trek.

Star Wars hit as a mass movement obsessed with the film and film series. Being a Science Fiction fan, that was a niche thing, and a bit nerdish. Being a Star Wars fan... well, there were toys and bedsheets and everyone was into it. Fandom changed, becoming acceptable, but also becoming narrower, breaking into niches. Suddenly you had the emergence of Star Wars Fandoms, Star Trek Fandoms, Buck Rogers and Battlestar Galactica Fandoms, Japanese Anime Fandoms, and Doctor Who Fandoms.

There was something else, something that made Star Wars different from Star Trek: Toys.

Ultimately, Star Wars was accessible to all ages, from grandparents to grandchildren, and for the children and grandchildren, there were all sorts of toys, action figures, spaceships, you name it. This was the thing: Star Wars encouraged children to play with it, its marketing was designed to be played with, to be interactive and user friendly. And because it was so hands on, what you saw were kids getting deeply, immersively into the world, making their own little Star Wars as part of play, and for some of them, with access to home movie cameras, that translated into making their own little Star Wars movies. That really started the ball rolling for everything.

It's no coincidence that the first fan film to get any broad public recognition was a Star Wars parody - Hardware Wars, from 1978, a bare seven months later. Or that a VHS release of Hardware Wars would showcase a whole series of amateur Star Wars productions, as well as other film parodies. Or that, decades later, in 1997, the Star Wars/Cops spoof, Troops, kicked off the modern fan film movement.

For Doctor Who, the fan culture started to gel in the mid-seventies as well. There had been Doctor Who fan clubs going back to the 1960s, and fanzines since at least the 1970s, but these had tended to be transient, local groups of pals, who really didn't have much access to fan culture.

In May, 1976, the Doctor Who Appreciation Society (DWAS) formed as a national, BBC approved fan club, with over a thousand members. With those numbers, the Society formed the foundation of a community, one which received attention and support from the BBC and from the actors, which published increasingly ambitious zines, organized meetings, and even supported the first Doctor Who conventions.

In turn, this fan community saw a series of short films, Threat of the Leviathans, The Destructors, Thosian Strategy, eventually culminating in the feature length Ocean in the Sky and the ambitious Image Makers, all by a relatively small group of enthusiasts in London – Marc Sinclair, Kevin Jon Davies, Paul Tams, Gavin French, Julian Vince.

Now, there were probably other Doctor Who fan films made or attempted around England during this era. But the presence of a fan community made a big difference, there was now an audience for these films, people interested to see them, to commit them to the collective memory, which is why Leviathans is remembered, and other fan films made outside London are not. There was a community of people willing to volunteer and participate, willing to commit time, work and resources. There was an audience in the fan clubs and conventions. Without that you couldn't have had productions as ambitious as Ocean in the Sky and Image Makers.

The other big development of the late 1970s was videotape, starting with Beta in 1975, and VHS in 1976, both of them really taking off from 1977-79 onwards. The simple existence of the Videocassette Recorder and player would prove revolutionary for both fans and fan films, because it changed fan culture.

Initially, all a VCR could do was enable you to record movies or television programs off the TV. But once you could do that, you could start collecting your favourite program. You could re-watch whenever you wanted.

If you were the sort that liked to make things you could freeze frame on props and costumes. That was significant, I used to have a friend who was into making props and models before the age of VCR's, and he would end up sitting in a movie theatre, watching a single movie over and over, tediously and meticulously, to make notes for his replicas. There was no freeze framing for him.

You could show these programs to friends and fan clubs, you could make copies of these programs, and start trading your copies for other peoples.

The limitation of Super 8 film was that you only got one copy, and that was it. That put a crimp in distribution. But by hooking two videocassette recorders together, you could make copies. Anyone could make copies. Lots of copies. This was a new channel of distribution which had never existed before.

Suddenly, copies could proliferate and travel. It was still infinitesimally small scale compared to commercial film or television. But now there was the possibility of distribution networks through conventions, through collectors, through the mail and hand to hand trading. It didn't happen overnight. Initially, VCRs were expensive. In the 70s, they could set you back a thousand dollars, very few people had them. They got cheaper, even so, through the 80s; these things were still a few hundred dollars a pop. It took time for the machines to become common household items, and for distribution chains to evolve. But once the technology was there, it was going to happen.

Of course, in the beginning, it wasn't about distributing fan films. It was about the show itself – there was a lot of Doctor Who out there being broadcast, which in turn could be recorded, treasured, copied and traded. Copying and exchanging videotapes was particularly important for Doctor Who, especially in North America, where the show was harder to get.

This was a show that had twenty years of history, a massive library of back episodes, of serials. Mostly what was being seen in North America was Tom Baker. What aired on television was only the tip of the iceberg. So for fans, there was this whole library of Doctor Who to share on videotape, to trade, to copy and collect.

In turn, Doctor Who was a gateway to whole new libraries of British cult and sci fi television - Hitchhiker's Guide to the Galaxy, Blake's 7, Sapphire and Steel, Blackadder, Red Dwarf, etc. that weren't available on American television. In America and England, a large part of the operations of Doctor Who fandom was exchanging and trading tapes back and forth. People put together amateur collections. Videotape bootlegger making a living off of rarities became a thing. So a fan film could actually be adopted into these networks of exchange and take on some kind of life.

Between 1983 and 1985, camcorders started coming onto the market. A technology which was far easier to handle than the Super8's, and we started to see fan productions on video. And the thing was that when these films started to emerge, there was a pre-existing videotape distribution and trading system to welcome it.

But even in the 1980s, all this really bought us was the possibility. You needed scripts, sets and settings, props, actors, costumes, cameras and lights, and you had to know what to do with cameras and lights. You needed to be able to edit film or video and mix sound, and you needed to be able to do it with at least some competence. It was hard to do, and hard to do well, particularly by young amateurs just starting out.

A great many fan films died in process as the inspiration faded, the work or organization required grew insurmountable, better ideas came along, or people simply found other, more satisfying things to do. It's not clear how many fan films actually managed to get made. A lot of projects probably died along the road, having become more work and less fun.

Of those that did get made, a lot of these are simply lost to us. That may not be a tragedy. Many of the lost fan films and videos were probably pretty harsh going.

As for the films that actually got made? Well, your mileage varied....

CHAPTER 2: CANCELLATION, CRISIS AND HIATUS

The Wrath of Eukor, from 1984, is the single most important Doctor Who fan film ever made.

To understand why, we need to go and look at what was going on with the BBC and Doctor Who, back in England, way back when...

Between January and March, 1985, Doctor Who was cancelled, then uncancelled, then postponed, then cut back. Through this period everyone was going out of their minds.

Let's rewind a bit further. In 1980, John Nathan-Turner, the new series producer, came on board. Flamboyant, outgoing, a cheerful extroverted man with bushy hair, a bushier beard and a penchant for outrageously colourful shirts, Nathan-Turner represented a changing of the guard, a new era for the show.

Tom Baker, by that time, had played the Fourth Doctor for six years. He was getting a bit tired of the role, the ratings were starting to drop, it wasn't as much fun for him anymore. He would do one more year as the Doctor, and then move on.

In 1981, Tom Baker had finished his seventh year, with some very well regarded serials and left the show on a high note.

He was replaced by Peter Davison, a well-known television actor. Davison had featured as Tristan in All Creatures Great and Small for years. Nathan-Turner knew him from his time as Production Unit Manager on that show. It was a safe choice. Davison's tenure as the Doctor been successful; the ratings had been good, the stories well received. Davison was well liked as the Doctor, his quiet approach contrasting effectively with Baker's.

By 1984, Peter Davison had served three years as Doctor, and decided it was time to move on. But with Davison leaving, Nathan-Turner, needed a new actor to play the Doctor. He found that actor in Colin Baker, the unluckiest man ever to take the role.

As the story goes, and there's some truth to it, Colin Baker got the role because he had been the life of the party at some function John Nathan-Turner attended. Nathan-Turner was so impressed with Baker's charisma and wit, he chose him for his new Doctor on the spot.

It's actually a little bit more complicated than that. There was a little more history. Baker had actually appeared on the show as the Time Lord Commander, Maxell, and he was relatively well known already. But why spoil a good story?

Colin Baker was going to be a major shift from the quiet Davison. This new Doctor was going to swing back towards Tom. He was going to be loud, extravagant and over the top. The new Baker was a big strapping man with a curly mop of hair, and instead of a twenty foot scarf, he was going to have a technicolour overcoat.

There might have been a little more going on. Over the years, comments have been made that Colin Baker's Doctor - boisterous, flamboyant and with appalling taste in clothes, was modeled on John Nathan-Turner himself, particularly his flamboyant, boisterous sensibilities. I can kind of see it.

Certainly Nathan-Turner seemed to really push this look. He fought efforts to tone down the wardrobe, and he seemed to want this Doctor to go broad and over the top. In turn, he put everything he had into trying to make the Sixth Doctor a success, bringing back classic monsters, famous historical characters, changing the format from half hour to full hour serials, and promoting for all he was worth.

Davison had been a safe choice, a conservative Doctor without a lot of risk. I think Colin Baker was where Nathan-Turner wanted to let loose.

Season 22 started off promisingly. Scripts were commissioned from January through March. Production began in May, 1984 and ran through into January, 1985. Season 22 began to air with Attack of the Cybermen, on January 5, 1985 with 8.9 million viewers, the highest in years, and would conclude on March 30, 1985 with Revelation of the Daleks.

But as the show was running, there was another drama playing out behind the scenes and Doctor Who's very existence would hang in the balance.

In January, 1985, the BBC decided to cancel the show.

There are a lot of myths about what was going on and why. I'd like to take a moment out to address them.

It wasn't about the drop in the ratings. There was no drop. Season 22 started off with the best ratings in years. While it did decline, its average ratings were about the same as Peter

Davison's seasons, which had brought no complaint. The ratings were well within the reasonable range for the series over its history. It wasn't as if the BBC had suddenly decided to institute a new ratings policy and the show just wasn't measuring up.

In any event, the key decisions were made before Baker's season had even fully aired, so you can't really make a decision based on ratings for episodes that haven't aired.

It wasn't about the quality of Colin Baker's stories. Those stories are often criticized, and rightly so. But John Nathan-Turner was a showman, and he had pretty much thrown everything, including the kitchen sink, into the mix to try and make the season a success. He'd introduced a new companion brimming with cleavage and legs for a bit of cheesecake. He'd brought back all the old favourites, Daleks, the Master, Sontarans and Cybermen. The Patrick Troughton Doctor was brought back as a stunt, to co-star in a serial. If Troughton's return was too much nostalgia, the season also introduced two major new villains, the Rani, another renegade Time Lord, and Sil, planned as a recurring adversary. For literary fans, he had a story with H.G. Wells. In the background, Robert Holmes, a star writer from the classic series came back.

It wasn't to do with cheap sets or lousy effect or bad acting - while the show couldn't compete with multi-million dollar movies, they were well within the acceptable range of what was on American television.

It wasn't that the show was too expensive. The budget had been frozen for years. With their overseas sales, the BBC was actually making a tidy profit on Doctor Who, though none of that made it back into the show's budget.

A Pirate's History, Page 22

The crisis had nothing to do with the show at all.

What it was about was two men: Jonathan Powell, the head of programming, who moved into his position in 1983, and Michael Grade, who became head of the BBC in 1984.

Michael Grade in particular was an outsider, he'd been hired on from an American television production company and had actually taken a pay cut to run the BBC. He had come on board to clean house and ring changes through the organization.

Between them, they had big plans. A major project was to launch daytime television. The BBC up to that point had not run a full daytime schedule. That meant that they were opening up several extra hours a day of new television. Through 1985, the BBC commissioned eight new series for the new daytime television schedule, at a collective cost of over thirty million pounds, and the schedule was dramatically revised. That was going to be very expensive.

The plan was that 1985 was going to be a bigger, better, brand new and improved BBC. The trouble was that the BBC didn't have an unlimited budget. So the money for these wonderful new initiatives had to come from somewhere.

It was the Thatcher era, the operating model of the BBC wasn't really in line with the free market ideology of privatization and free enterprise, there wasn't a lot of new money coming into the BBC's budget. So if Grade and Powell have ambitious plans to shake up the BBC, bring in daytime television, launch a soap opera and all these wonderful things…. Well, they weren't going to have extra money to do it. The pot wasn't any bigger. So the money has to come from somewhere.

It came from other programs. Over a dozen programs were cancelled or in a few cases postponed in order to free up their budgets for daytime television and the slate of new programs. Doctor Who was just one more show ending up on the chopping block, one of the shows that Grade and Powell figured the BBC could live without.

EastEnders is often cited as one of the shows that killed Who. Not quite. EastEnders premiered in February, 1985, literally in the middle of the cancellation crisis, so in people's minds it's the symbolic cause of the fall of Doctor Who.

A soap opera is not a cheap thing. A regular television show had a small cast, a few sets and played once a week for a short season. EastEnders was going to run daily, which required a huge cast of thirty or forty characters, dozens of sets interior and exterior, it was going to be a huge commitment of time and resources.

Actually, EastEnders had been proposed in March, 1983, production had begun in 1984, concurrent with Colin Baker's first season, so there's no real connection – not in the sense of EastEnders stealing Who's budget. The money for East Enders had already been allocated before the big purge.

It simply represented the winds of change.

John Nathan-Turner, in an interview from 1993, said "I think the real reason was that they needed a certain amount of money by cancelling many programmes – 'Doctor Who' was one of them – to establish daytime television on the BBC, and it was an attempt to suddenly demand this money because the BBC wished to pull forward their launch date because the independent companies were pulling forward theirs. So there was a sudden and dramatic attempt to get this money by cancelling a lot of shows, "

This simply included Doctor Who.

So there you have it. Bureaucracy, accounting, spreadsheets, budget allocations and 'bold new visions' were going to kill the Doctor.

There were a few other reasons why Doctor Who ended up on the hit list.

Neither Grade nor Powell liked science fiction at all. Powell is on record as saying he would have never allowed Star Trek: The Next Generation on BBC1. Given the Next Generation's popularity, production values and critical acclaim back in the 90s, that really speaks to a dislike of sci fi.

Fair enough, it's a matter of personal choice, and people are entitled to have preferences. Of course, some might say that personal taste or prejudice shouldn't get in the way of doing your job professionally. Powell and Grade thought sci fi was lowbrow, even when well produced. They thought it was for kids, even when critically acclaimed. They thought the BBC needed to do more elevated stuff... like soap operas.

In particular, they didn't think much of Doctor Who.

"I thought it was rubbish. I thought it was pathetic," Michael Grade would say later, *"cardboard things probably clonking across the floor, trying to scare kids. You just sit and laugh at it."*

At different times, both men publicly criticized it for cheapness and shoddy production values. They just didn't think it was competing with American science fiction movies, which had fantastic and expensive special effects and production design.

Of course, they were setting the budgets and schedules, so if it was a bit cheap and shabby - well that kind of came back to their decisions, but that's neither here nor there.

Then there was personal dislike. Jonathan Powell despised John Nathan-Turner, Doctor Who's producer. He didn't like the show. But he really didn't like the producer. He just didn't care for any of it at all.

At one point in an interview decades later with Richard Marson, printed in Marson's book, *'The Life and Times of John Nathan-Turner.'* he said *"What was I going to do with fucking John Nathan-Turner? I didn't want him doing anything else; because I didn't think he was good enough. You didn't want to give him stuff because you didn't trust him. And the worse the programme got, the less you were going to trust him. I wanted him to fuck off and solve it – or die, really."*

Let's acknowledge that quote is thirty years later, with a lot of water under the bridge. What's striking is not just the deep loathing for Nathan-Turner undiminished even a decade after the man's death, but the underlying sense of petulant grievance. Powell feels angry and put upon even to be discussing Doctor Who and Nathan-Turner, as if, somehow, he's the victim.

Michael Grade, on the other hand, wasn't a fan of Colin Baker. Grade was used to a more naturalistic American approach to acting. He found Baker's acting style too theatrical. He found Baker's portrayal of the Doctor unlikeable and bullying.

Grade would tell the Daily Telegraph in 2003, that he had fired Baker because he thought his portrayal of the Doctor was *"utterly unlikable, absolutely god-awful in fact."*

Ouch!

Grade was on to something there. Nathan-Turner's decision was to play it theatrically, and to make the Doctor unlikeable and then soften the character over time, in order to have the audience fall in love with him. Kind of like Mister Darcy in

Pride and Prejudice. So in the first serial, *Twin Dilemma*, he goes a bit mental and tries to murder his companion by physically strangling her. That's a really bad start, and frankly, I don't remember Mister Darcy doing that.

There's also the fact that a lot of Baker's stories were simply, genuinely, bad. Eric Saward, the Script Editor, seems to have actively disliked Baker, and peppered scripts with insults to him. So: Bad start, bad stories and a Script Editor that goes out of his way to slam him. None of this was Colin Baker's fault, but it certainly didn't help him or the show.

Grade also seems to have disliked the man personally. There was the thing with Colin Baker's ex-wife Liza Goddard.

"There's a history between Michael Grade and Colin. Liza Goddard was Colin's wife. And she was Michael Grade's best friend. The divorce was acrimonious and she moved into Michael Grade's house while she was getting over the divorce. And I'll say no more," revealed Gary Downie, former Doctor Who Production Manager, back in a news interview in 2004.

It's true: Baker went through a very nasty marriage breakdown, and his spouse had moved in with Grade, her best friend and supporter in the marriage breakdown, and according to some sources, ended up dating him. Well, that definitely raises a few eyebrows.

But actually, Downie's being a little bit disingenuous, because he leaves the impression that this was happening while Colin was the Doctor. Not quite. Looking up Liza Goddard online, it appears that her marriage to Baker was from 1976 to 1978. Goddard remarried in 1981, to a glam-rocker named Alvin Stardust, and remained so until 1989. So the Liza Goddard thing, while not ancient history, wasn't that fresh either. It wasn't like Grade was gunning for him over stuff that had happened last week. But yeah, there could have been a long buried grudge, seething in the background.

The divorce seems to have been messy and painful. Michael Grade was definitely in the middle of it. It does seem like the sort of thing that would leave a deep well of bitterness for years. So, I'll say this: It probably didn't help Colin Baker. Not in the least.

All these factors meant that when Michael Grade was looking around for things to cut… Well, it didn't look good for Doctor Who.

Somewhere around January, 1985, the decision was made to cancel the show. Within the senior management, it was known and accepted. BBC Managing Director Bill Cotton and Brian Wenham, Director of Programmes, were both aware of Grade and Powell's decision to cancel the show in 1985.

The rumours began to leak out. In February, John Nathan-Turner was informed by series writer, Robert Holmes, and by a fan, Ian Levine, that the show was being cancelled.

From there, the news spread like wildfire.

These rumours sparked outrage throughout the British fan community, covertly supported by Nathan-Turner, and an avalanche of angry letters and petitions to the BBC.

It also attracted attention from British news agencies. Doctor Who, with 22 consecutive seasons on air, was an institution. The imminent cancellation produced newspaper headlines. There were weeks of daily coverage.

Imagine being the head of the BBC and waking up in the morning to headlines like that. Caught flat-footed, Powell and Grade were forced to retreat, and announced in February that

Doctor Who was not cancelled after all, but simply 'on hiatus' for 18 months. The show would be postponed until the 1986 fiscal year.

It was a major personal humiliation for both men. They got thousands of angry letters. They were pilloried in the media. What had seemed like a minor administrative decision had blown up in their faces in the most appalling way.

This kind of thing wasn't supposed to happen.

Men like Grade and Powell were Masters of the Universe, at least as far as their own little world in the BBC went. They made things happen, they decided things, they set the world to spinning, and ordered the firmament as they pleased. Criticism, if there ever was any, was a muted soft thing, to be aired in boardrooms or over genteel lunches. So it's traumatic to suddenly be accused of conspiracy by daily newspapers, pilloried in parliament, to be inundated by angry letters, to be publicly embarrassed for weeks on end.

Payback would be forthcoming. From that point on, the BBC Senior management did everything they could to slowly wreck the show.

At this point, my lawyers advise me to wedge a little nuance in here.

It is only my opinion that the BBC Senior Management were out to kill the show in revenge. There's no actual proof or smoking gun. There's no memo saying 'Aha, our evil scheme to screw the show into oblivion is working!' Memos like that generally don't get written, or if they do get written, they don't get released.

Even the events leading to the hiatus have been debated over the years, and there's been controversy over whether it was really cancelled or intended to be cancelled. On that front, I can point to several people who were privileged observers who were saying 'yes it was cancelled or going to be cancelled' at the time events were happening. And for the record, I think that Marson's book about Nathan-Turner lays the subject to rest.

As to post-1985? Well, it's a fact that Powell and Grade were publicly humiliated and embarrassed. It's a fact that they were forced into an appalling about face. Their quotes about their dislike of the show and of Nathan-Turner are facts on the record. Grade's prior friendship with Baker's wife is a fact on the record. It's a fact that the show bounced through several bad time slots, and suffered budget and episode cuts. And so on. All these are facts.

The conclusion that the BBC was out to punish and wreck a show, after being humiliated by their attempt to cancel… That's just my opinion. But I'll stand by it.

Of course, even with the reversal, fans didn't trust Powell and Grade further than they could throw them. Even if the mainstream media lost interest with the de-cancellation of the show, the fan community remained up in arms. The angry letters kept coming in to the BBC. There were protests. Fan clubs had angry meetings, and people yelled and argued. There was even an embarrassingly bad 'Save Doctor Who' song recorded by Ian Levine, in February.

They were suspicious, belligerent and angry. And they were without a Doctor... the show was postponed for 18 months. Would it really come back?

American fans were largely on the outside looking in. The show continued to gain popularity in America, the volume of conventions and convention appearances continued to grow.

But they weren't sure what was going on over there in England.

What exactly was the hiatus? Was it just cancellation by another name? A lot of American fans had just discovered the show. To them it was brand new, and the apparent extinction or rescheduling, cancellation or the hiatus, the whole controversy was disturbing and mysterious. On the other side of the Atlantic, the American audience was only dimly aware, and American fans had only a distorted vision of events. They only knew things had gone horribly strange and unpleasant.

In a sense, Doctor Who, during the hiatus period, had become Schrodinger's cat - it was neither alive nor dead. No one outside the BBC knew what was going on.

Basically, from March, 1985 to September 1986, fans in Britain and the United States were in a state of controversy, of flux. They were suspicious of the hiatus and mistrustful of the BBC. They were looking at the end of Who. No more new Who, no more new episodes or adventures. They wanted more. They wanted more stories. They wanted new stories. They wanted news about the show and things to talk about. There was a vacuum and nature abhors a vacuum.

It was the perfect time for a well done, polished production to rush into that void and make a huge splash. That's when the Wrath of Eukor caught fire.

CHAPTER 3: THE STRANGE TRUE STORY OF THE WOMAN DOCTOR

Wrath of Eukor is the first great Who fan film, and perhaps most important Doctor Who fan film ever made.

Technically, it wasn't the first Doctor Who fan film, that was probably the Super 8 *Son of Doctor Who*, from somewhere around 1975. During the latter half of the 70s there was a whole run of Super 8 fan films, and even early attempts at video, now mostly lost.

Nevertheless, it's certainly one of the earliest, and definitely one of the most easily available. Indeed, thanks to the efforts of its Producer/Director, Ryan K. Johnson, it's probably one of the most widely seen Doctor Who fan films ever before the modern era. It's practically ubiquitous, showing up at multiple locations on YouTube, Vimeo, Dailymotion, as a download, circulating among clubs and collectors on tape or DVD, and even having a career on public access television.

It was certainly the first professional looking Doctor Who made up until its time, and for ears afterwards, shot on 16 mm film when the original series was mostly shot on videotape. It utilized real technical equipment and crew, was and looked and felt thoroughly professional. It featured real performances by real actors, it was shot on impressive locations, and it ran long enough to tell a coherent story.

It's one of the first to feature a genuinely original Doctor, rather than re-creation of a canonical Doctor. By 1984, there had only been six official Doctors, each one distinctive. The notion that you could just ignore them and create a whole new persona to be a Doctor was nothing less than shocking for its time.

It's also the first story, amateur or professional, to feature a female Doctor. That is a choice which remained controversial for the BBC series thirty years later, until the casting of Jody Whittaker.

Most importantly, *Wrath of Eukor* is important because of its release and circulation at a critical period during the history of the show.

Now, let's take a moment out because there's some historical context we need to explore, in terms of both the American and the British history of the show.

Doctor Who in America has its own history. In England, Doctor Who had been around since 1963. But, except for the mostly unremarked Peter Cushing movies, it was unknown in America. The show appeared for the first time on American television screens in 1978, mostly on public television stations. The American first Doctor Who convention had only taken place in December, 1979, and it would be a few years before the American conventions ramped up.

Tom Baker had been the Doctor for seven years. He had produced an impressive body of forty-one serials and a hundred and seventy-two episodes.

That meant that Public Television stations could pick up the Tom Baker package and run it through most of a year before needing to rerun anything. For several years, that was all they ran. They didn't need to deal with the baggage of other Doctors. They didn't need to wrestle with the black and white or missing serials of the Troughton and Hartnell years, or the shorter runs of Pertwee and Davison. With Tom Baker you had a full package. It was straightforward.

Tom Baker was also a good choice, cheerful and unforgettable, with his toothy grin, curly mop of hair and twenty foot scarf, he had massive charisma, a profound stage presence, and his long run had included many of the best stories in the shows history. He was tailor made for a cult audience, and that cult audience formed quickly.

The series steadily picked up momentum into the 1980s. PBS stations eventually purchased more of the Doctors, buying Jon Pertwee's and Peter Davison's eras. Fan clubs began to form, a cult audience grew rapidly. They were never as numerous or vocal as Star Trek or Star Wars fans, but they were dedicated.

We see this in the explosion of Conventions. In 1980 and 1981, there had been one North American Doctor Who convention each year. In 1982, there were six Doctor Who conventions. In 1983, there were twenty conventions wholly or partially about the show. In 1984, there were thirty. In 1985, there were sixty, either about the show in whole or in part, or featuring stars from the show.

This exponential growth didn't go completely unnoticed. John Nathan-Turner, the producer of Doctor Who, wholeheartedly embraced American fans, giving interviews and access to fanzines, attending conventions, and doing everything he could to promote the show in America. Along with him came a torrent of guests - Tom Baker himself, Patrick Troughton, Jon Pertwee, Peter Davison, Nicholas Courtney, Liz Sladen, John Levene, Louise Jameson, Terrance Dicks and Terry Nation. Practically everyone connected to the show was crossing the ocean to appear at conventions. People who hadn't appeared on Doctor Who for ten years were suddenly signing autographs and telling packed rooms about their experiences.

For the British actors and writers it was a novelty. They weren't Hollywood culture; they weren't invested in stardom or making big money. The culture of acting in England was very much a workmanlike thing. There wasn't nearly the same aura of celebrity. For them being invited to America to sign autographs was a novelty. They'd assayed a minor role years before, and suddenly, people were treating them like movie stars. They enjoyed it and so they were accessible and friendly. Best of all, from the Conventions and fans viewpoints, they could be brought in relatively cheaply.

Most importantly, they were fresh. Star Trek had been in reruns for twenty years. Its stars were as familiar as the next door neighbor. But for American audiences, the twenty or so years of Doctors and Companions were all brand new, all seen and discovered for the first time within the last year or two.

One of those people caught up in the explosion was a young Seattle resident named Ryan K. Johnson who became a diehard fan in 1983.

Johnson was an aspiring film maker. He'd already shot his first short, a thriller called *Kill Roy*. He decided to enter a short film contest being held at the upcoming World Science Fiction Convention in Los Angeles in August, 1984. Among the judges were industry professionals such as Gary Kurtz, who had produced Star Wars. This seemed like a golden opportunity to break into Hollywood.

Johnson decided to do a Doctor Who fan film. He was dead serious about this. It wasn't a lark. This wasn't fooling around in the backyard. This could well be his chance to break into Hollywood, so he was going to give it everything he had.

At this point he made several very good decisions.

Johnson was captivated by Tom Baker, but he was also canny enough to realize that he couldn't replicate him. Baker was unique, and his charisma could not be reproduced. He could stick another actor in a fifteen foot scarf, but it just wasn't going to work. So instead of trying to simply imitate Baker, he went with a completely new Doctor.

A female Doctor.

Believe it or not, a female Doctor had been discussed publicly as early as 1980, when Tom Baker speculated on television that his successor could be a woman. It's been said that Baker was just having it on, but it was out there.

But it hasn't ever been much more than a farfetched idea. Later on in October of 1986, when Sidney Newman, Doctor Who's creator, was brought back for his ideas to save the show, he too suggested that the Doctor should be a woman. Newman had a lot of wild ideas at the time, so he didn't get much traction.

Thirteen years later Joanna Lumley actually appeared briefly as the final Doctor in the comedy spoof, *Curse of Fatal Death* in 1999.

Then when the series rebooted, it was eventually suggested that Time Lords could change their gender in The *Doctor's Wife,* under Matt Smith. In *Night of the Doctor*, in 2013, Paul McGann's Doctor is told he might regenerate as a woman. Then in 2014, the Master eventually became Missy. All this amounts to tap dancing lightly around the subject. It's out there.

Thirty years later, the notion of a female Doctor is still controversial, sufficient to send both hard-core fans and BBC executives into vapours. Thirty years of progress since 1984, and fans are still flipping out at the very idea, while legions of bureaucrats squirm at the thought. It's kind of appalling.

When you look at it like that, a woman Doctor, back then, was bold and remarkable. Thirty year later, it was still controversial and terrifying. Johnson's decision really was revolutionary.

But Johnson reasoned that if he couldn't imitate Tom Baker, he needed something else to make a splash some other way.

His third very good decision was Barbara Benedetti, a dyed blonde, slender, elfin featured, thirty-one year old actress. Benedetti was not a sci fi fan of any sort. She didn't even know what Doctor Who was. But she was a serious actress.

Originally from Portland, she'd moved to Seattle at 21, studying theatre and earning a fine arts degree. In 1982, she won a starring role as a housewife/punk guitarist in A.M. Collins '*Angry Housewives*', a musical comedy about four financially strapped women who decide to form a punk band. In 1983, she relocated to Chicago to repeat the role for a

Midwestern production. The next year, she returned to the role in Seattle and would continue to play for four more years. Along the way, she distinguished herself as an actress, a musician, dancer, writer and director.

Angry Housewives' playwright, A.M. Collins recommended her to Johnson for the Doctor.

He asked, she said yes, simple as that.

So what you had was a mature trained actress stepping into the role. Someone who knew how to say lines, someone who knew how to inhabit and breathe life into a character, someone with the confidence to walk the stage or go before a camera.

In turn, Benedetti recommended one of her co-stars, Randy Rogel, for the part of Carl, the chimney sweep. That was another professional, confident actor. Someone who could bring something to the role and someone who could work off of Benedetti.

From there, Johnson opted for as professional a shoot as possible. That included having the script reviewed and refined heavily. The story was developed, embroidered, revised, polished. Characters were deepened. Rehearsals allowed the actors to craft real roles.

Johnson's decision included shooting on 16 mm film. That's significant. In Doctor Who's entire twenty year history up to that point, over something like five hundred episodes and a hundred and twenty serials, only one serial had ever been shot completely on film - Jon Pertwee's debut, Spearhead from Space. Film had been used for special effects shots, for outdoor location shots, as inserts. But mostly the series was simply shot on video. So with that one stroke, Johnson was shooting at a technical level beyond much of the series.

Making a film, even a fan film, is an exhausting and expensive proposition. Wrath of Eukor probably cost somewhere between $3000 and $10,000 in 1984 dollars – 16 mm film, that's not cheap, and neither are processing and lab costs. The IMDB listing shows about fifteen people working behind the camera. Figuring sweat equity, you're looking at anywhere between $35,000 and $50,000 as the real price of the production. That's for the *Wrath of Eukor* alone, and there were four Benedetti stories. That's stunning.

The project proceeded through production in about sixty days, including ten days of principal photography, and some further second unit work. That's very nearly professional speed. Many fan films, simply because of the volunteer nature of the production, can take months or years.

The finished film had its first showing in Timecon, in San Jose, August 3-5, 1984. Jon Pertwee, Nicholas Courtney and John Nathan-Turner attended that convention, but there's no indication that they ever saw the film. According to Johnson, it was shown early on a Sunday morning with no publicity.

Then on to the Worldcon, August 30-September 3, 1984, where it played to a packed house as the first film on the schedule. Then, two and a half hours later, someone else won the competition. That was it. Ryan K. Johnson did not have his great Worldcon breakthrough.

For the next six months, Johnson's film lapsed into obscurity. Nothing much happening and no one much interested. The Wrath of Eukor was on its way to being forgotten, and, all else being equal, it might very well have ended up as a negligible footnote, no more remembered or noted than *The Thosian Strategy.*

In March, 1985, in Norwescon, a Pacific coast convention, suddenly, people went wild for it. Suddenly, it was huge. In Ryan Johnson's own words, from his website: *"The audience went nuts and I was immediately asked if I was going to make a sequel. Bogged down with trying to finish Kill Roy, a sequel was the last thing on my mind. Little did I know what lay ahead..."*

That timing is not a coincidence.

Basically, here we are at the beginning of 1985. Just a month before, in February, the cancellation crisis had broken in England, with the show being cancelled, uncancelled, on hiatus. The classic series is in turmoil, on the edge of the abyss, everyone's looking at the end of Who. As of February, 1985, the show is up in the air and no one is quite sure what's going on. There's a sense of crisis, of impending doom.

Suddenly, in March, 1985, there's this extraordinary fan film, shot on actual film, polished, professional, about the length of a typical serial episode, making the rounds. It's got a brand new Doctor. A female Doctor! Better yet, her first appearance is in Colin Baker's technicolour coat, practically a statement that she's the next one right there.

And this is the most important thing – she's a good Doctor. She's got that combination of wit and charm and presence that makes the Doctor a force to be reckoned with.

So of course, there has to be sequel. Everyone wanted a sequel. Johnson had gone from relative obscurity, to something near fame. There was a huge incentive to follow this up.

Visions of Utomu comes out in January of 1986, also during the 18 month hiatus, and it's another strong story. So now it's not a one off. The female Doctor is a body of work at a time when the real series is in limbo. This is when the Benedetti Doctor starts playing regularly on regional cable access.

This was followed up by *Pentagon West-Doctor in the House* in May 1987. The hiatus is over, but the crisis rolls on. The Trial of a Time Lord has aired and failed with critics and audiences; Colin Baker has been fired; John Nathan-Turner's tried to resign; Sylvester McCoy's the new Doctor but no one knows him; the season won't begin until September 1987. So basically, Doctor Who is in limbo, when Benedetti's third adventure comes out. No one really knows what to expect.

While the real show is in chaos, the female Doctor series becomes a trilogy, and the release of *Pentagon West* revives both *Wrath of Eukor* and *Visions of Utomu*. Even if *Pentagon West* is a weak offering, it's still new Who, to fans who are desperate.

Finally, there comes *Broken Doors* in March, 1988, a strong surrealist entry which ends the Benedetti run, even as the real show finds its feet. The original show is still wobbly. Sylvester McCoy's first season has run from September to December, 1987, receiving poor ratings and decidedly mixed reviews. Now Benedetti and Johnson have four stories. You have an actual series.

This is astonishing. For the first time ever, there was actually an entire alternative series of Doctor Who. There was a full-fledged alternative Doctor. This was unheard of.

Sure, some fans might get together and do a one off, some single adventure. But this was a whole run of stories. Call it unofficial, or non-canonical, call it a pirate series, or a ghost series, but it was a series.

Benedetti's run finished with Sylvester McCoy's first season as the Doctor, and it comes off well in comparison. McCoy's first season of four stories were pretty dubious, the show and the Doctor struggling to find its feet.

Essentially, the Woman Doctor comes along when the mainstream show is at its weakest, cancelled and uncancelled, gutted, its creative team in disarray, floundering technically and professionally. The show literally vanishes, and then when it comes back, it lurches incoherently.

In contrast, Benedetti had four stories, most of her stories are at least comparable, and arguably better, better written, better acted, better looking.

They're shorter, yes. Single-episode half-hours amounting to two hours collectively, in contrast to the BBC's series multi-episode serials.

But they're solid stories with production values, real stories with beginnings, middles and ends, with real actors and real characters in Barbara Benedetti's Doctor and Randy Rogel's Carl, who are genuinely charismatic and engaging.

Remember, back in those days, it was all by hand – no computers involved. So making one, particularly back in the day, that's reasonably impressive. Making four stories? Essentially creating an entire coherent series of strong, diverse stories? That's incredible, and it's significant, particularly in the 80s.

There was something more. Ryan K. Johnson's series were made in era where it would find actual distribution. A copy of the first two stories made its way to Seattle Public Access TV, and ran there regularly until 1995, in the Pacific Northwest. You could actually turn on the television looking for Doctor Who and end up watching episodes of the woman Doctor. Meanwhile, Ryan K. Johnson played and premiered at conventions,

This was the era when VCRs were coming into their own. Fans were taping their episodes, making copies, trading back and forth. Ryan K. Johnson was incredibly generous in that anyone who asked, and sent him a blank VHS could get their own copy. Of course, those copies made the rounds at Conventions, were shown at Fan club meetings, copied and traded. Another prominent fan video group, the Federation, promoted Johnson's work. When the internet became powerful enough to upload videos, Wrath of Eukor uploaded. It can be found now on a half dozen locations.

Over the last thirty years, probably tens or hundreds of thousands of people have watched the Wrath of Eukor. We have no way of knowing how influential it was. Did it inspire the fan films that came subsequently? On the one hand, it's hard to say, the show was there, the technology to do it was there, people were going to come up with the idea on their own. But something remarkable and well done; something ground-breaking, that comes into a community? That's definitely going to inspire more people, and it's going to inspire greater ambitions than either a complete absence or a poorly done work.

In the case of at least one other major fan film, 1999's *Time and Again*, the *Wrath of Eukor* has been cited as a direct inspiration. I suspect that there were many more.

Benedetti's Doctor certainly wasn't seen nearly as much as the real Doctor Who. This was still mostly underground, a cult thing, among fans. But the female Doctor circulated to Doctor Who fan groups, in ways and in numbers that simply hadn't been possible or even imaginable even a few years previously.

All of which combines to give us something unique and special in the history of Doctor Who. Literally, for a brief window of time, at the time of crisis and crossroads, when Colin Baker's tenure of the Doctor seemed to have come to an ignominious end, when the show was on ice, it's future uncertain, when a generation of American fans had discovered the show… just in time to lose it.

For that strange sideways moment in history, in a very real way, Barbara Benedetti was The Doctor. She was the Doctor of the gap, the Doctor of the hiatus, she was the alternative.

Review: The Wrath of Eukor (1985)

The Rise of the Benedetti Doctor

STORY: London, 1910, Carl, a cockney 'chimney sweep' is walking home on the fog shrouded streets. Suddenly, a figure in a hideously mismatching coat looms out of the darkness at him, babbling incoherently about getting back to their ship. Dragging Carl back to a police box, she announces that she is the Doctor. Cut to, a verdant forest and a trio of Vietnam vets are threatening a photojournalist, while unknown to all an alien menace gathers in the woods…

REVIEW: The first time I watched *Wrath of Eukor*, it was at the Centennial Library in Winnipeg, in a crowded audio-visual room. The chairs were uncomfortable; the television was an old 20 inch set. The room was dark and crowded with fans. I was amazed.

So what about the *Wrath of Eukor* today?

I'll be honest, I was reluctant to review this again after a couple of decades distance. The things that you enjoy in a younger day, sometimes they're embarrassing when you go back and look critically. All those flaws and mistakes you overlooked, suddenly, they loom large, and the whole thing gets painful.

I'm glad to say, that wasn't the case. Watching it again, I'm thrilled by how well it stands up, how polished and effective it is. If anything, I appreciate it more today than the first time I saw it. Trust me; I don't enjoy watching amateurish dreck. I wade through it, searching for the gems.

First up, the visual quality is exemplary. It's shot on real film. The image is clear and pristine, the sound mix is professional, and the editing is sharp, the composition of shots, lighting, you name it. On a purely technical level, it stands up very nicely; it plays like a real production.

The performers are all real actors, they say their lines and hit their marks, when they speak, it comes across as spontaneous and natural, as if they're saying what they've just thought in that instant, rather than reciting a line that they've rehearsed. They're mature adults. There's no sense of kids in the backyard playing grown up.

Wallace the photojournalist, played by Tom Lance, really does come across as a photojournalist snooping around, someone cosmopolitan and observant on the hunt for a story.

The Vietnam vets/survivalists, led by Jim Dean as Grant, convincingly portray veterans with a chip on their shoulder, hanging out in the woods playing war games because they just can't fit into the regular world any more.

The characters bounce off each other in a natural way. How they react to and interact with each other is a direct outgrowth of who and where they are. Their actions feel organic, rather than them arbitrarily doing things because the plot needs it. There isn't really a bad performance or a bad characterization in the bunch, except possibly the alien force 'Eukor' in full villain mode. But alien villains always come with a slice of ham. It benefits from a very strong supporting cast, and very well drawn supporting characters.

What really makes the production come alive is Barbara Benedetti's performance as the Doctor and Randy Rogel's turn as Carl, the new companion. They don't get to be natural characters. They're the outliers – they aren't playing the people you could meet on the street corner, and so they have to sell it even harder. This is the Doctor; she has to be larger than life.

She is. Benedetti takes to the role as if she was born for it, and she inhabits the character completely.

Barbara Benedetti, thirty-two at the time, was a well-known and well respected stage actress in the Seattle cultural community. She wasn't a Doctor Who fan, had arguably never heard of it. She was a working professional, she knew her stuff, and she gives a marvelous performance as the Doctor, mercurial, brilliant, sardonic, witty and eccentric. She's a slender, short haired blonde, dressed in a band leader's uniform and swinging an umbrella, but she is "The Doctor." If there ever were any doubts as to whether a woman can handle the role, she puts them to rest immediately. We enjoy watching her.

Randy Rogel's Carl Evans, a cockney fish out of water keeps up with her nicely. He's more a Dick Van Dyke type of cockney, and he highlights the anachronisms of a chimney sweep in 1910 who somehow knows what a police box is, but don't worry about that. Benedetti and Rogel make a terrific team, bouncing off of each with an understated comic timing. Their chemistry is unforced and a pleasure to watch. Interestingly, they'd co-starred together on stage in Desperate Housewives just before this production.

Both came from a stage tradition, and it shows. One of the things you get with stage actors is business. Basically, if you're doing a lot of television or film, it's about hitting your mark, standing in the right lighting, and not strolling around out of frame or doing anything that's not specifically called for in the script. So one of the things is that the foreground characters tend not to be spontaneous, and the background characters tend not to do anything – no one wants a shot ruined by an ad libbed line or gesture that doesn't fit the next shot or by an extra who comes up with a funny bit of business.

Stage actors though, they're often stuck on stage for quite a bit of time, the audience sees them, watches them, even if they're not foreground. You have to hold that attention, both with words and actions. So stage actors, good ones, will tend to be physically expressive and interesting. They do 'business' – throwaway bits that are just meant to keep them going onstage. We see a lot of that between Benedetti and Rogel through their episodes; they play off each other, not just verbally, but physically as well. Benedetti and Rogel are simply the best Doctor/Companion duo in fan films.

There's another aspect to this though - American television grew up in Hollywood, in the shadow of the movie industry, the acting styles of American television were formed by the acting styles of the movies. In England, however, the theatrical tradition dated back to Shakespeare and beyond, it was very strong, and it shaped British television, particularly in the 60s. The actors on Doctor Who were stage actors, and their acting was shaped by the theatre. Benedetti and Rogel came from a theatrical tradition in Seattle, so their acting, their style of acting, feels very 'right' for Doctor Who.

As for the story, I was prepared to dismiss as standard fare. Basically – alien menace poses a threat, but the Doctor sorts it out. On rewatching it, I was pleasantly surprised. There's actually a lot of plot going on – the initial conflict between the Vietnam Vets and the Photojournalist sets up nicely, allows us to deliver exposition, and then neatly blindsides us when the Photojournalist dies and the real menace arrives onscreen.

Characters that start out as bad guys turn into good guys, the Doctor, the monster, and even the supporting characters move and countermove. We get surprised. You're never quite sure what's going to happen next. Eukor as a disembodied energy being on the hunt even has a bit of a swerve going, when the Doctor frustrates his original plan, he adapts and tries to steal the Tardis. That's nice, most villains/monsters aren't so flexible.

One of the things I love about classic Doctor Who is its storytelling. The serial format meant that you couldn't do a simplistic three act structure, but you had to have multiple storylines weaving in and out of each other, coming to resolutions, taking surprising turns. Despite only being half an hour, roughly the length of a single episode from a serial, the Wrath of Eukor has a very good grasp of the wonderful serial twistiness that is a hallmark of classic Doctor Who.

It's witty. The story is full of fun moments, both visual gags and clever lines in exactly the right places and delivered the right way. The scene where the Doctor confronts a group of angry survivalists and simply overcomes them with the force of her personality is brilliant. Later, after a trip through time and space, the Tardis materializes outside a power station, smoke pours out, and Carl and the Vet angrily complain that the Doctor can't drive the thing, kvetch about all the Indians and while they argue, the Doctor casually plucks an arrow from the Police Box shell and flicks it away.

It's is a vital thing. The Doctor is witty, the Doctor is fun, it's an essential quality of the Doctor. There are serious turns, of course, but wit is one of those defining aspects of Doctor Who. The sly lines, the moments of subtle or unsubtle comedy, the straight-faced lunacy of the situations. If you don't have that, you really don't have Doctor Who. The Wrath of Eukor has it, and more importantly Benedetti's Doctor and Rogel's Carl have it.

A key but subtle strength of *Wrath of Eukor* is in the settings. Again, that's something that separates the unwatchable amateur from the near professional. Settings as expressed in locations or sets, or even sometimes in major props, bring the visual quality to the story. They drive and define a story. We focus on what's in the foreground, but it's the background that often shapes the experience for us. A good location or set make the story come alive. A dull one can suck the life out of the story. That's why James Bond never goes to Cleveland.

No sets were built for Eukor. But they did build a pretty respectable Police Box shell, and despite missing a few details, it works, and using it in different locations conveys a lot.

Mostly, they shot outdoors on locations. In the opening scenes, old Seattle makes a nice double for turn of the century London, and they're smart enough to shoot at night, using shadows and a fog machine to cover up any flaws. The result is really nice production values, it's very gothic, even antique, it makes for a very strong visual opening for the actors to work in. Shadows and darkness are used to excellent effect.

It's when the action shifts out of the city that it really gets going visually. Seattle is in a temperate rain forest belt, and you don't really get what that means until you've been in one. There are ordinary forests, we've all seen them. But a rain forest is something different. Some places in Washington

State average as much as 150 inches of rainfall a year, that's a lot of water, and the green goes into overdrive.

The main part of the *Wrath of Eukor* is shot in the temperate rain forest outside Seattle, and it's practically a character in itself. A rain forest isn't just some woods or meadow. I'll put it this way, a rain forest to an English wood is like a Bengal tiger to a beagle. There's an overwhelming lushness to the green, a proliferation of shades and plant species, giant leafs, a profusion of vegetation crowding into every inch of the frame. It gives a real vibrancy and intensity to the story, at once familiar and alien.

The final location, the power station, is forbidding industrial gothic, a shift from the organic lushness, to angles, transformers and machinery. It's not a great location, particularly in terms of what's come before. But the production benefits from the diversity: 1910 London - rain forest - power station. Wisely, the production doesn't spend much time indoors – I think there's only one interior shot in the whole thing.

The consequence of that is that we're mostly seeing stuff that's not familiar or dull looking, and that has its own life. Amateur film makers take note – a good location is its own production value.

It's amazing how well it holds up some thirty years later. It's not surprising at all that some of the fans back in the 1980s could mistake it for the real show, or that it could attract its own cult following as a worthy successor or alternative series.

Particularly when you recall the hash that had been made of *Timelash*, the entire *Trial of a Time Lord*, *Time and the Rani* or *Delta and the Bannermen*.

Is it perfect? Of course not. If you want to be a nit-picker, look at the windows on the Police Box. Just for the record, there weren't any police boxes in 1911, so Carl shouldn't recognize it. Speaking of Carl, what's a chimney sweep doing in 1911? And let's not dwell too much on Carl's 'cockney accent' or Benedetti's British accent.

Eukor's little pyramid? Pretty tosh stuff there. When Eukor possesses one of the Vietnam vets, all talent leaves the actors body. The lightning bolts, the explosion effects? Actually, they were remarkably professional for the films of the time, but perhaps haven't aged well.

Honest to god though, look through the classic series — there's no shortage flaws and foibles to overlook there. If we love the classic Doctor Who and forgive its occasional shortcomings because the rest of it is so well done, then shouldn't we forgive Fan Films working with so much less?

But surprisingly, there's not that much that we really need to forgive here.

This is the secret of the female Doctor's success: It's simply well done, and well done in almost every way. As I've said, it is one of the best Doctor Who fan films ever, very nearly professional, with a ground-breaking concept in the woman Doctor and a solid performer in Barbara Benedetti. Indeed, Barbara Benedetti is match for Jody Whittaker, inhabiting her Doctor instantly, where Whittaker constantly struggled.

Wrath of Eukor came along at the perfect time to break into fan consciousness at a critical point in the show's history.

CAST: *Barbara Benedetti as The Doctor, Randy Rogel as Carl Evans, Tom Lance as Wallace, Jim Dean as Grant, Kevin McCauley as Harris, Michael Smith as Tate, George Catalano as Francis, Mark Schellberg and Karl Krogstad as bound workman.*

CREW: Ryan K. Johnson - Producer/Director ; Cheryl Read (credited), Ryan Johnson, Deborah Walsh and Linda Bushyager - Script; Mark Schellberg - Production Manager; Mills Rhiannon - Editor; Karl Krogstad and David Crowther - Camera; Greg Carlock and Tom Burden - Sound; Alex Gonzalez - Boom; Henry Gonzalez - Assistant Camera; Gordon Erickson and Paula Cox - Script Supervisor; Brian Loomis - Props; Eric Thomas - Sound Effects; Mark Lorge and Coenraad Abas - Sound Editors; Linda Bushyager and Deborah Walsk - Script Editors; Mike Bentley - Creative Consultant; Janice Findley - Designer; Blackwood Laird - Music;

Review Visions of Utomu (1986)

Gotta Sing! Gotta Dance!

STORY: On the planet far, far away, two medieval Kingdoms are attempting to seal a peace treaty with a royal marriage between Prince Germain and Princess Aldriana. It's not working out well, the Princess is kind of butch, the Prince definitely isn't. Things go wrong when the evil Wizard Utomu's henchman, Formor, breaks in and kidnaps the Prince. The Doctor is enlisted to rescue the Prince, with the aid of some song and dance…

REVIEW: *Visions of Utomu* is the sequel to *Wrath of Eukor*, which is both a strength and a handicap. *Eukor* is so groundbreaking, so well done, that we've built up an affection for the characters, we're willing to be forgiving, but it also sets up expectations. It defines what comes after. As a result, *Visions of Utomu* gets left in the shadow of *Eukor*. *Utomu* suffers a bit from little brother syndrome, it's always going to be seen as the lesser work. That's just the way that people are.

But for sheer creativity and charm, Utomu might well be the superior film. It is arguably the more original of the two, full of wit, life, inventiveness and sly goodwill. *Utomu* breezes through with the effortless charm of an Astaire and Rogers, or a Hope and Crosby, movie. In the sixty years of Doctor

Who's official history, and the thirty years of unauthorized films, there is simply nothing else quite like it. It's a perfect Doctor Who story, and yet it's unique.

Utomu, in terms of production values and cinematography is a less polished work. Sometimes a lot less polished. I think it's because they got ambitious here, and their ambition outran their money and abilities. Utomu had several key swerves from Eukor that, I think, undermined it.

It switched from 16 mm film to 3/4 commercial videotape, for instance. That saved a lot of money on lab and processing costs, but possibly lost a bit in image quality. I'm not criticizing, this is a volunteer production funded out of Ryan K. Johnson's pocket, and thousands of dollars in lab and processing costs are a big bite. The BBC shot the original series on the same sort of video format, so it's not a big deal. Still, Eukor, shot on film, stands out visually, so Utomu shot on video suffers a little, although it remains on par with the BBC show of its era.

They also decided to shift from a location backed story to a set-based production. Building sets is hard. Building good sets is harder. The cast is larger, and while the central cast is strong, there's a large number of extras who are sometimes used poorly.

On the other hand, *Utomu*'s timing was perfect. Filmed November, 1985, and released January, 1986, the future of the Doctor was still up in the air. The hiatus would not end, and *Trial of a Time Lord* would not begin until September, 1986, nine months later.

What makes *Utomu* work for me is its sense of fun. Its tongue is firmly in its cheek. It's a light comedy, good hearted, with a wink and a smile.

Eukor was a serious story with a few comic touches – let's face it half the cast dies and the story is about a body snatching alien criminal intent on murder and conquest. That's pretty grim stuff, no matter how many comic lines you throw in.

Utomu, in contrast, is light as a fluffy white cloud on a summer day; it's buoyantly weightless in the best ways. The opening scene is a clip from *Singing in the Rain*, and it's full of sly comic touches like that. The climactic battle is outright slapstick. It's got just enough darkness, in the form of the wizard Utomu to keep it grounded and moving, otherwise it might have floated away on its own lightness.

There's a strong sense of fun – people are dressing up and going in disguises, and seeing through each other's disguises. It's reminiscent of some of Shakespeare's comedies or a classic Hollywood screwball caper. Everyone's got a smart line they're tossing off, there's double takes, and 'oh whoops' moments, and a whole series of visual gags.

What can you say when the plot hinges on sneaking into the Wizard's castle disguised as a song and dance duo? Or when the Doctor uses hypnosis to turn Carl into a dancing virtuoso to win a contest. This is Hope and Crosby territory and Benedetti and Rogel travel it effortlessly. The script is equal parts witty and convoluted. But it works.

The actors acquit their roles nicely. Benedetti and Rogel as the Doctor and Carl have some really nice chemistry going on. It's amazing to see how well they work together, putting in all these little visual gags and witticisms. They really are the consistent highlight of the whole series. Although Benedetti is one of the best fan Doctors, there are still a few others that might compare with her.

But the Doctor/Companion thing she has going on with Rogel, that's unparalleled.

Wesley Rice as the evil wizard Utomu is also a standout. He manages to convey intelligence and menace, and he's got some very nice bits of stagecraft going on, despite not moving around too much. That's the lovely thing with stage actors. They know how to work business.

There's a nice bit of gender role reversal that's almost Shakespearean – the Prince, played by Robert Eustace, is in the essentially feminine role. He's quiet, bookish, all about feelings, physically tentative. When the bad guys bust in, it turns out he's the one who gets kidnapped. The Princess, played by Stasia Johnson, is active and outgoing. After the kidnapping, she sets out to rescue the Prince on her own, disguising herself as a dancing girl to enter the talent competition, and reaching for a sword when danger is afoot.

The performance of Jim Dean as the King is a mirror opposite of Rice's evil wizard – he's doing a light comedy character with a very deft touch. Dean, by the way, played the survivalist/Vietnam Vet, Grant, in Eukor. His performance here is so different, so light; it takes a minute to realize it's the same guy.

The cinematography is uneven, particularly at the outset, but it does pick up as we move along, with increasingly effective use of light and shadows. You can almost see them learning as they go, and this is the handicap of productions like this, you have to learn as you work. Quite often there isn't the time or the resources to apply that learning, to go back and reshoot the scene that you could have done better once you'd figured it out later, or to get those extra takes. It makes the production overall seem a little uneven.

Despite this, there are shots and scenes and transitions that are amazingly good. The zoom in on Utomu's henchman as Carl does his dance routine shows us a man being captivated – that's beautifully done. Almost every scene or shot where Rice is playing the villainous Utomu stands out. In the first scene between the Prince and Utomu, there's a wind sound foleyed in, it's subtle, but chilling. The background music is well used, never so loud as to call attention to itself, and almost always just right for whatever they want to convey in the moment.

Major strengths are the costumes and props. We got medieval stuff coming on strong here. Initially, I looked at the great costumes and the fake set flats, and thought maybe he'd hooked up with some kind of stage company that had done Shakespearean production.

Close. Johnson managed to link up with the Society for Creative Anachronism, so the result is that we've got some very sharp, nice quality costumes, and an impressively large cast of extras. Sadly, the extras are not used to full effect; a lot of them just end up running awkwardly in front of the camera.

The Bad: Those sets! Ouch! What it looks like is a handful of flats, painted in a stylized manner to suggest brick work, with some styrofoam blocks thrown on here and there. What it reminds me most of is a theatrical set, stylized, lightweight, moveable and designed for a stage, and a more forgiving stage audience.

Except that we aren't a stage audience, and we're expecting a higher degree of cinematic realism. The artificiality of the flats really is jarring. It's like biting on tinfoil. To make matters worse, initially, it is shot in the worst possible way, just glaring lighting, flat and bright, that really makes it impossible to see it as anything but fake and artificial. It's heartbreaking to think of how hard they must have worked to make something that looked so crap.

The BBC Doctor Who, of course, was infamous for its wobbly sets. Not as often as you'd think but yes, it did have its share of tosh sets that it would have to dress up or work around. So we live with these things.

It's particularly damning here because this is actually the sort of sets or locations that the BBC was good at. England is lousy with castles and immense brickwork monstrosities, so they have a lot to choose from, and even when they're shooting in studio, they have enough experience with how they look and how to shoot them effectively, that they carry it off. So Utomu is falling afoul of our subconscious expectations, as much as if they accidentally painted the Police Box orange.

Oddly, as the story goes on, the production does seem to get better at it. Johnson becomes increasingly assured as he plays with the lighting, darkens the flats, focuses on foreground characters and blurs the background, films the action to emphasize movement. It's as if we're watching him learn how to shoot these flats. I suppose we are.

Over time, the sets, for the most part, stop being disconcerting and jarring. Possibly we've been beaten into submission. Or more likely, the whole crew is just doing it better – shooting and lighting them properly and focusing better on the story and characters, so that it's generally stronger later on. But still, getting better later on only buys you so much, when you set your foot badly wrong on your first step, it's hard to recover.

To be really fair – remember that mostly, this was being shown on mid-1980s, 12 to 24 inch colour television sets, not high def or high resolution, and often being shown in crowded rooms at gatherings of fans. So it may not have been as jarring back then. There's a lot of stuff from the Hartnell and Troughton eras, or for that matter from the Pertwee and Baker eras, that looked okay on the old scan line/cathode ray televisions that is now pretty blatantly awful on higher resolutions and higher definition.

What else? Randy Rogel's choreography: Sorry, it doesn't come off. The story requires that he be a brilliant dancer, and the henchman's zoom shot almost sells it. But it doesn't come across strongly. It's one of those things where they bite off more than they can chew, when what carries in the script can't carry on the screen. What hurts is that Randy wanted to do it. He was pushing to do a song and dance number. Kind of a mistake there.

Inexperience hurts: Kinetic stuff, fight scenes, dance numbers, they're tricky to shoot. You can't actually just have the camera sitting there. It has to almost be a character, and the dancer or the fighter has to play to it as much as they simply do their stuff. From what I understand of the shooting, they didn't really have the time or resources, and were working under pretty brutal conditions. Frankly, I don't think they understood what they were getting into. Time to dip into that pocket of forgiveness.

So that's a pair of harsh flaws to get caught between, and you have to make the decision to let them slide in order to enjoy the story. Ultimately, these flaws are no worse than some of the things we've seen and opted to forgive in the BBC series. I dunno though, maybe I'm too critical. I could see some people not even noticing these things, just delving right into the story and grooving to the light, breezy touch.

Visions of Utomu finishes up as a singular Doctor Who story. On its own merits it has real strengths. It's imminently watchable. Utomu doesn't do everything well, but it does a lot well. For me, the cheerful amiability rules, it's a Gene Kelly sort of story. *Eukor* you appreciate, but somehow it's *Utomu* that puts a smile on your face.

CAST: *Barbara Benedetti as The Doctor, Randy Rogel as Carl Evans, Wesley Rice as Utomu, Stasia Johnson (no relation) as Princess Aldraina, Robert Eustace as Prince Germain, Jim Dean as the King, Randy Dixon as the Carnival M.C., Joseph McCarthy as Formore, Eric Barney as the Magician, Dameon Willock as the Kings Guard, Michael Kemmir as Prime Minister, Aaron Lewis as Servant, Gareth Davis, Marshall Hunter, Brian Loomis, Dean Sepstrup, Patrick Sonlin as Utomu's Guards, and an orange.,*

CREW: *Produced, Directed and Written by Ryan K. Johnson; David Cameron, Howard Carson, Sue Egan - Camera; DJ Driscoll - Assistant Director; Ian Smithers - Sound; T. Brian Wagner - Make Up; Robert A. Johns, Sally Woehrle, Ian Smithers, Lisa Hennes, Nancy Jean Hewes, Sharon Demuth, Darryl Bratz, Carla James - Set Builders; Pat Mitchell - Lighting; Michael Cain - Best Boy; Lori Hillard and Shelley George - Costumes; Howard Carson - Designer; Thanks to Friends of the Doctor, and to The Society for Creative Anachronism; 32 minutes. 3/4" videotape. Filmed November 1985, released January 1986.*

Review: Pentagon West (1987)

A Doctor in the House?

STORY: The friends and associates of Doctor Komar are worried. The Doctor's been acting more and more strangely, even while he mumbles about a radical new breakthrough. Meanwhile, a mysterious police box appears in the park and there are disturbing glimpses of a woman in a red jacket and a man in a black suit....

REVIEW: The third, and the weakest, of the four Benedetti-Johnson stories

Oddly, the Doctor and Carl are barely even in the story. There's an appearance of the Tardis at the very beginning. There's a series quick shots of the Doctor and Carl lurking, 8.5 minutes, 9.5 minutes, 11.5minutes and 13 minutes, into the 28 minute run – no dialogue, no action, just kind of there… watching, no more than a few seconds at a time. They're just a presence that the main cast keeps noticing.

The Doctor doesn't actually get a line or become an active character in the story until 19 minutes in, when she shows up and explains the crisis to the other characters for two and a half minutes.

It seems that Komar, the mad scientist, is breaking down the dimensional barriers, which isn't a good thing. Not a good thing in this case equals kaboom! The Doctor suggests believing her and stopping Komar would be a good idea. Then she steps out for a couple of minutes while the rest of the cast has a debate over it. They eventually decide to go with her.

After that, though, the Doctor is part of the crowd, has a few more lines, but really, she's just a bystander. Count it all up, Benedetti and Rogel are maybe in for 7 minutes of a 28 minute running time, and they don't get to do a whole lot. There are some nice physical bits between them, and Benedetti has a good line or two, particularly in the end. But that's it.

Instead, the lead hero or villain is Doctor Komar, played by Michael Santo. It's Komar that the plot revolves around, he's one the rest of the cast are connected to – he's the glue that connects them to each other. He's the one whose actions precipitate the conflicts and he's the one that the Doctor is interested in.

It seems that Doctor Komar is working on a cancer cure, urgently so, given that he's got cancer (represented by an awful prosthetic tumor on his bald spot). Komar, feeling desperate, has zapped up his intelligence to evil genius levels, pierced the dimensional barrier releasing cancer-curing radiation. The trouble is that it really will blow up the universe. The Doctor and Komar's friends try and stop him, but bungle it all up, literally falling over each other. Komar knocks them all out with a stun ray or something.

Then, left to himself, Komar has a soliloquy over the big moral quandary: *"Should I keep trying to cure my cancer and blow up the universe, dying myself anyway and killing everyone else?"*

A Pirate's History, Page 66

Which isn't actually a moral quandary, when you stop to think about it.

I mean: *"Hmmm, my course of treatment will not work, in that it will kill me and lots of other people."*

How is that a dilemma?

If that pulpy premise wasn't enough, Santo plays Komar with a fake European accent and a sense of theatrics channeled from Bela Lugosi's performance at the hands of Ed Wood in *Bride of the Monster*. Santo is a decent actor, his turn as Captain Picard in *Star Trek: The Pepsi Generation* is spot on and hilarious. But here he's wrongheaded as hell. He's handicapped all sorts of ways; he doesn't have a chance to carry the weight.

Then again, maybe it's a deliberate choice. Faced with a *Bride of the Monster* sort of story, Santo opted for a campy *Bride of the Monster* sort of performance? If so, it misfires, because no one else in the production seems to be in on the gag. If you're going to go there, you can't go alone.

A big problem with Komar is that despite being central to the story, like the Doctor, he's off stage for most of the production. He really only shows up as a force at the end. This gives us a peculiar situation in which both the apparent protagonist and apparent antagonist are absent for most of the film, leaving the rest of the cast to flounder.

The rest of the cast isn't a strong group either. Five less able amateurs get the lion's share of dialogue and action, what there is of it. Unfortunately, due to the story mechanics, they're hamstrung. They literally have nothing to do but stand around and talk about the absent Komar, as if this was *Waiting for Godot*. Worse, they don't really know what's going on, until the Doctor shows up to explain the plot to them.

They're not really able to advance the story. Instead, they literally get in each other's way. None of them have enough to do, none of them establish an identity. They sink the story like a lead weight.

Structurally, it's simply a tough script, and it doesn't do the actors, any of them, any favours at all. Sure, there's an occasional good line. There's a nice interlude where two of the cast members speculate mockingly about alien life coming to earth. But a few light spots aren't enough.

What was going on, was that Ryan K. Johnson, after doing two Doctor Who stories, was actually trying to move forward and launch his own sci fi series. This was a pilot for that series, and the Doctor and Komar were essentially guest stars. That's why the production has two titles: *'Pentagon West,'* the apparent series title, I guess, and *'A Doctor in the House'* the episode title.

The production history, unlike *Eukor* and *Utomu* was pretty tortured. The *Wrath of Eukor* was essentially Ryan K. Johnson's effort to break through at the World Science Fiction convention in Los Angeles. *Visions of Utomu* was a direct response to the *Wrath of Eukor*. But I don't think that Johnson particularly wanted to stay in a Doctor Who niche. Rather, his next step was to try and launch his own series, to do his own thing. He wanted to move from the Doctor to his own original work. Johnson had an idea for a pilot; a sci fi soap opera titled *'Tripp in Space'* and was able to get a small grant. The pilot was to serve as the first two episodes

Meanwhile, a friend of Johnson's, Howard Carson, was trying to produce an ambitious Doctor Who script for Benedetti and Rogel, which would also feature Michael Santo. That project fell apart when Carson had a car accident and subsequently went bankrupt.

When Carson's project died, and Benedetti, Rogel and Santo were available, he recruited them. Meanwhile, the original version of the Johnson's project wasn't working out. He decided to throw the Doctor and Carl into this story.

There's a certain political economy going on at these levels. There's no money to speak of, everyone is volunteering and you really have to work with and motivate people. This means a level of personal commitments to people. You gather a group of volunteers for a project, the project falls through and you end up doing something else. It's just hard to drop those people. You want to find something for them.

That's probably why the Doctor and Carl found their way into Johnson's pilot. There were other reasons. Benedetti's Doctor was a recognized and recognizable character, with a connection to an established audience. There was the potential to use her Doctor as a lead in to help launch the series.

Unfortunately, the script was too expensive and ambitious for the resources. The production collapsed about half way through, and Johnson had to consolidate a story and cobble something together mostly with what they already had. This became *Pentagon West: Doctor in the House.*

Tripp in Space didn't go any further. I suspect that Johnson was exhausted and frustrated by the whole experience. To his credit, he finished and produced something. The world is littered with abandoned projects, films and pilots that died or were orphaned somewhere along the way.

It's a shame. Johnson's works consistently show enough promise and flair that there was the potential there for something interesting and worthwhile in *Tripp in Space.* But it doesn't really show in *Pentagon West.* Crippled by limited funds, a run of bad luck, and the struggle to do too many things with too many people, the A-story doesn't unfold well and the A-characters never really gel. The effort to establish a viable pilot for a series largely fails.

The whole thing would have been a wash except, ironically, for the presence of the Benedetti Doctor in a supporting or guest starring role, included almost casually during the production process, which made Pentagon West part of the Female Doctor story cycle.

Seen strictly as a Doctor Who story, this plays as almost an experimental, avant garde piece. Moving the Doctor into the background, making her a supporting character, allows us to see the Doctor through other people's eyes, as a mysterious, sometimes arrogant, sometimes dangerous figure. The classic series never did anything like this, but the new series has dabbled with this, particularly in parts of Rose, with Christopher Ecclestone, and Blink and Love and Monsters with David Tennant. In this sense, Pentagon West is almost prescient.

There's an interesting wrinkle or two on the Doctor here, there's a suggestion of her as a Machiavellian force, glimpsed but not understood. She plays the Doctor darker, she's not going to cure cancer for us, the world has to save itself sometimes, and her one decent line 'I can live with what I've done, can you?' is almost cruel.

Some people feel this draws on the portrait of the McCoy Doctor in the Cartmel years. The Doctor with the hidden background, the chess master and manipulator. But this version of the McCoy Doctor wouldn't appear for another year. So Benedetti's Doctor is really doing it first, an interesting coincidence.

This is a version of the Doctor we seldom see. This is the outsider who intrudes into the known world, the unknown quality whose very presence is an omen of bad things. The Doctor may not be trouble, may not be evil or the source of trouble. But when the Doctor comes, you know that trouble is around, and the safe, normal world you've enjoyed so much, that's over with. There's a sense here of the Doctor not as someone who stumbles into situations, but is actively policing threats.

It almost raises *Pentagon West* to a near miss. Sadly, there's just not enough of the Doctor and Carl. And without them, there's not enough going on with the foreground characters to make up for it.

Benedetti's Doctor has a nice physical gag or two, and she and Rogel work with what the script gives them.

There's a scene that the two of them have with an easy chair that reminds you just how good they are together. Overall, despite a nice shot or two, this is the least visually innovative and interesting of the four. Some of the scenes and dialogue aren't too painful, but overall, it's slow and awkwardly structured.

Pentagon West - A Doctor in the House didn't get the same reception that *Eukor* and *Utomu* got. It couldn't, it's just not nearly as good as the first two and whatever cachet it had was riding their coat tails. Then there's the fact that this is the third female Doctor story, and you know, it's just not new and shocking any more as an idea. It's established now. The inherent novelty is worn off. It makes a wave as part of a trilogy, but that's probably it.

Meanwhile the hiatus was over. The real BBC Doctor, is back, sort of. Colin Baker's completes the Trial of a Time

Lord. But this is followed by chaos - Baker is fired. There's going to be a new Doctor, no one knows who just yet, and there's a new season coming up soon. The attention of fans is elsewhere. There's a sense, perhaps that the time of the Female Doctor is over. There's no void left for her to step into.

As for Ryan Johnson? Reading between the lines of his 'making of' essay, I had the sense that it was one of his most dispiriting projects. This production had been very hard to get off the ground, it had been frustrating, it had morphed continually, it was just a headache. This seemed to have been much more of a struggle, and a struggle in negative ways — overcoming obstacles to get something done is one thing, overcoming obstacles to be allowed to try and do something can be disheartening. The final product could not have been satisfying to him. The reception was certainly poor; *Pentagon West* was not knocking anyone on their ass.

With *Eukor*, and with *Utomu*, he had hit a moment, but that moment had passed, was passing. It just wasn't fun anymore. Maybe it was past time to move on and do something else.

CAST: *Michael Santo - Komar; Laura Kenny - Iz, Laura Sweany - Robin; Josh Conescu - David; Jonathon Stewart - Alex; Eric Anderson - Simon; Barbara Benedetti - The Doctor, Randy Rogel - Carl.*

CREW: *Directed by Howard Carson, Written and Produced by Ryan K. Johnson. Ryan Halfhill - Director of Photography; Kathy Schickling - Editor; Daniel John Willken and Wesley A. Galloway - Musicians and Sound Effects; Gordon Davison, Richard Elmore and Steve Bishop - Sound Recorders; Andrew Lowder and DJ Driscoll - Assistant Directors; Carla James - Script Supervisor; EJ Fadgen, Mary Whitlock, Ian Smithers, Sharon DeMuth, Sally Woehrle, Tony Case, Rosanne McLees, Ed McLees - The Production Crew; T. Brian Wagner - Make Up Artist; Location Supervisor - John Whitmore;*

Special Thanks to Marvin and Vicki Sindt, John Eineigl, Nancy Morris. Production made possible with a Grant from Kings County Arts Commission. 28 minutes. Betacam videotape. Filmed September 1986, released May 1987.

Review: Broken Doors (1988)

The Final Benedetti Doctor Story

STORY: The Tardis breaks down in mid-flight, stranding the Doctor and Carl in a strange otherworldly realm. They make their way to a forbidding castle, where a bouncing ball leads them into danger…

REVIEW: Among fans, the consensus seems to be that this is the best of the Benedetti stories, and it's cited as one of the best fan films ever. Personally, I'm not sure I buy into that. *Broken Doors* is good. But then, so is *Eukor* and *Utomu*, in their respective ways. In the end, the three are so different that I don't know how I'd rank them against each other. But *Broken Doors* definitely seems to have won followers.

The good: We have a small cast, very effective use of location in terms of the creepy old house and the outdoors, and as always, great chemistry between Benedetti and Rogel.

Freed from the requirement of naturalism or realism, the production was at liberty to do some interesting work. There's an impressive 'room of mirrors' set, which is very effective. It is genuinely surreal and arresting, altogether unearthly. Sets of any sort are very hard to do, as we saw in *Visions of Utomu*. And a set consisting of mirrors should be just hellish – hint – mirrors reflect back, which is not good if you want your camera and crew out of sight. But they pull it off: Good lighting, good placement, good camera-work, all work to create an environment which is trans-dimensional and otherworldly.

There are other things to like – there's a scene in a quarry, which is accompanied by some rather nice matte shots. According to the notes by Ryan K. Johnson, the crew were absolutely thrilled to finally be shooting in a quarry. I gather that thrill faded as they schlepped around props and equipment. The interior locations, as I've said, are well chosen. They've mastered some very effective smoke/pyro effects which adds a lot of production value.

Of course, Barbara Benedetti shines as the Doctor, although in this story she's looking a bit worn. Actually, Benedetti looks very worn. In some shots you can see bags under her eyes, she looks physically tired. It's possible she was beginning to suffer the effects of the lymph node cancer which would be diagnosed next year in 1989, and kill her a few years later in November, 1991.

Her character comes alive though, particularly in her scenes with Rogel, who plays Carl. Half way through the story the characters are separated and must face their own trials. Even without Rogel, she turns in a strong performance. Her scene in the room of the 'hopscotch of death' is brilliant. With no one to act off of, and a fairly neutral environment, she still manages to convey the Doctor at full force, fishing through various pockets for different gadgets, fiddling with things and throwing them away, and then finding a bag of jelly babies which she ingeniously uses to solve her problem. She's the quintessential Doctor in these scenes.

Meanwhile, Carl, wherever he is, copes rather more frantically with his own strange events, and this is done engagingly.

On the down side: This is the shortest of the Ryan Johnson Doctor Who videos. Nineteen minutes isn't really enough time to develop a story fully. It's the shortest of the Johnson/Benedetti stories. This economy tells on us. It feels like it's rushed through, hitting all its beats, but you sort of want a bit more, perhaps some plot swerve, perhaps just more of Benedetti being the Doctor, or her Doctor kvetching with Carl, or even a few minutes to see what the Michael Santo Doctor is going to be like.

It could have been worse – Johnson wanted fifteen minutes. It's pretty clear he was just tired of doing Doctor Who. The plot is linear to a fault, there's no sub-plots, no side trips, no real swerves. It lacks that 'twistyness' that's a hallmark of good Doctor Who, or of Johnson's previous outings.

Instead, the Doctor and Carl end up in a strange dimension where a godlike being inflicts pranks and forces them to play a series of lethal games. The godlike being shows up late to the party spends a little too long explaining itself and doesn't make a whole lot of sense.

Now admittedly, the godlike being showing up late is good storytelling. I always hated it when Q or Trelayne or Apollo or whoever showed up right at the beginning of a *Star Trek* story and said 'I'm going to screw you around now.' There's rather more mystery and intrigue if the nemesis shows up later, is a little more coy, then you can milk dramatic tension and keep the audience guessing. So I don't actually mind the late appearance.

But when he does appear… wow, does he talk a lot. And wow, does so little of it make sense. Parsing it out, the entity

A Pirate's History, Page 77

is saying both *"Hey, I am my entire dimension, I'm a conscious universe in here, and you're just talking to my hand."* And *"Hey, I'm actually you, the dark side of you."* Can it make up its mind?

It says a bunch of other things, including how it likes to play cat and mouse games and kill its visitors. Then it does an about face, saying the Doctor has won and can go free, but it turns out, that's just another trap, one in which Carl is tricked into killing the Doctor.

Its final line is *"The Game is Never Over, the Prize is Never Won."*

It's actually a good line, although it is pretty dickish. But then, it's actually fitting for a godlike entity whose hobby is screwing with people.

It seems to me that the basic concept of the confrontation with the entity is good; certainly the surreal setting of the room of mirrors is excellent. It's hampered by the fact that a lot of key information is the entity monologuing. There should have been more back and forth. Certainly, Benedetti was a strong enough actress that it could have been carried off.

The final trick by which the entity kills the Doctor is also well done, both as a concept, and in execution.

So what's the bottom line for *Broken Doors*? It fits into the surreal genre of Doctor Who, it's of a piece with stories like the *Mind Robber*, the *Celestial Toymaker*, *Warriors Gate* or Timebase's *Paradise in Chains*. If you like those, you'll like this, and as I've said, some web sites and reviewers see this as, hands down, the best of the Benedetti stories.

Yes, I gave away the ending. My bad. Michael Santo was an enthusiastic young actor and hard core Doctor Who fan who desperately wanted to play the Doctor. He was actually the driving force behind this film, pushing and possibly funding Ryan Johnson to take one more outing. The script was written by T. Brian Wagner, and Steve Hauge directed. Johnson himself sat back sticking to the role of producer.

Oddly, for all Santo's enthusiasm to be the Doctor, this single minute or so of footage at the end was the only time he would play the Doctor. He never got to play the role again.

By this time, Johnson had done four Benedetti films in four years, plus a couple of Who spoofs, the *Tardis Home Companion* and *Dona-Who*. This last film, *Broken Doors*, had been done reluctantly, he just wasn't up to doing it one more time.

Brian T. Johnson did write a script for a Michael Santo Doctor story, but it took so long that whatever impulse or energy to do it dissipated. Michael Santo ended up slumming doing Shakespeare, which made it harder to find the time to work on Johnson's projects. It just never happened.

Frankly, I don't mind. Barbara Benedetti was something special. The whole concept of the woman Doctor was ground-breaking. For all his enthusiasm I'm not sure that Santo was going to bring anything more, or that Johnson had any new places to take him. Would it really have been worth it to be known as '*the guy who came after Barbara?*'

In an ironic twist, Santo made his big mark in fandom, working with Johnson and making 'Star Trek: The Pepsi Generation' where he parodied Picard. Ironic because he disliked the new *Star Trek* in its early, wobbly years.

Michael Santo continued to act, accumulating credits for films, video games and stage. His most recent film project was 2006's *Drifting Elegant*. Notable stage roles include

Leonarto in *Shakespeare's Much Ado About Nothing,* in both Connecticut and Washington D.C.

Ryan K. Johnson was tired and ready to move on. He'd put in a lot of time and money. *Eukor* had cost somewhere between three and ten thousand dollars out of pocket, the other films had been cheaper for being shot on video, but still, you were looking at thousands of dollars in real money, and tens of thousands in sweat equity. He was done. If not for Michael Santo, there probably wouldn't have been a *Broken Doors.*

Ryan K. Johnson would go on to do one more Doctor Who story, *Death Takes a Holiday,* roughly sixteen years later. That seventeen minute short would feature Colin Baker and Frazier Hines in cameos, and give us Wendy Padbury, and Nicholas Courtney actually frolicking around genuine Mayan ruins.

Johnson remained active and engaged as both a fan and a film maker, producing a pair of his own *Mystery Science Theatre* episodes, a brilliant Star Trek parody, and a long list of short film and stage productions. His most recent work includes the feature length *House of Glass* web series and *Flesh of my Flesh,* a Lovecraftian zombie movie.

As for the stars: Randy Rogel, who had played Carl through four episodes, moved to Los Angeles in the early 1990s, where he became a writer for *Batman,* the *Animaniacs, Tarzan* and *1001 Nights,* among many other shows. He accumulated a long list of story credits, as well as working as story editor, producer and even as a composer. One of his scripts for the *Batman* animated series won an Emmy award.

Barbara Benedetti collaborated with Ryan K. Johnson on one more film. A half hour production called *The Wolfe Project.* In it, Benedetti dyed her hair black and played a supernatural researcher investigating a mysterious haunting.

Barbara Benedetti passed away after a two year battle with lymphatic cancer in November, 1991, at the age of 38, only three years after *Broken Doors*. Although an active and talented actress, and performer, most of her work was on stage. A multi-talented performer, she was involved in music, writing and directing. At her funeral, the stage community of Seattle turned out to give her one last standing ovation. In mainstream film, she had small parts in *Shredder Orpheus*, *Bomb's Away, Dogfight* and *Waiting for the Light*, all shot in the Seattle area.

Outside of the Seattle community, her work on Doctor Who, a show that she'd never heard of, and a role that she was never paid for, are probably her most famous and well known performances.

Benedetti was one of the finest fan film Doctors ever, one of the few that deserves a place with the real Doctors. She took the role and she was The Doctor from get go. Her Doctor was witty, unconventional, eccentric and unflappable, smarter than anyone around her and ready to do the unexpected.

So how do the four Benedetti/Johnson stories stack up? Well, it's an actual body of work. Four stories, 108 minutes. Among other things, it's an actual series which in itself is astounding. Up to that time, and for years afterwards, that made the Benedetti Doctor unique. Fan films were single productions, you didn't have a series.

Even now, the vast majority of fan films tend to be one-offs. Any kind of film is just brutally hard to do. Most stop at one. A few stubborn folk do two. But usually no more.

To have an actual series of four stories or videos was unheard of at the time, and impressive even today. The last four seasons of Doctor Who had been four stories or serials per season, albeit multiple episodes per story. The Benedetti Doctor with four stories was working very close to the same plateau as the classic series.

Or perhaps above? Both Colin Baker's last and Sylvester McCoy's first season had been pretty wobbly affairs. Of Benedetti's four, I would say three brilliant or near brilliant ones, and one interesting misstep. There's a range to the female Doctor – she goes from adventure, to light comedy, to experimental to surrealism. The Benedetti stories don't sit still and just do the one thing, tell the same kind of story. Rather, Johnson chose to tell not just different stories, but different kinds of stories in different ways.

A lot of it looks and aspires to professional quality, in both the story, the acting, the shots and settings. There's the usual glitches and hiccups, and some things definitely need to be forgiven.

I think that one of the strengths that Ryan Johnson brought to his Doctor Who stories was that he was a film-maker first, rather than simply a fan. An amateur film maker, but still a film maker. That's no small thing. He has a broad appreciation, both of fandom and pop culture, as well as film making, and that allows him both to make better films, and to be willing to experiment more. In this sense of being willing to experiment, I'd rank Utomu as his best – not even the Timebase people dreamt of crossing Doctor Who with a Crosby/Hope yarn. Of course, the downside of being willing to experiment means that you have to be willing to fail, which gives us Pentagon West, but at least it was an interesting failure.

A Pirate's History, Page 82

Johnson also seemed willing to share the load, which both helped and hurt. I think his most polished scripts were Eukor and Broken Doors, both credited to other people. Being willing to solicit help, and respecting the ideas and contributions of that help gave him Benedetti and Rogel.

While the Benedetti stories don't really fit into an overall narrative arc, they do chronicle the beginning and end of this Doctor Their strength is their diversity. It's held together by the continuing characters in the Doctor and Carl who together bring a consistent identity and sensibility to the productions. But each story is unique. Nevertheless, as a body of work, the whole is somehow greater than the sum of the parts, particularly for being diverse.

Barbara Benedetti broke new ground and lead the way for a number of women, including Sharon Crookes, Lily Nelson and Krystal Moore, to try their hand at the role of the Doctor in fan productions, some of them quite remarkable.

Out in the mainstream, thirty years after Barbara Benedetti took on the role in 1984, the notion of a female Doctor remained controversial until Jody Whittaker took on the role in 2019.

CAST: *Barbara Benedetti as The Doctor and the Manager; Michael Santo as The Doctor; E. Kim Tonas as the Manager, Randy Rogel as Carl Evans, Gareth Davis as the Soldier.*

CREW: *Written by T. Brian Wagner. Produced by Ryan K. Johnson. Directed by Steven Hauge; Ryan Halfhill - Photography; Bill Corrigan - Editor; Wesley Galloway - Music/Sound; Jennifer Hauge and Sally Woehrle - Script Supervisor; Ian Smithers - Models; Paul Johnson, Elinor Fadgen, Doris O'Connor, Tony Case, Gary Watts, Nancy Powell, Steven Powell and Sharon Demuth - Production Crew; Bruce Derocher III - Computer Graphics; Holly Forbis - Costumes; Mike*

Raabe - Masks; Lach Loud - Designer; Special thanks to Friends of the Doctor; 19 minutes. Betacam video. Filmed November 1987, released March 1988.

CHAPTER 4: THE SUPER-8 SEVENTIES

Initially, we focused on the *Wrath of Eukor*, and on the hiatus. But *Eukor* wasn't the product of the hiatus, and wasn't even the first. It was simply the best and the most innovative of that early generation where fan films came of age, and the one that ended up in the right time and place to have an impact.

But before we examine rest of the fan films of classic Doctor Who's declining period, let's take a moment to look at some of the earlier films, now mostly lost to us: The *Son of Doctor Who*, circa 1970-1975, an animated short from 1977, *Doctor Hoo, – Threat of the Leviathans*, *The Destructors*, *The Thosian Strategy*, *Ocean in the Sky*, *The Image Makers*, all from the mid to late 70s.

Now, Doctor Who had been around since 1963. And it wasn't the first sci fi TV or movie series to have a fan following. On television we had *Space Patrol* and *Rocky Jones*, and before that *Captain Video*, *Flash Gordon* and *Buck Rogers* in the serials. *Tarzan* was in newspaper comics, novels, and serials. *Doc Savage* ruled the pulps, the *Shadow* dished out justice over the radio, and *Superman* flew through the comic books.

But we didn't really see fan films much at all, except for a few enthusiasts like Don Glut.

So what changed in the 1970s? That was when Super 8 came along. Technically, it was 1965 when Kodak released Super 8 millimeter, but it took a few years for the format to go widespread.

Super 8, compared to this, was revolutionary. A Super-8 camera was small that it could be held in one hand, a child could use it. It was durable enough to be dropped on the floor. The film came in cartridges no larger than an audio cassette, you could pop a cartridge in and out in literally two and a half seconds, and you could get them processed at the neighborhood drugstore. It was super easy, user friendly.

A few years later, in England, between 1970 and 1975, a couple of teenagers were making their own fan films, of everything from Doctor Who to *Gerry Anderson* to *James Bond* culminating in their epic fifteen minute *Son of Doctor Who*.

A whole subculture of Super8 film makers emerged in the 1970s, making movies for their own pleasure, or showing them to each other at gatherings or festivals. There were books and magazines devoted to the Super 8 enthusiast, with tips and techniques for making better movies, mastering everything from cinematography to script writing and special effects.

Of course, Super8 filmmakers were hamstrung in a lot of ways. Let's be honest; it didn't look terribly good. Super8 cameras were by no means professional or semi-professional instruments. The image wasn't great to start with, the film quality was grainy and the machines were often quirky, durability and ease of use took priority over precision.

Sound, after 1973, consisted of a microphone mounted in the camera itself, so the sound quality was generally poor - full of camera noises, pops, glitches, ambient omnidirectional noise, you name it. The sound recording was eight frames out from the film image, so simple editing could get choppy sound. They kept improving of course, with separate sound microphones that could plug in, and technical improvements to synch sound tracks up.

 Processing was done by regular photo labs, who weren't doing a lot of attention to finesse, if you were trying to edit a scene together from multiple cartridges, then tints, colour correction, the fine details that professional film development houses did... that was hit and miss. You didn't get to see rushes, you had to shoot and hope you got what you got when it came back from the drugstore. That was totally fine if all you wanted was an uninterrupted three minute film of your daughter's birthday party. But it could get difficult if you wanted to edit a scene together.

One of the biggest handicaps was distribution. Supposing that you actually made yourself a little *Star Trek* or Doctor Who fan film? Well, what do you do with it?

In 1974, John Cosentino, a carpet installer in Michigan made his own feature length *Star Trek* film: *Paragon's Paragon*. Loosely based on James Blish's original Star Trek novel, *Spock Must Die*, Cosentino's film ran over sixty minutes. Cosentino built himself an optical printer for effects; he used stop motion, glass mattes, miniatures and superimpositions. He created the costumes and props, even re-created the bridge of the Enterprise. It was an epic. It was an astonishing. It was legendary.

If even a thousand people saw it, I would be surprised. You can see fragments of it on YouTube, and I recommend looking it up. It's an interesting mix of special effects, impressive costumes and sets and seventies hair styles. We can't really speak to the acting. But the original full length film, on Super8 is now mostly lost. It was ahead of its time, a sort of masterpiece without an audience. Or more properly, a sort of masterpiece without a way to reach its broad audience.

All *Paragon's Paragon* could really do was occasional showings at fan clubs and conventions before the film finally wore out. Even that wasn't easy. There weren't that many conventions, barely a handful compared to the explosion of fan clubs and conventions in the 1980s. And to show it at a convention, you actually had to physically travel, bringing the film with you, and bringing or making sure that there was a projector and screen arranged and available on site. Who was going to pay John Cosentino to drag his movie back and forth across the country?

Before VCRs came along and got cheap you couldn't really make or distribute copies. Most Super 8 fan films existed as single copies, shown mostly to friends. That's pretty limiting. Good, bad, it just didn't have legs. Super 8 had been revolutionary because it was user friendly, but that user-friendliness had limits.

There was something else missing. The community that would watch and support these films was only barely coming into being in the 1970s. *Star Trek*, of course, was ahead of the curve in the late 60s and early 70s in America. The move to cancel the show had galvanized fans lead by Bjo Trimble, and a coherent and activist fandom was emerging. But emerging slowly. *Star Wars*, and its overnight fan base, wouldn't even be a thing until after 1977. Through the 60s and early 70s Doctor Who fandom was only a handful of short lived clubs and single enthusiasts.

Somewhere between 1970 and 1975, we had *Son of Doctor Who*, a twenty minute epic. But they had no audience or community for it, beyond their circle of friends. There are other films around this time - *Threat of the Leviathan, The Destructors, The Thosian Strategy*, made on Super 8, around London by local fans, for local fans, and it's mostly luck that we even know about these. The films themselves are mostly lost.

The first national Doctor Who Club wasn't established until May of 1976. The first Doctor Who convention held anywhere in the world wasn't until October of 1977.

One of the early Super 8, film was a three minute animated short called *Doctor Hoo*. You can find it on YouTube now, because it played at the first ever Doctor Who convention, held in Battersea, England, back in 1977. It only succeeded and survived because it was made for and played at a convention, one of those rare occasions back in those days, possibly the first occasion, when a fan audience was possible.

Super 8 offered the possibility of fan films, and inspired the first wave of fan films. But the end, the Super 8 the limitations of the format posed too many challenges and it just wasn't enough to sustain a culture.

The high marks were 1979 with the *Image Maker* and *Ocean in the Sky*, both of which struggled with major technical handicaps. The fan film boom of the 1970s never managed to catch on, and died away, all but forgotten. Super 8 film would linger on into the 80s and 90s as a format for artists and experimental film makers.

In the end, the fan film boom of the 70s ended up stillborn, and forgotten. There were a few people connected with it who went on to prominence – Kevin Davies, Paul Tams, Mark Ayres. But mostly, it was overlooked, a false start.

In contrast, the 80s boom would sustain itself, continuing and evolving to the present day.

Review: Son of Doctor Who (1970-1974)

Super 8, 20 minutes, Live Action

STORY: It begins in the laboratory of the evil Professor Mad, who invents a time disappearing gun. No sooner does he do so, then the villain, the Son of Doctor Who arrives to steal it. From there, the story moves through a killer robot, a caveman, a spaceship, a mob of children, a planet that looks suspiciously like earth, and a cast of thousands.

PRODUCTION: In the early 1960s, William Hartnell, the first Doctor, apparently pitched a story to his producers called 'Son of Doctor Who.' The Doctor's son would be a villain, flying about in his own Tardis, identical in looks to the Doctor, and to be played by Hartnell.

I suppose spending 40 weeks a year playing the Doctor, Hartnell wanted to change things up a little, or maybe he just wanted to get paid twice for two roles – both Hartnell and Troughton would play dual roles as look-alikes. Hartnell in The Massacre of St. Bartholemews Eve, and Troughton in Master of the World.

The BBC never went for it, but Hartnell would relate the story in a letter he wrote to a young fan years later. It's tempting to wonder if Hartnell's idea for a villainous son of Doctor Who inspired this film, but as far as I can tell, it's entirely coincidental.

Son of Doctor Who was the brainchild of two teenagers living near Newcastle, Peter Davis and Derek Browell, 47 years ago. Peter Davis recalls *"In 1970 I bought a Super8 movie camera and for the next five years made a series of home movies, mainly with Derek. We were influenced, in no particular order, by Gerry Anderson and his TV puppet series, TV sci fi particularly Doctor Who and Star Trek, James Bond movies and Stanley Kubrick and Ken Russell."*

After cutting their teeth and learning the craft on a variety of shorts, they decided to make an ambitious 'full length' production. By full length, we probably mean fifteen or twenty minutes or so. Short in one sense, but in another, the equivalent of a handful of Super 8 cartridges, or a full sized exhibition reel.

"We wrote the script, drew storyboards, acted in it with a cast of friends, relations, etc. … All the props were cobbled together, the robot suit was made from plastic ice cream tubs stuck together which fitted over Derek's little cousin. A spaceship model was filmed to look enormous using parallax vision effects." Peter remembers.

Derek Browell recalled *"We used members of a Church holiday and ourselves as the cast, and set the film at Patterdale Hall in the English Lake District. We edited it pinning the cuts to a broom shank with dress making pins and numbered labels."*

In the early 1970s, Super8 didn't yet have sound. So they recorded live piano music for a separate sound tape track.

"It was great fun and I learned so much about the art of moving visual images, framing camera angles, etc. and still have that interest today whilst watching movies. In another life, I would have liked to have been a film director. It was one of our longest movies," Davis recalled.

The film still exists; gathering dust in Derek's garage, but it's never been uploaded or digitized. It's likely though, that for all intents and purposes, it is or will be lost to the general public. We may never see it, and our only record are Peter's and Derek's recollections.

There's something endearing and precocious about *Son of Doctor Who*. It's really about these two enthusiastic kids, playing with the camera, making short movies about everything from Gerry Anderson puppets, to Bond, to Ken Russell, really just reflecting a wide variety of cultural influences. I suspect most 70s Super8 film makers were like this, taking their inspirations from everything in sight. If they happened to make a Doctor Who film, it was because it was part of the landscape.

There was an entire world of Super8 film makers like Derek and Peter, and mostly, it's lost to us. Perhaps that's not a great loss – most of it probably wasn't high art. But a lot of it was of value to the people making it, even home movies of family gatherings and birthday parties had a lot of emotional resonance. For the people that put the effort into making it, I can't help but believe that there was a lot of love and creativity there. Over the years, I've been lucky enough to see some of people's old Super8 work, stop motion films, or cartoons, or little dramas, and it has always been naively charming.

But the world moves on, when Camcorders came in, Super8 went out. It was so much more convenient. You didn't have to send film cartridges for processing; you just plugged the camera into your VCR or TV. Editing became a matter of pushing buttons on a pair of decks, rather than painstakingly cutting pieces of film. Watching it was just putting a tape in and pressing the button, rather than painstakingly setting up a screen, threading a film, adjusting focus. So a lot of Super8 just ended up sitting in closets or in garages, gathering dust and being forgotten. A vast amount has been simply lost, thrown away or forgotten about.

We've seen this with Camcorders as well, as new formats and new generations of technology have come along, a lot of the older stuff simply ends up falling by the wayside, whatever was on them, eventually lost.

Reviews: Seventies Super-8

A Grab Bag of Mostly Lost Films

PLANET OF THE SLEEPERS, THE DESTRUCTORS, THE THOSIAN STRATEGY (1975-1977, Mostly Super8, short films)These were a handful of short films produced in the London area by young fans.

Planet of the Sleepers, autumn, 1975 was Kevin Jon Davies abortive first effort at a Doctor Who film, on black and white reel to reel video.

"It was about some astronauts who land on an alien planet and discover humans in cryogenic sleep. The building (the school!) was patrolled by a Dalek for some reason. The Doctor, Sarah and Harry arrive and get embroiled in the action. There was a sequence where the Doctor leads the characters across a minefield. Elements of Ark In Space and Genesis of the Daleks - it was that golden era! The girl who played Sarah Jane eventually became my wife. Very little was filmed and we did not have the ability to edit properly, so it was never completed. I still have the reel we made. I should put it on YouTube one day."

"The main problem we faced in 1975," Davies recalls, *"was a lack of editing or post production facilities. Compare it to nowadays. Fans have a host of professional software at their disposal which makes me green with envy."*

The Thosian Strategy and *Destructors*, both shot on Super 8, were the work of Gavin French. Very little is known about them.

Paul Tams appeared as the Fourth Doctor in the *Thosian Strategy,* with a model Tardis supplied by Julian Vince. Vince also contributed props or effects work to the *Destructors,* creating the city rising from its underground base in long shot. Kevin Jon Davies also helped out on both films, and appeared in one of them.

Most of these films are lost now, but clips from several of them can be seen on the *'Before Wartime'* extra of Reeltime's *Wartime* DVD. Those extras can be found uploaded to Vimeo.

From the very little we see in the documentary, they're pretty rough. There's a lot of cardboard and duct tape in play. But there's a precociousness to them that's engaging. You can't help but smile when you're looking at a Tardis that only has one side, or is an obvious miniature, or a K9 that is clearly cardboard and tinfoil being dragged around on a visible string.

Julian Vince, a participant in many of these films, sums up the era best, *"It's important to remember that in the 1970s, new Doctor Who episodes were on television every week, but not expected to be repeated, or really ever seen again. Rather like a soap, you always moved forward in the Doctor's adventures with each new story. Video recorders were rare, and only now with DVDs can you travel back in time and revisit those television times that passed by so quickly, like a view from a bus window. But the fans wanted to relive the sense of fun and adventure that Doctor Who created each week on television. It was the next step up from playing with your trainset."*

"The only visual way to attempt that was with 8 mm home movies. Cameras and equipment were very expensive then, but someone at school usually had a Dad with a camera, so they became the way of getting your adventure captured on film! They were fun and exciting to do, but were hardly realistic, with school friends or neighbours being dragged in to play

characters, and monsters. It was not unusual to find 12 year-old UNIT soldiers, or Doctor Whos with beards in these films."

"A strong gust of wind could whisk away your cardboard box K9, or topple your one-sided Tardis! Daleks had to turn on the spot, as they couldn't handle moving along a footpath in your local park. You might only know who the Doctor was because he was six months older than everyone else around him!"

"The plots and stories were whatever you remembered from previous tv episodes, and wanted to copy, or could afford to make with your pocket money budget of £3.75. But they were fun to do, and allowed you to learn and grow in your next attempt, after you had bored, amazed, or been praised by your fan based audience of fellow Who-ies, in the starving years of early Timelord adventures."

&&&

THREAT OF THE LEVIATHANS (1976, 25 minutes, England, live action, Super8 film format)

STORY: The Time Lords snatch the Tardis out of the Time/Space vortex and tell the Doctor he must use his skills to destroy both the Daleks and the Master. These are trying to take over the Earth, using the RSS Leviathan, designed by the Doctor. Contacting the Daleks, the Master begins to call allies to his cause – the Ocupoids under Commander Stygron as well as Yttrium's race. Although the Thals try to interfere, the Master eventually appears to have humanity on the edge of defeat. Then in a corner of the Invasion HQ, the Doctor's Tardis materializes. The Doctor is able to save the Earth, though the Daleks and the Master get away. (Synopsis taken from Owen Tudor's fanzine, Beka 40, 1976)

PRODUCTION: An early Super8 film by Mark Sinclair. According to the review in Owen Tudor's fanzine, it seemed a bit seat of the pants *"The actors are mostly children though the* *leads are adults… The actors were having to read from scripts learnt only minutes before the shooting took place. "*

On the other hand, some care does seem to have gone into it. Tudor refers to *"…a wonderful piece of animation, showing the time/space vortex, a swirling mass of colour, where* planets oscillate *and change hue."*

A brief clip of Threat appears to show a rather amateurish homemade robot and an alien. In the clip, the cast is writhing around and falling, as they're zapped by a disintegrator ray. The disintegration ray was simply directly scratched onto the film, but it actually makes an effort at a special effect. Sinclair already owned a Dalek and a Police Box by this time, so they probably made appearances, boosting the production values.

It's not great art. The clip looks crude, if enthusiastic. Sinclair acknowledges that back then they didn't know to do much more than point the camera and press the button.

The organized fandom that would be the audience for fan films didn't really exist then. The national Doctor Who club was barely getting off the ground. The first Doctor Who convention was at least a year away. So typically, outside a small circle, there was no one to watch these, and no real fan venue for them.

Sinclair, however, reached out and began to show the new film to schools, community centres and youth clubs where it was a resounding success. This may have been the first time that a Doctor Who fan film attempted to find an audience beyond the immediate circle of film makers. People loved it, or at least appreciated it.

Back in the day, most places like that had a Super8 projector as part of their standard equipment, but mainly what were given to show were home movies from someone's vacation, educational or documentary subjects, or old cheap or public domain shorts. Pretty dire stuff.

Threat, even with its clunky production values, would have been a fresh new adventure about a current pop culture phenomenon. It would be absolutely different from the usual stale fare. People loved Doctor Who, especially younger people, so if you had a Doctor Who based product, you count on an enthusiastic reception.

Seriously, it would have gone over like gangbusters. That success inspired Sinclair towards Ocean in the Sky.

CAST & CREW*: Mark Sinclair, Nigel Woodley, Philip Collins, Julian Chapman, Andrew Shenton, Simon Dingemans.*

&&&

1977 - DOCTOR HOO (4 minutes, England, animated, 4th Doctor)

STORY: The Fourth Doctor is fixing the Tardis when he accidentally pokes a hole through the floor. The Tardis is propelled like a balloon with the air escaping, looping through space, knocking into a Sontaran ship and eventually crashing down on an unnamed planet, next to a Pyramid marked 'property of Mars.' Sutekh is spotted, and it turns out his throne is a toilet. The Doctor and Leela make their way to the Dalek disco, where a Zygon arm issues a ticket. Inside the Disco the Bay City Daleks play, and we see a dancing Robot, Sea Devil, Cyberman and even a dancing Davros, lifting up his skirt. Disgusted, the Doctor and Leela decide to leave by teleporting away in a red phone booth, but it vanishes leaving them behind.

REVIEW: It's all a bit juvenile, but it's short and moves fast, and that gives it a certain amount of cheeky charm. Roughly three or four minutes, without sound, it is the earliest known Doctor Who fan film generally available. You can find it on Youtube.

Shot on Super8 mm, without sound, by the students and Tottenham School, *Doctor Hoo* premiered at the world's first Doctor Who convention in Battersea, London, 1977.

Kevin Jon Davies, was the Director, and guiding force. He received five pounds to pay the processing fees, his first paid job. Davies would go on to be an essential figure in fandom and over the years produced a number of interesting fan films. Among these were a *Spitting Image* puppet style fan film *Auf Wiedersin Doc* about Colin Baker looking for work during the 18 month. Hiatus; The Few Doctors in which all the former Doctors are forced to leave their retirement home and compete with villains in a sort of sports tournament/reality show, a *Corridor Sketch*, and a mythmakers parody about *Barrington Black*, the unseen, forgotten Doctor.

He would would direct *Shakedown: Return of the Sontarans*, reviewed here, as well as two seminal Who documentaries: *Dalekmania* and Thirty Years in the Tardis, among many many projects. He's one of the fans who went pro, accumulating a long list of IMDB credits, including work on *Roger Rabbit*.

CREW*: Animators - Kevin Davies, Andrew Harlow, Steven Harlow, David Beasley, Mark Fuller. Artists - Kevin Davies, Steven Harlow, Andrew Harlow, Mark Fuller, Ning Lee. (Producer/Supporter – Keith Barnfather)*

Review: Ocean in the Sky (1979)

The Lost Fan Film Epic (Super8, live action, DWAS, British, 69 minutes)

STORY: The story opens with the fourth Doctor being pursued and killed by a Wirn. After regenerating into his next form, he acquires a new companion, Gina, a psychic alien.

Meanwhile, the Daleks have opened a 'blue hole', a wormhole in space, connecting our universe with that of the planet Ancholus, as part of a scheme to destroy both worlds. They enlist agents on both worlds, Layfe from Ancholus, and two high level Earth officials, Perdue and Regerski.

Back on earth, two 'out to pasture' scientists, Brigger and Green studying satellite telemetry, discover the blue hole - a black hole emitting blue light, but can't get the government to pay attention.

Meanwhile, two astronauts, Barry and Ardweiler, on a space mission, find themselves trapped by the gravity field of the blue hole. As they try and figure out what to do, the Tardis is also dragged into the field of the blue hole. Acting on Dalek's orders, Perdue and Regerski order the astronauts to destroy the Tardis with a bomb.

The bomb doesn't work, although the Tardis is shaken. One of the astronauts Barry, who planted the bomb, is hurtled through space. The scientists, witnesses the explosion, and one of them, Green, and hijacks a spaceship to rescue Barry.

Both the Tardis and Kaft 6 are drawn through the blue hole to the planet Ancholus. There, the Doctor and Gina meet the astronaut, Ardweiler. The Daleks, however, are active on Ancholus, and they enlist Layfe in a scheme to separate the Doctor from his Tardis, and send him Earth in Ardweiler's ship, where he can be captured.

Perdue and Regerski are then ordered by the Dalek Emperor to send a battleship, run by Commander Mueller, to destroy Kaft 6, and hopefully the Doctor and his friends. However, Kaft 6 is protected by a gravity beam from the blue hole, and the battleship, drained of power, ends up in orbit around Mars. The Doctor decides to go down to an abandoned Mars base to try to investigate the blue hole. Commander Mueller goes down to Mars after the Doctor, but the Doctor and Gina escape to earth using a teleport. Unfortunately, they're captured almost immediately by Regerski.

Green manages to rescue Barry, and they rejoin with Ardweiler. The two spaceships head for Earth. Green's ship is captured by Daleks, who interrogate and then kill him. Barry and Ardweiler make it to Earth, where they're imprisoned and thrown in with the Doctor and Gina.

The quartet escapes, and after a battle, Perdue and Regerski are killed. Barry and Ardweiler fly out to the blue hole, but they are killed by psychic attack of the Ancholi. The Ancholi begin a campaign to destroy the human race with a neutron beam through the blue hole. Once Earth is devastated, the Daleks reverse the beam to destroy the Ancholi.

The Doctor builds teleports to jump back to Mars, where they meet Commander Mueller and his lieutenant Stevens. The four of them jump through another teleport back to Ancholus, where they finally encounter the Daleks. The Doctor tricks two Daleks into destroying each other, and the four survivors reach the Tardis.

Mueller and Stevens hold Gina hostage, demanding to be taken back to the devastated Earth, where the Daleks are taking over. The Doctor tries to talk them out of it, but eventually relents, setting them free. Gina and the Doctor travel through the universe alone.

PRODUCTION: *Ocean in the Sky* was a near feature length, fan film produced between 1977 and 1979, through the Doctor Who Appreciation Society (DWAS).

Ocean was the brainchild of Mark Sinclair, a teenager whose parents were well off enough to own a fairly high end Super8 film camera.

Mark was a hard core fan from early on. The Dalek 63*88, a prop history site, mentions him: *"In the summer of 1974 one lucky fan, Marc Sinclair, who lived locally to Terry Nation, was given a treat when he was invited to tea with his family and Matron from his school at the Nation home in Lynsted. Although Nation was away on business, Marc recalls having tea with his wife Kate and meeting Dalek AARUII 12-9 and Dalek AARUII 9-11. Both were kept in an outhouse in a walled off part of the garden and both were starting to look well worn. Marc was able to play with the Daleks all afternoon and remembers the lights on Dalek AARUII 12-9 were still working. "*

Sometime in 1974, Sinclair managed to get his hands on a police box shell, when Elstree-EMI Studios was downsizing.

This was an actual movie/television prop, originally built in 1965, for a police show called *Gideon's Way*. The Elstree prop wasn't actually from Doctor Who, but it became a fixture at Doctor Who conventions, public events and even appeared in a parade float with Peter Davison. It eventually ended up in a little shop in England, where it's labeled, falsely, as being from the Peter Cushing movie.

Sinclair, sometime around 1974-75, also acquired a Dalek. According to Kevin Jon Davies, this particular Dalek was actually semi-famous. Back in 1973, the *Radio Times Magazine* published plans to build your own Dalek. As proof of concept, they gave the plans to a group of high school students at Highbury Grove School – so this was the world's first homemade Dalek. That was just the start, everyone started building their own, and nowadays there are enough homemade Daleks in England to legally qualify as an ethnic minority. That original Dalek, eventually named 'Fred,' was painted a couple of times, made frequent appearances, but was eventually stolen after participating in a parade in 1981.

With a Dalek and a Police Box, Sinclair first experimented with amateur stage plays. Then in 1976, Sinclair, with the assistance of his best friend, Nigel Woodley, made their first fan film - *Threat of the Leviathans*. It was a success. Sinclair got ambitious. Ambition doesn't necessarily get you anywhere, but things were lining up.

In May, 1976, the Doctor Who Appreciation Society had formed. It was the first national, even international, Doctor Who fan club, and one with strong ties to the BBC. Suddenly, overnight, its membership burgeoned to a thousand, all over England, as far away as Canada and Australia. It had newsletters; it brought fans together, inspired conventions and created a community. What this meant for Mark Sinclair, was that suddenly, he wasn't some kid on his own; he had access to a community, to an audience.

Mark Sinclair talked his way into being the head of DWAS Drama Department, quite possibly a position created for him because he had a camera and wanted to make a film. Apart from lending their name, and occasionally mentioning it in their newsletter, DWAS doesn't actually seem to have had much to do with the production. But DWAS was the forum that allowed Sinclair to recruit fans willing to participate, willing to donate props, work on sets, etc.

Owen Tudor and Paul Howden-Simpson, had written or would write an epic three hour, nine episode script, that eventually got cut down to *Ocean in the Sky*. It would evolve a bit - the original version featured an android and was written for the 4th Doctor and Leela with not a single Dalek in sight. Sinclair embraced it.

From there, recruited his friend Nigel Woodley, and Nigel's sister, Diane Woodley to act in it, and engaged a few other friends and fans.

Leo Adams was recruited to play the 5th Doctor, years before Peter Davison came along. Apparently, he was the second choice. Adams, 69 year old at the time, was veteran actor and member of the Manchester Theatre Repertory company. According to a contemporary article, he had appeared in films with Robert Mitchum, James Cagney and Richard Harris. If true, it was probably small roles, since he doesn't appear on the Internet Movie Database. Adams would live to the ripe old age of 92. But in the late 1970s he was spry and active, with the charisma to carry off the central role of the Doctor.

Arrayed against the Doctor were not one, but a small army of Daleks - no less than four separate Daleks would appear in the film.

We've already heard of Fred the Black Dalek. There was also a prominent Red Dalek, nicknamed George, was built by Eddie Thomas. Originally blue, it was painted for the production to contrast with Fred.

There was a third blue Dalek, visibly different from Fred and George, of unknown provenance, which appears for an interrogation scene.

The final Dalek was the Emperor, a golden monster, with a great imposing Dome for a head. Again, this was another unknown build, but there are photographs elsewhere of it at conventions with Jon Pertwee.

Emperor and Supreme Daleks had been seen in the television series. But the golden Emperor took its inspiration from the comic strips. Back in the 1970s, there were no VCR's, no freeze frames, the only reference guides were scattered photographs from books and magazines... and the comic strips. Doctor Who comics had evolved its own version of an Emperor Dalek, in the form of a Dalek Chassis with a huge globe for an upper half, representing a super-sized Dalek brain. So this is what they used. Interestingly, the 'big dome' version would eventually be used by the television show a decade later in Remembrance of the Daleks.

This was how it was happening. Sinclair was the driving force, but he was part of this community, where other people had their own home-built Daleks and were willing to a loan them to the production, people who just wanted to build things or have these things, which were then available to be part of the film.

A Wirn prop, the insect-like race from the *Ark In Space*, was used for early scenes. Again, no idea who built it, and it's only used briefly, but it's cool.

Another monster was Layfe, the Ancholi, which was a really effectively ghoulish costume, sort of a cross between a catfish and a ghost, worn by Mark Sinclair.

Locations included a Canterbury university computer science lab, Canterbury university exterior grounds, a garden, a picturesque industrial ruin, and a hospital corridor which doubled for part of a Mars base.

It also included Mark Sinclair's family garage, and a lot of scenes were shot in and around that, notably the spaceship cockpit, with bucket seats stolen from Sinclair's mother's car. Other sets, a Mars base laboratory, were somewhat thrown together, Ed Wood style.

The crown jewel of the production was a Tardis Interior complete with console built by Reg Spillett for three hundred pounds. In modern rates, that's somewhere between $1800 and $2500 dollars. This was an amazing set, large enough for the actors to move around in freely, to shoot from multiple angles. It had working doors on either side of the set, flashing light panels in the background, an authentic console, and the rotor even lit up.

Kevin Jon Davies another fan had just premiered an animated short - *Doctor Hoo*, at Panopticon in 1977. Sinclair recruited him, and Davies brought some like-minded friends in. Davies went on to build miniature sets as well as construct five separate spaceship models, and show them taking off, landing, docking and flying through space, itself a remarkable achievement, and complementing Spillet's Tardis interior. This was literally an entire fleet.

He and his friends, Jon Saville, David Beasley and Peter Cox, rigged an explosion with two model Daleks, and did an animation dissolving from Leo Adams face to the title, and built their own Dalek voice modulator. They brought a level of ambition here that you didn't see in some professional movies.

In this they were helped by BBC special effects technicians who dropped by to offer pointers. In fact, BBC staff even loaned them a miniature Tardis from the series, seen in productions like Horror of Fang Rock. That's just cool!

Davies would go on to be a professional film maker as we've already noted.

Mark Ayres was another contributor who would go pro. Studying music at Cambridge University, he ended up doing original music using an 18 channel mixer, and a 'twenty piece orchestral, this in a time when many films used existing tracks. Ayres would go on to compose for Sylvester McCoy serials in the 1980s, and work steadily in the industry.

Even with Ayre's participation, sound was a massive challenge. Super 8 cameras came equipped with sound, and some cameras even had plug ins for external microphones. But the sound wasn't very good, and the sound strip was six frames removed from the film image, so that made editing a tricky proposition. Editing, whether film or sound, was a manual effort, and determining where to begin or end or how to cut a scene was almost a stab in the dark.

The sheer scope of the production was astonishing. Super8 film came in cartridges of about two and a half minutes. Simply filming one cartridge after another in continuous takes would take up almost thirty cartridges. But add in complex editing of shots, effects shots, etc., the real total must have been anywhere from sixty to a hundred cartridges. Each cartridge had to go to the photo-lab and be developed separately. They shot so much that one camera actually wore out, and Sinclair had to buy another. Sinclair was mainly funding it out of his own pocket, and often they could only afford one take.

Not everything went smoothly. Leo would forget his lines, and try and cover with annoying whimsy. Wrangling people was a permanent challenge. According to Owen Tudors' fanzine, some 400 feet of footage was lost. I'm not sure it was ever recovered, or if not, how that loss was compensated. It feels like there's gaps in the finished product.

There's some indication that Sinclair could be a bit tumultuous. There's a section of the DWAS newsletter that wryly notes of the Drama Department that Mark himself was the source of some of the Drama.

I tend to be forgiving though. Fans have never had a shortage of drama. The reality is that many far less ambitious fan films, art house productions, and even professional productions have fallen by the wayside as less driven or committed people wandered off or found more interesting things to do. Even a modest production can demand an astounding amount of work. This production was extraordinary on every level, from sheer length, to the complexity and demands of the story, to the production values and challenges, and stretched across two years, from September, 1977 to August, 1979.

This is an amazing level of commitment, and somehow, Sinclair and his friends persevered across two years and got it done, entirely as a volunteer project, with barely any resources beyond Mark's own pocket. Difficulties and frustration are inevitable, but they got it done. And that was truly remarkable.

A Pirate's History, Page 109

Even the BBC was supportive. DWAS was a BBC sponsored club, so they knew what was going on, including this film. Their effects technicians gave advice and loaned props.

They seem to have given express permission to exhibit it within DWAS activities and conventions. A newspaper article from the time indicates that the movie would be offered to Children's homes, schools and hospitals to raise money for charity, implicitly with BBC approval. So oddly, it was almost semi-official.

This was well before Fan Films were even recognized as a genre. I suspect that the BBC simply didn't know what to make of it. It wasn't for television, it wasn't for theatrical release, so.... what was it for? They couldn't get their heads around it. So they just went 'where's the harm?' and said 'Ok.'

Finally, after two years of practically herculean struggle and effort, *Ocean in the Sky* was finally premiered for the first time, on Saturday, September 18, 1979, at Panopticon Convention, in London, England.

And never shown again.

REVIEW: For forty years, it's been a lost film, all but unknown, occasionally whispered about, a kind of hidden legend, in a series with its own great mythos of lost works. In its way, it's almost like the lost Hartwell and Troughton serials, this film and the story of this film are like some fabulous epic, known only from fragments.

The audience on that night was not kind.

Reports in DWAS publications mentioned 'mixed reviews.' The closest we have to an independent assessment is from Bruce Barnes, an Australian fan who attended Panopticon. *"Another production in 8mm was Ocean in the Sky. We were told at*

Julian Vince and Paul Tams were openly disparaging, their own rival film, the *Image Makers*, unfinished and without a sound track, got a standing ovation.

Marc Sinclair in the Wartime DVD extra refers to it as being known as *'Puddles on the Ceiling.'*

Kevin Davies remembers Sinclair promising a restless audience that there was only one reel left to go. I can imagine him, sweat pooling down the base of his spine, his face permanently blushing, watching his child sink like a stone on its first outing, wanting it to be over, wanting to be elsewhere and having to stick it out through the whole thing. To work so hard, and to fail so completely? It must have been excruciating.

Since then, recollections of *Ocean in the Sky* have usually been embarrassing. Usually it's referred to as being of minor historical significance, but not very good.

Was it actually that bad?

No. Not even close. It's not brilliant, the script gets away from the film, there's cinematic gaps in its visual language. The whole is less than the sum of its parts, I think. You can see there's more enthusiasm than skill. And perhaps, in the end, more bloody minded determination to just finish the thing and be done with it, than enthusiasm.

But it is still something genuinely remarkable.

But before I get into that, let me talk a little about why it flopped that night.

First, the conditions weren't optimum. In fact, they were pretty harsh. Super 8 came in 20 to 25 minute reels. For a seventy minute film that meant you had at least three reels. Now unless you had two Super8 projectors lined up, ready to go alternately, what that meant was that at the end of the reel you'd have to turn on the lights, take the old reel off, put it away, put the new reel onto the projector, thread it through, turn off the lights and run it. That's a ten minute exercise, you're going to do it at least twice through the movie, and that's going to kill the momentum of your film stone dead.

The projector was right in the room, so it would be its own noise source, making a racket. The image would be grainy, shown on a medium sized screen. It would probably be shown in a conference room, with people sitting on uncomfortable hotel chairs, in a venue not really meant to comfortably watch a feature length film. As a viewing experience, it would be pretty harsh in just about every respect.

And there was another problem. Leo Adams wasn't Tom Baker. This was premiering in Baker's penultimate year, arguably around the height of his popularity. Baker had been the Doctor for six years, an unheard of duration. He was the epitome of the Doctor. Even the BBC weren't sure that the show had a future without him, so closely entwined he'd become with the role. That was damned near insurmountable.

And there was more - it didn't look like Doctor Who - the television Doctor, the screen image, the image quality, were all dramatically different from the stark, saturated grainy look of Super 8. It didn't sound like Doctor Who; the music wasn't like the show at all. It didn't feel right.

In a sense, it had landed right in the middle of Uncanny Valley - that creepy feeling you get when you see a face that's almost human, but not quite human enough. Ocean in the Sky was like that, it had all the elements - the Doctor, the Companion, Daleks, the Tardis, Spaceships etc., but it wasn't quite right. It was simultaneously too close and not enough. Too polished for an amateur film, and too rough for a pro film.

The audience just didn't know what to do with it.

In 1979 there was no real tradition of fan films, there was no culture for them. That culture, that appreciation of fan films, the network and the fan audience hadn't evolved yet. It wouldn't evolve, the traditions, the tolerance, the acceptance and interest wouldn't really gel until the mid-80s and 90s when suddenly it exploded.

In this sense, I think it was genuinely ahead of its time, and given its ambition and production values, had it found its way back into fandom in the mid-80s it would have been more readily embraced, perhaps even a cult item, at least for that period.

But in 1979, it's shown to a community that barely knows and doesn't accept anyone but Tom Baker, it's in a difficult venue with lengthy interruptions, and it's just too unusual. So, there you go.

It does have deeper problems, some of which hamstrung it then and drag it down now, and we'll discuss those as we go along. But let's take a second, deeper look.

For me, it's been a great white whale, and after a couple of years of knocking on heads, I was lucky enough to finally be shown a copy for review, and was able to watch it a few times. Knowing how obscure it is, I've made a point of posting a fairly detailed synopsis, elsewhere, my story segments are usually teasers to encourage the reader to find it themselves. Normally, almost every fan film can be found if you search hard enough. But this one's been essentially lost for forty years, and it may never be widely available.

The first time through, I liked it, it was visually impressive, but seemed aimless and running out of energy. The second time, I didn't really like it, but I understood it a lot more and could see what it was about and where it went wrong, not quite the sum of its parts, continually reaching beyond its grasp. Third time... brilliant and badly flawed, continually struggling struggles against its limitations. In the end, I can't help liking it, even acknowledging its flaws.

There is a lot that is simply extraordinarily well done.

Leo Adams is a charming and distinctive presence as the Doctor. He doesn't have Tom Baker's instant charisma, but then he's not trying to be Tom Baker, or any previous Doctor. He still manages to bring that distinctive 'Doctor' quality to the role, he's almost like the Cushing Doctor in his innate gentleness, but with a whimsical streak reminiscent of Troughton.

Diane Woodley, playing his companion Gina, is a good match, at times flighty, they share a playfulness. They work well together. Woodley's acting is sometimes a little stiff, but she comes off well. They're easy to watch.

Green and Brigger, two older scientists, also play off each other well. Other performances are at least tolerable.

In terms of production values, there's some amazing stuff. Reg Spillett's Tardis control room is brilliant, a huge set large enough to shoot from multiple angles, with flashing background lights and a convincing console. When I showed this to a friend, he initially thought the BBC had allowed Ocean to film on the actual Tardis set.

The shots of the garden, of the industrial ruin, of the abandoned Mars-base corridor, are each standout location shots, beautiful and effective. There's a profusion of sets and locations.

Kevin Davies and his friends effects work is also a highlight. Davies has literally built a space fleet, five ships, each one radically different from the others, and he does a lot with them. It's nowhere as kinetic as Star Wars. But it mostly looks good. The shots of the space battleship orbiting stationary above a rotating Mars are wonderful.

Also they had four Daleks! Four! Including an Emperor! That's a veritable Dalek army! For the original television Daleks, they only made four, and didn't make an Emperor.

Sadly, the Emperor doesn't do much. Mostly, it operates as an exposition machine in cutaways, as it and the black Dalek explain the Dalek's plot or fill in bits of the script that they weren't able to shoot, or that went astray. That's not necessarily a bad thing, but there's a sense of missed opportunity - build something like that and you sort of want to see a little more done with it. You want it to be shot with a little more grandeur.

In fact, you want to see more done with the Daleks period. They're not really central to the action, apart from exposition to each other; the Daleks are operating behind the scenes as puppet masters. It would have been nice to see them interact more with the characters, particularly the Doctor.

There's also Ancholi alien, played by Mark Sinclair. It's a good costume, genuinely creepy and unhuman, if rather cheap. But his interactions with the cast are limited, mostly confined to showing up, doing some weird body language straight out of the Web Planet, and portentous speeches done with a nasal drawl. The character moves the plot along, but doesn't really participate in it much, if that makes sense.

Early on, we see a Wirn, an ant-like creature from Tom Baker's '*The Ark in Space*'. It's just a quick shot of the prop.

On top of all that, we get a multitude of sets and locations depicting scenes on Earth, Ancholus, and inside spaceship. Not all of the location or set work is brilliant. Shots of woods and grassy fields... ho hum. And given that Sinclair owns a police box, we see very little of it. There are spaceship cockpits or Mars base radio rooms that are basically thrown together. It's not great, but it's not distractingly awful. There's sort of charm to it. It reminds me of the aeroplane cockpit in Plan 9 From Outer Space, it's just a couple of folding chairs and doodads with the actors pretending. There's some tosh stuff, but mostly, it doesn't drag things down. Maybe with a fan film, or a low budget film, we're willing to let more stuff go by. Give them credit, they really pack it in.

The camera is mostly stationary, but there is effort at art. We see pans or zooms, complex scenes edited together, deliberate sound bleeds, transitions and establishing shots. There's an effort to use cinematic technique, even hampered by the limits of Super8, and overall lack of experience.

There's also a certain amount of pedestrian stuff. Sometimes its inexperience and learning. Other times, you can tell they had seventy pages of script and were just trying to get a page done. Not having the option of multiple takes hamstrings you. Lack of money, exhaustion, it drags you. But there's not a lot that's explicitly terrible that we can't forgive, and in a mixed bag, I think that the good elevates the whole, rather than the dull dragging it down. At most, we just let the pedestrian pass through unregarded.

There's no shortage of glitches. I count at least three times when a boom mike operator or other crewperson is glimpsed at the edge of a frame. There are shots that you want to linger. There are shots that drag on. There's edits that are abrupt, scenes that begin or cut off in mid-sentence. Mismatches of focus or colour balance. There's a lot of this stuff, and technically, it's almost inevitable with the format.

Super 8 was meant for long take, single reel, family birthday parties and suchlike. It was never meant for anything this ambitious. The cameras were made to be crude and durable, rather than precise and delicate. The lab was the chemist down the street. The film and sound tracks were six frames out of synch. Editing was done by eyeballing and guesswork. Through it all, they've got one take, and they're working with no money and no time, trying to get it done. So it is what it is.

They were literally fighting beyond the physical limitations of the technology. They did their best, and quite often, they did very well, or at least passably well, and sometimes it glitches. You get past it, and maybe have an affectionate laugh when you spot the boom mike operator at the edge of the frame.

Technically, the biggest weakness is sound. That's always the biggest weakness, and it's the hardest to get right, particularly with the technology to hand.

Robert Rodriguez, the Mexican film maker, is famous for launching his career with *El Mariachi*, a gangster movie shot on video for Five thousand dollars. What gets left out of that rags to riches, is that when a major studio bought the movie, they spent a quarter million redoing the sound. J.R. Bookwalter in the 1990s made a zombie epic on Super8 for peanuts, and then Sam Raimi came along and invested over a hundred thousand dollars on a sound mix. It's the big overlooked part of amateur film, and it's almost always crucial. Mistakes there always get noticed. Paul Tam's fan film, *The Image Makers*, may have actually done better as a silent film with no audio track.

In this case, even more so, since so much of the story rests on and relies on the dialogue. Having characters often barely legible, or outright illegible, really undermines a story that turns on nuances of dialogue it makes it difficult, if not tiresome for the audience to follow. You almost want subtitles.

Then there's the musical score. I'll credit Mark Ayres with this; he clearly put a lot of work into it. There are a number of different instruments in use, there's a clear effort to match the music with the visual action. But it's almost too much, the use of different instruments keeps it from having any unified feel, it just keeps changing. Sometimes it's not bad. There were moments where it almost felt like silent film music, and other moments when it was reminded of the poverty row productions of the 50s and 60s, both of these were kind of cool. But then it shifts again, and you're listening to something else, that's distracting. Sometimes it doesn't balance off well against the dialogue.

Still, going by Rodriguez or Bookwalter, all they needed to fix this was a rich patron to throw in fifty thousand pounds. Short of that, they did the best they could, and you learn to take it or leave it.

The musical score doesn't sound like Doctor Who though, and that hurts it. I'm sure that put fans off back in 1979. Doctor Who is show that often relies on very distinctive musical cues. A lot of fan films borrow those cues and can end up feeling very much like the original show. Carving your own musical path? The risk is that you're in uncanny valley; it can look like Doctor Who, but just won't feel like it. I think audiences are broader now, more accepting.

Overall, the story hangs together. It's a complicated story, weaving in and out of a half dozen pairs of characters, producing a huge number of scenes. The story is conveyed through dialogue and encounters between characters, and it packs a lot in, with a 'blink and you'll miss it' quality. Despite that, it all fits together neatly. The handicap is that it can be difficult, even exhausting to try and follow the story, given the difficulties with the sound. I can see why people, crowded into a viewing room, on uncomfortable chairs, with long intermissions, got annoyed with it for that reason, and they had a point. If this is ever made publicly available, then I have one word: Subtitles.

But the story, although it hangs together, is also the central the weakness, the core flaw.

As ambitious as this project is, the story they've chosen is even more ambitious, almost impossibly so: A Dalek conspiracy to foment interstellar war, an attempt to chronicle the destruction of two whole planets; a space-walk to plant a bomb on the Tardis; a daring rescue of a marooned astronaut in outer space; the fall of the human race to an Ancholi neutron beam assault; a group of Daleks furious assault on the Tardis on Ancholus....

The trouble is that none of these things are actually depicted. It's only referred to and talked about rather than shown. The characters watch it and just tell each other, and by extension, tell the audience about it. The Daleks are particularly bad for being exposition machines.

But there's the problem - it's all but impossible to show these things. A super-Dalek plot to engineer the destruction of two worlds? The ambitions of the script, the epic scale utterly outstrips the production. Frankly, it would have outstripped Tom Baker's era. Graham Williams, Doctor Who's producer back then, would have taken one look, shaken his head and walked away. Even with the extraordinary production elements, the script is just too big, the spectacle is too big and it's impossible to convey visually.

The result is that the drama gets attenuated. Key plot points, key events aren't shown, they can't be, but instead, are related in exposition by Daleks shrieking at each other. It's a cheat, and it undercuts the story, but it's an honest cheat. There just isn't the time or the ability to show these things, you have to convey the information some way.

This is also really dark story, pretty much the entire cast, good guys and bad guys, are killed off steadily through the narrative.

We saw this now and then in the show - *The Horror of Fang Rock,* for instance, has no survivors except the Doctor and Leela. But this is bleaker, the end, the Daleks have succeeded in their scheme, the Ancholi are wiped out, Earth is devastated, and there's a reference to Robomen which suggest that this is the beginning of the era of the *Dalek Invasion of Earth*. But afterwards, you're thinking, "Wow, downer."

Another problem is that overall, the Doctor doesn't seem to be all that effective, he doesn't actually do much, or succeed in doing much - despite travels to the blue hole, and then between Ancholus, Mars and Earth he has little impact on the narrative. He spends most of the story being led astray by an Ancholi who is actually a Dalek agent. He doesn't even realize the Daleks are involved and manipulating events until the very end. The Doctor does succeed in destroying a couple of

Daleks on Ancholus, but the Dalek Emperor isn't particularly disturbed by the loss, focusing instead on a devastated Earth, clearly a lead in to the Hartnell serial, Dalek Invasion Earth. The Doctor regains his Tardis and escapes.

But this makes the Doctor almost a bystander in his own story. This sort of passive bystander quality would start to show up in stories in the 1980s, with Davison and Colin Baker, but again, it's a little jarring. We tend to expect more from the Doctor, more action, that he's more engaged in the story and moving events.

In a sense, it's almost less of a Doctor story than a Dalek story. They're the manipulators driving events. The entire story amounts to a Dalek victory lap. In hindsight, it's disturbingly grim.

But having said that, it doesn't necessarily make it bad. It's not what we're used to and not what we've come to expect. It may be off putting, but it's not necessarily illegitimate. Bleak stories where everyone dies and the hero is clueless and ineffectual? Sometimes that's just literature. Hell, that describes 80% of Canadian literature. It's a staple of literary fiction.

So what does it all come down to? I feel that in trying to evaluate it, I've been diffident, Wandering back and forth between the good and the bad, I might seem to be lukewarm. But I don't think I am, really.

I can see why it failed on that night in 1979, I can't argue with that. I can't avoid the flaws and the missteps, sometimes that's inexperience, and sometimes exhaustion and simple limitations, and sometimes it's simply working far past what the technology was meant to do. It is inherently imperfect, and the imperfections are written across it everywhere.

A Pirate's History, Page 121

It's also utterly brilliant, for every bland shot of grass, there's an elegantly cut scene. For each flaw, there's something extraordinary. There is so much that is done so well, and so much else that's basically acceptable. It doesn't quite add up, it doesn't come together. But watching it, going through it carefully, I think its flaws can be forgiven.

This is equivalent to a three episode serial. In the 1970s, a bunch of fans actually made a Doctor Who movie. The professionals had been trying and failing to make a Doctor Who movie for forty years. But Sinclair and company pulled it off. That's amazing. It was ahead of its own technology, it was ahead of its own culture. It would be a decade and the 80s before fan films reached a similar level of ambition, and perhaps another decade into the 90s before productions like Millennium Trap, Phase Four or Resurrection of Evil actually pulled it off.

It's huge and heartbreaking on so many levels. Both the film, Ocean in the Sky, and the story of its production, march in tandem. On every level it's great tragic epic.

CAST: *THE DOCTOR (Leo Adams); GINA (Diane Woodley); GREEN (John Smith); BRIGGER (Peter Rae); BARRY (Mark Sinclair); ARDWEILER (Nigel Woodley); MUELLER (Reg Spillet); STEVENS (Pat Spillet); ANPE (Elizabeth Kelly); REGERSKI (Pat Wilkinson); PERDUE (Geof Bailey); LAYFE (Mark Sinclair); EMPEROR DALEK (Adrian Tute); RED DALEK (Edward Thomas); DALEK VOICES (David Beasley, Peter Cox, Kevin Davies); VOICE OF EARTHBASE - (Julian Chapman)*

CREW: *Mark Sinclair (Producer, Director, Stills Cameraman, Set Dresser, Special Costumes, Sound Mixer); Owen Tudor (credited) and Paul Howden-Simpson (uncredited) (Writer); Tom Marshall (Story Editor, Director); Nick Kelly, Leo Adams (Directors); Kevin Davies*

(Art Director, Director of Photography, Special Visual Effects, Models, Effects, Animation, Artwork; Mark Ayres (Music and Sound); Elizabeth Kelly (Wardrobe Mistress, Special Costumes, Assistant Director, Continuity); Jon Saville (2nd Unit Art Director, Special Visual Effects); Peter Cox (Special Visual Effects, Special Props); David Beasley (Special Visual Effects, Lighting Cameraman, Dalek Voice modulator); Peter Bentley (Hair Stylist); Reg Spillett, Pat Spillett (Tardis Console Room); Eddie Thomas (Red Dalek); Highbury Grove School Students - (Black Dalek), Doctor Who Appreciation Society (Producer); British Broadcasting Corporation (prop).

A Pirate's History, Page 124

Review: The Image Makers (1979)

A Silent Adventure, 25 minutes, live action, Super8 film, British)

STORY: The Doctor and K9 meet a new companion, Sheena, a futuristic policewoman. Arriving on a strange planet an alien, attacks the Doctor using a series of familiar past enemies, including a Cyberman, an Auton and an Exillon (a creature from Death to the Daleks), against him using a mind ray to project them from his memory. The Doctor deactivates the memory sucking device from the Aliens' ship and turns it against the creature summing up the creatures own worst nightmares causing him to crash his ship.

PRODUCTION: Shot in colour and on Super8 film, the *Image Makers* played only once, at Panopticon, on Saturday, August 18, 1979, before an audience of Doctor Who fans, where it received a standing ovation. The twenty-five minute film was incomplete at that time - the sound track wasn't finished. Following the single exhibition, the film was shelved and the sound track never completed.

This was the same convention where *Ocean in the Sky* encountered a harsh reception. It's interesting to examine why one failed and the other succeeded.

Overall *The Image Maker*s seems to have been a faster paced, more straightforward and more lively film than *Ocean* which instead opted for a complex story with multiple viewpoints. Instead *Image* seems to have been a much simply and more straightforward story. Given the limitations of Super 8, this was the better choice.

Ocean was a long three reel production, and the length alone, together with ten minute reel changes would have made it tough. Image was a shorter story, under half an hour, on a single reel so less likely to wear out its welcome.

Finally, not having a sound track probably helped – sound is hellishly difficult to get right, and if the narrative was simple enough to be understood visually, it would have worked much better as silent than with a distractingly flawed track of illegible dialogue and erratic music.

From what we can tell of the surviving clips, it seems to have been a lively production. Julian Vince plays a Cyberman, and you can tell it's a skinny teenage version of a Cyberman. But this is a fast dangerous Cyberman, he sprints, and it gives the performance life. Overall, the production, as long as a regular episode, seemed to have a fast kinetic feel. Vince also supplied the Auton costume. Another artist, Sue Moore, created masks for the Exillon and Alien. Between Vince and Moore, perfectionists both, they gave the film unusually impressive production values.

Pat Thomas, who played Sheena, would be the first ever black companion, something the BBC show would not manage for twenty years. She was an American Army Lieutenant attached to the US Embassy at the time, and had been a member of the *Blake's 7* fan club. David Howe played the Exillon, while Owen Parker rounded out the cast as the Alien.

Paul Tams played a lanky, teenage, but rather engaging
version of the third Doctor, and also produced and directed.
He had previously played a version of the Fourth Doctor in
The Thosian Strategy. It was Tams, who funded most of the
costs out of his own pocket,

Vince recalled, *"…with a few pounds budget, we kept it local to where
we all lived, which was London. So there was filming on Wimbledon
Common, in parks, at Earls Court, and on The South Bank, by the
Thames at Waterloo. My accurate (metallic green) K9 was used there,
and I was dressed in my Cyberman costume, being zapped by my own
dog! We filmed usually when we were all available at a weekend. I recall
that Owen Parker, was dressed up in a latex mask as the alien at the
heart of the adventure, controlling things. My model Police Box, K9,
Cyberman and Auton costumes were all used for the filming."*

It is recorded in travel diary of Bruce Barnes, an Australian
fan who attended a Doctor Who convention, Panopticon 3,
in England: *"There was another 8mm Doctor Who film (apart from
Oceans) called The Image Makers. It looked better than the other
production, but I can't make much more comment due to the fact that the
sound track was not yet complete and so was not presented at all. Pretty
pictures though. Paul Tams – producer of The Image Makers –
displayed the actual K9 model built for his film."*

The Image Makers, along with *Ocean in the Sky* represented the
pinnacle of the fan film movement around DWAS in London
in the late 1970s. They were both extraordinarily ambitious
films, aspiring to professional levels – real stories, with real
plots, performances, costumes, props and effects. They
represented what was almost certainly an extraordinary effort.

Many of the people involved, would go on to professional
careers in the entertainment industry. But DWAS, and the
London fan community, seems to have lost interest in fan
films after this.

A Pirate's History, Page 127

And why should they? There wasn't really a need or a niche for them at this time. The real thing was appearing regularly, right there on television, more regularly, with all around superiority in visual quality, production value and talent. That was the standard that *Ocean* and *Image* were compared to, and it was an impossible standard to meet.

Because they were working in Super8, not video, it seems that they had little influence and provided little or no inspiration to the later fan film groups that emerged in the 80s and 90s, taking advantage of new technology and an evolving fan culture and network.

The Image Makers still exists, possibly. Paul Tams has a copy on VHS, although he notes that he hasn't watched it in over thirty years. Clips from the Image Makers also appear on the Wartime DVD extras, and on the K9 Unleashed documentary.

Paul Tams would go on to be an industry professional. One of his most notable productions was the Doctor Who spin off series of *K-9* produced in Australia.

CAST. Paul Tams as The Doctor; Julian Vince as a Cyberman; Owen Parker as the Alien, Pat Thomas as futuristic policewoman/companion Sheena, and David Howe as an Exillon alien.

CREW: Paul Tams & Julian Vince/ Stephen Payne (south bank sections) – Directors. Paul Tams – Producer. Production: Shot in London, Wimbledon Common, in parks, at Earls Court, and on The South Bank, by the Thames at Waterloo. Julian Vince's K9, model ,Police Box in space and used at South Bank borrowed from Mat Irvine, 1/4 size Police Box used in Wimbledon Common scenes made by

Paul Tams, Cyberman & Auton. Ray gun effects. Running
time 25 minutes

Review: Mission of Doom (1979-1985)

Daleks versus Mechons

STORY: An attempt is made to assassinate the Earth President by the Korvens, a race of giant frog like creatures. This murderous act forces Earth to declare war against Korva. However, the Doctor, and his companion, Amber, who are attending the conference, are abducted and forced to flee in TARDIS at the hands of the alien assassin. Landing a short time in the future on the planet Tao V, the Doctor, Amber and Korven discover that they are not alone. They soon encounter the crew of a crashed earth Warship, the Vanguard, together with their spherical robot servants, the Mechons, and a series of mine workings belonging to the Doctor's most malignant of metal monsters, the Daleks! Once again, the Daleks were going to hollow out the Planet's Core and use the Planet as an organic "Death Star type base for their galactic conquest, (after failing to do it with Earth)! Can the impending war between Earth and Korva be averted? Will the Doctor finally be discovered by his arch enemies and EXTERMINATED? "

REVIEW: Claimed by some to be the 'the best amateur Doctor Who film of all time.' High praise given that it was never finished, scenes from the movie and an interview with creator Julian Vince were featured in *Dalekmania*, a documentary about the Peter Cushing movies. There's also four minutes of scenes available on Myspace and YouTube, as well as still photographs and articles online.

"After a few years away from fandom," Paul Tams recalls, *"I was approached by Julian after he had made several 24 inch tall Dalek Puppets in the style of the Peter Cushing films. They looked superb and were a testimony to his skill as a prop maker. He wanted to do a semi-pro film in the style of the Cushing films. This would have served as a great portfolio for him to find work after leaving College. I considered it and thought, 'go on why not!' Especially as everything was going to be screen accurate. I wrote the script and bought the full size Tardis console and space ship model from a model maker called Malcolm Gibb who was renowned for his accurate Gerry Anderson scale model making. I also had costumes made by a friend who was a professional. We did a display of the Tardis interior and some photo blow ups of cast etc at a convention in the early 1980s and it caused quite a stir, Colin Baker posed with the console and JNT asked me where the costume I was wearing for the film had come from. When he discovered I designed it and had it made he asked me to work on his annual Pantomimes from that point on a freelance basis."*

Paul Tams, from photographs for the production, now a bit grown up and looking like a young David Bowie, would have starred as a rather garishly dressed Doctor. It would have been his third appearance as the Doctor, although he seemed to play a different Doctor each time.

"There were no live action scenes shot," Tams recalled. *"We had a cast ready at one point, all of who were semi-pro and looked great! It would have looked like the TV 21 Dalek Strips come to life! We did a couple of script run-throughs that's all. The Earth president was female and going to be played by an actress who was one of Mari Wilson's*

A Pirate's History, Page 133

Wilsations backing singers. I forget her name. The Spaceship Captain was going to be played by my friend Lionel Robinson who was the writer of a song used by Gerry Anderson in Terrahawks called 'SOS' The Korven never got finished, I had my costume lady ready to make the space suit it would wear under its Sontaran-like collar but as Julian wanted to do everything himself it was just too big a strain for him."

Intended as a sequel Cushing's Dalek Invasion Earth 2150, the Daleks are clearly modeled upon the movie versions, with some influence from the comics.

It was insanely ambitious. Julian Vince, the creator, manufactured at least twenty miniature two-foot-tall Daleks, built miniature sets, used stop motion to animate a Dalek armada and produce impressive visuals impossible at full size. In addition, Vince built full sized Daleks, a police box and other full sized props for the live action actors. He even managed to get a very restricted permission from Terry Nation (limited copies and could only be shown at the Doctor Who Appreciation Society), which makes it almost official. It was the pinnacle of the early generation of fan creators.

Ultimately, ambition and exhaustion overcame the project; it was just too much money and work for the tiny crew who eventually got caught up in other things. *"It was John Nathan Turner who convinced me to stop spending money on the project,"* Paul Tams recalls, *"by this stage it had cost hundreds if not a few thousand pounds. JNT said I needed to concentrate on my career and grow out of making Fan Films."*

"We wanted a pro looking end result and it was decided to use Video for the live action, VHS cameras were all that were available at that time with shoulder recorders, the results just would not have done justice, unlike today's digital."

It did have a small legacy. The Korven would reappear, in name at least, in Tam's Australian K9 series. *"The Korven in the K9 series were not frog like they were more Lizard-like creatures. We needed a series villain alongside the Jixen Warriors, so during a script brainstorming session I said how about 'Korven' and we used it. As I had written the Mission script and with what had happened 3 decades earlier I thought it a little tongue in cheek. ..... Also Julian's versions of the Dalek Hoverbouts were used by artists in the DWM (Doctor Who Monthly) strips, so what we had done did have a lasting influence"*

The online clips are mostly of Daleks and miniatures with an accompanying music track. Originally shot on film, the imagery is very well done, and despite the lack of human presence, the scenes are full of moody grandeur.

CAST: *Paul Tams - The Doctor ....*

CREW: *Julian Vince*

CHAPTER 5:
REVENGE OF THE BBC

The Hiatus passed in 1986, but the show that came out the other side was mortally wounded. The reality is that the BBC's top executives, Comptroller Michael Grade, and Programming Head, Jonathan Powell, had been humiliated by the cancellation crisis.

They had their own plans for the BBC, they were launching daytime television, launching a major soap opera, commissioning a raft of new shows, and as part of that process, they'd cancelled a half dozen other series. They hadn't started out as enemies of the show, they certainly hadn't been fans, but there was no profound animosity - Doctor Who just hadn't been important enough for them to care about.

But this was the one that had blown up in their faces. This was the one that had been reported on television and carried in the newspapers; that provoked a hostile reaction from the public and a flaming outcry from a legion of what Grade disparaged as *pointy headed fans.*

There'd been embarrassment, and journalists, parliamentarians and thousands of letters. Something innocuous, a simple administrative decision, had turned into a blistering nightmare. Powell and Grade had been accosted, insulted, upbraided, they'd been forced to back down, to come up with a new story, that the show had never been cancelled, just rescheduled. People don't forgive humiliation.

Over the next few years, the BBC senior management engaged in a campaign of passive warfare against the show.

This began immediately. Shortly after Doctor Who was 'uncancelled' and put on hiatus, the postponed second season was cut in half. Previously, the show had averaged 24 to 26 half hour episodes. But half hour serial drama was an obsolete format by the 1980s.

The producer, John Nathan-Turner, after experimenting with the Davison serial, *Resurrection of the Daleks*, had launched Baker's first season as thirteen hour long episodes, effectively the same as twenty-six half hour episodes. Now it was winched back to the half hour format, but reduced to only fourteen episodes. This left the show with not only a reduced schedule, but a drastically reduced budget.

There were knock on effects. Doctor Who was a profitable show for the BBC, but those profits didn't go to the show, they went into the BBC's general coffers. Doctor Who's actual budget had been frozen or declining since the Tom Baker years in the 1970s. This had resulted in some decline in production quality during the Davison years. Sci Fi series are not like regular television. Fixed production costs are higher. Cutting the budget in half didn't just mean half the episodes; it meant that you were forced to do a lot less with those episodes. The show was hamstrung.

To add insult to injury, it was rescheduled to play opposite the second half of the American hit series, the *A-Team* at 5:30. Potential viewers would have already committed to the first half of the A-Team before they could even begin to decide whether or not to switch to watch Doctor Who. Most didn't bother.

John Nathan-Turner had taken the attempted cancellation as a personal humiliation and a vote of non-confidence. He attempted to resign but was asked to continue for one more season. Ironically, Grade and Powell had cited creative exhaustion as their reason for wanting to end the show, but in continuing, they'd insisted on keeping the same creative team in place through the hiatus into the new season.

Behind the scenes of Colin Baker's second season, anarchy, mostly self-inflicted, prevailed. All the pre-production work that had gone on before the hiatus, including finished and commissioned scripts was thrown out. It was paid for, and abandoned, so much for savings.

Instead, Nathan-Turner and story editor Eric Saward, with half the episodes and a gutted budget tried to mount a bold experiment - a fourteen episode story, the *Trial of a Time Lord*, mirroring the fact that the show itself was on trial with the BBC. Did I say bold? Perhaps it was merely self-referential.

On the framing structure of a trial, they decided to do a version of the *Christmas Carol*, with the Doctor encountering his past, present and future, a conceit that went absolutely nowhere.

Meanwhile, the rocky relationship between Nathan-Turner and Saward was falling apart rapidly. The two men had begun to clash frequently during the Davison years, with Saward feeling increasingly overlooked and disrespected.

Saward had intensely disliked Colin Baker from the start, but his opposition had been overridden. Bitter, Saward took his revenge in the scripts for Baker's first season, the Doctor was played for a nasty fool, and practically every episode featured supporting characters insulting him. It was unprofessional of course, and it hurt both Baker and the show.

Saward was upset again with the casting of Bonnie Langford. Unhappy with Turner, unhappy with Baker, and unhappy with Langford, Saward increasingly withdrew from the show, preferring to work from home rather than come into the office, less and less willing to even speak to people.

For his part, Nathan-Turner's paranoia, vindictiveness and micromanagement increased. Despite the budget being gutted, he decided to commission the show's most expensive special effect ever, in a display of pointless recklessness. Sadly, the effect wasn't even particularly memorable, and didn't actually contribute or add to any of the stories; it was just a showpiece without context.

Robert Holmes, arguably the finest writer the series had ever seen, was tapped by Eric Saward to write the first four and the last two episodes. This should have been a good move, except that Grade meddled with Holmes script, forcing a rewrite. Grade had demanded comedy, when he received it, he decided it needed to be more serious. Holmes, in failing health, overworked and under stress, fell behind.

Meanwhile, Nathan-Turner and Saward couldn't agree on satisfactory stories for the middle episodes, and it turned into a power struggle as they undermined or fired each other's writers and stories. The middle episodes became a revolving door of recruited and abandoned stories and writers. This was only resolved when Nathan-Turner hired Pip and Jane Baker, two writers that Saward loathed, at the last minute, without even consulting him.

It reached the point where the two men were no longer speaking, and Holmes had to act as the intermediary. In the midst of this, Robert Holmes died. Holmes last commission, the final serial, was only half written. Saward would be forced to write the other half.

Shortly after this, Eric Saward, up and quit. His resignation letter was incendiary, *"I have put the best writer (Robert Holmes) the series ever had in hospital and, out of sheer desperation, I am now working with two of the most talentless people (Pip and Jane Baker) who have ever had the nerve to set pen to paper. What's more, I will be expected to "fix " their appalling drivel so that it will appear less like the pile of trash it is - a task I fear beyond Jehovah himself. "*

Saward followed it up almost immediately with a brutal interview in Starburst Magazine. *"I was getting very fed up with the way Doctor Who was being run, largely by John Nathan-Turner — his attitude and his lack of insight into what makes a television series like Doctor Who work. This had been going on for a couple of years and after being cancelled and coming back almost in the same manner as we were before…the same sort of pantomime-ish aspects that I so despised about the show. I just think it isn't worth it."*

To add insult to injury, Saward forbade them from using any part of his script for the final episode of the final story. As a result, Pip and Jane Baker were called in again, given Robert Holmes first half, and told to write an original ending with no other information. After being publicly slagged by Saward, I'm sure it must have amused the Bakers no end to be replacing him on the final episode.

During the show's moment of crisis, when people should have been pulling together, things were practically falling apart behind the scenes, as death, bad decisions and a bitter and public fallout between Saward and Nathan-Turner poisoned the waters.

The general audience didn't pay much attention, mainly. They watched the show and that was it. The fans, on the other hand, paid attention and were divided and dispirited. Many of the fans who had lined up on Nathan-Turner's side began attacking him, and fandom split.

The results were predictable. The ratings for Baker's first season averaged 7.6 million. For his second season, the *Trial of a Time Lord,* those ratings dropped to 4.8 million. More than a third of the audience had vanished. A large part of the drop was almost certainly due to scheduling. But part of that reflected the backstage chaos, and the wandering and incoherent serials of the season. Rather than play it safe, he'd gambled on an ambitious, but poorly conceived and badly executed experiment. Of course it failed.

Interestingly, viewer satisfaction with the series increased. It seems that what was left of the audience was loyal.

Again, Nathan-Turner tried to resign. Instead, Grade and Powell promised him an assignment to a new series, on one condition: That he fire Colin Baker. On October 29, 1986, Baker got the axe very publicly, leaving the series without a Doctor. To be fair, Baker wasn't technically fired, he had a three year contract to play the Doctor, and although he'd only played two seasons, his contract was up, and was simply not renewed.

But niceties aside, it was definitely a firing.

As we've noted, Grade had a very personal relationship with Colin Baker's wife in the midst of and following their very difficult divorce back in 1978. Was there something personal?

A Pirate's History, Page 142

My impression is that people of Grade's class make a big deal
out of impartiality and professionalism, they talk a good
game. But they also nurse their grudges and they keep their
knives very sharp, and somehow, sometimes those knives end
up in backsides.

Was this one of those times? Hard to say. What happened to
Colin Baker was unprecedented, in terms of BBC
management intervening against a star. Draw your own
conclusions.

Colin Baker's anger was very public, he said in an interview in
the Sun newspaper at the time, "*I couldn't take (being sacked) in,
it was such a shock. I'd fought so hard for the show, I was stunned.
What I couldn't accept is that Grade didn't have the guts to tell me
man-to-man....Many people believe, as I do, that I have been treated
shabbily. Grade didn't want me to say I had been fired. My boss,
Jonathan Powell....strongly suggested to me that I should claim to be
leaving for personal reasons. How could they expect viewing figures to rise
when (Trial of a Timelord) was slotted in at such a bad time? Even so,
five million viewers isn't so bad. The Wogan show doesn't do much*
better than that, but you won't find Grade moaning about a
show that's his brainchild. "

Despite doing the dirty work of firing Baker, John Nathan-
Turner was not allowed to resign. Grade and Powell welched
on their promise to assign him to a new show. He had no
other option but to stay with Doctor Who. He had no place
else to go.

At the same time, no one else was willing to take on the
series. Given its disrepute with the senior management, that
would be career suicide. With no one else, to step up, the
BBC made it clear that it would be cancelled if he left.
Nathan-Turner, burned out and demoralized, would keep
trying to resign each year. But would end up staying with

Doctor Who until cancellation, whether he or anyone else wanted him to or not.

The production crew was demoralized and the talent pool of writers and directors was simply gone. Nathan-Turner and Saward had made a determined effort to make a break with much of the older talent, in favour of bringing in new people. That creative old guard from the Pertwee and Baker eras of the 1970s was long gone. With Saward's messy departure, Nathan-Turner was unwilling to rely on the stable of writers favoured or cultivated by Saward. The new guard were no longer welcome.

With a next Season counting down rapidly, Nathan-Turner had to literally start from scratch, finding a new Doctor, new writers, and eventually a new story editor, all increasingly late in pre-production, who had to try and rebuild the show from scratch, with nothing but handicaps and liabilities. This was the beginning of the Sylvester McCoy era.

The new Story Editor would end up being Andrew Cartmel, hired on the basis of a lunchtime meeting. Cartmel was a computer programmer who had taken a script writing course, but had never actually had a script produced. It was a sign of how devastated the show was, and how its talent pool had thinned or become demoralized, that Cartmel became the major creative force for the show during his tenure.

Not that Cartmel was untalented or didn't have ideas, but this was a young man without history or experience, and suddenly he was catapulted into the second most important position behind the scenes... based on little more than a good interview.

The ambitious productions of the Jon Pertwee or Tom Baker, or even the Peter Davison era were now mostly out of reach.

They simply didn't have the budgets. Michael Grade had ordered the show to focus on comedy.

The new Sylvester McCoy era of Doctor Who with Cartmel, began to develop an absurdist style, showcasing it's cheapness to reach for surreal or satirical material. Serials like *Delta and the Bannermen, Greatest Show in the Galaxy, Paradise Towers, The Happiness Patrol, Time and the Rani* and even *Dragonfire*, played as farcical, loud, brash, deliberately in your face with its cheapness, trying to make the most with a gutted budget, a burned out producer and a largely inexperienced series of writers and directors.

As bold as these shows were, they didn't go over particularly well with fans. They, and much of the audience, tended to prefer the traditional stories. Avant garde absurdist serials with candy villains, or settings in tents, apartment blocks and beach holiday resorts left fans and audiences baffled and annoyed. This wasn't the show they loved. In terms of audience attention and approval, the highest rated shows in a season tended to be the ones closest to the series traditions - the *Remembrance of the Daleks, Silver Nemesis* with the Cybermen, and Survival with the Master, were the highest rated of their seasons.

The budget for the upcoming season was again frozen or cut. In the inflationary times, it didn't make much difference. The show was moved to Mondays at 7:30, to go head to head against Britain's most popular soap opera, Coronation Street. McCoy's first season would limp along with an average rating of 4.9 million viewers. That set the tone for McCoy's tenure: Budget cuts, bad scheduling and executive meddling applied punitively - the classic weapons of any television executive out to kill a show.

Michael Grade had moved on in 1987. Jonathan Powell stepped into Grade's position. But that didn't help the show. He'd been just as badly embarrassed as Grade, and if anything, he'd loathed Turner even more. In bureaucracy, attitudes are set from the top, and at the top Grade and Powell disdained Science Fiction in general and disliked Doctor Who in particular. Two consecutive BBC heads had had it in for the show. The rest of BBC management towed the line; they knew which way the wind was blowing. If a BBC manager or executive had any fondness for Doctor Who, it was probably best to keep that to themselves.

McCoy's second season was shifted from Monday to Wednesday nights at 7:30 against *Coronation Street*, an even worse time slot. When the director for the serial's first season, *Remembrance of the Daleks* went twelve thousand pounds over budget, he was blacklisted from the show by BBC management.

Despite this, McCoy's second season did have one thing going for it - it was now the 25th Anniversary. The British were fond of anniversaries, which made it hard to drop a hammer on it. That guaranteed at least one more season. The show actually hung on, bringing back the Daleks and Cybermen for some of its most traditional and expensive productions. McCoy's second season averaged ratings of about 5.3 million viewers.

The third season remained on Wednesday nights against *Coronation Street*, but the ratings fell dramatically. The opening serial averaged 3.1 million viewers. The serials were repetitive - *Battlefield* and *Curse of Fenric* were virtual clones of each other, as had been the Cyberman and Dalek stories of the previous year. With a mere four stories, somehow, it seemed that the series couldn't help being repetitive. Or if not repetitive, then obscure - *Ghostlight* was incomprehensible, *Survival* almost so. Production quality was a mess. The show did steadily increase its ratings, until the final serial with the return of the Master reached almost 5 million. Still, the average audience was down to 4.1 million. Over 20% of the McCoy audience had faded away; the show was down to roughly half of its pre-hiatus viewing figures.

That was the end. In its last five seasons, the show had earned the vengeful hatred of two consecutive BBC heads, been moved through four time slots, each worse than the one before. It had seen two Doctors, three major format shifts, a massive reduction in episodes, brutal reductions in budgets, and a lot of very messy dirty laundry aired very publicly.

At the end of the 26th season, it was announced that the show was going on hiatus again. Not cancelled, just another hiatus, one with no return date.

This time, no one cared.

A Pirate's History, Page 148

CHAPTER 6: THE MID-80s, THE RISE OF FANDOM

Even if the mid-eighties saw the long decline and fall of Doctor Who on British television, elsewhere, things were taking off.

In Britain, Doctor Who fandom was literally exploding, with conventions, fanzines, costume play and prop making. Through fan clubs, conventions, zines and letter writing, fans were making contact with each other, gelling as a community and reinforcing their interests and activities, and this produced a flowering of creativity.

Meanwhile over in America, thanks to Tom Baker, Doctor Who was breaking through. No one had ever seen anything quite like Tom's quirky brand of time travelling adventures; his mixture of eccentricity and heroism was compelling. The networks of fandom that were establishing around *Star Trek* and *Star Wars* expanded for this new perspective, and lead by Who, British science fiction, from *Gerry Anderson* to *Blake's 7*, became a cult thing of its own

And as in the 1970s, there was a new technology on the way, opening the door for a new wave of creators: Videotape.

Now, videotape had actually been around for a long time, since the 1960s. But through the 1960s and 1970s, it was mostly around as a commercial format. The original videotapes were reel to reel, the cameras were huge and expensive, the equipment complicated and finicky. In the early days of Doctor Who the show was shot on video, and as an example of how crude things were back then, when they wanted to edit, they physically cut and spliced.

The thing with technology though, is that as time goes on, it becomes cheaper and easier to use.

In 1971, the U-Matic videotape format came along, recording and playing video on bulky cassettes. U-Matics caught on with businesses like car dealerships for playing videos to customers or trainees, and with schools and universities.

In 1975, Betamax emerged, and then VHS in 1977. Suddenly, you had a Videocassette player and recorder, and videocassettes which were small enough and cheap enough for the consumer market. Of course, it's not as if in 1975, everyone went out and got a VCR. As with Super 8, there's always a lag time of a few years from the introduction of a technology to the point where it's widespread and commonplace.

But by the early to mid-eighties, the VCR was well established in most households. It was a versatile product, not only could it play movies that you rented or bought, but you could buy blank tapes and record off television - so now, with a little programming, you could watch your favourite programs whenever you wanted, rather than just when it aired. Or you could re-watch your favourite program as many times as you wanted. Or, if you happened to have two VCR's to hook together, you could make copies of your favourite programs.

Nowadays, we live in an era of immediacy. Between Netflix, streaming services, PVR, DVD and Blue-Ray collections, we can watch or obtain the entirety of almost anything at any time. But back then this new capacity was mind blowing!

The ability to record and make copies added a brand new dimension to fandom. Suddenly, you could collect episodes of *Star Trek*, or *Star Wars*, or *Doctor Who* or *Monty Python*. You could collect whatever you wanted. You could build your collection by trading with other fans for missing episodes.

For the first time, it was possible to have all the Star Wars movies, or to build a complete run of Star Trek, or to own Doctor Who from any era.

A lively network of traders and collectors emerged. Conventions hosted television rooms where collectors could show hard to find movies and TV series. Bootleg dealers became a thing. Movies and television became as portable, as reproducible, as exchangeable as print.

It was a quantum leap over Super 8. For that you needed a projector, you needed to carefully thread the film through the projector, adjust focus and elevation, turn off the lights, set up a screen. As for making a copy of a Super 8 film? Good luck. That was a conversation you needed to have with the local chemist, and even if you could, each copy would cost, possibly significantly.

With a VCR all you needed to do was press play. A television, a VCR or two, a cassette, and you were in business. It was user friendly taken to the next level, and it transformed fandom and fan culture.

In 1983 the first camcorders hit the market, and this was the final piece of the puzzle. Now they could create, not just copy, not just trade and distribute and exhibit.

It was easier than ever before. Super 8 had film cartridges, but it still required film processing, you had to take the cartridge to the drugstore and wait to have it developed, it was limited to three minutes at most, editing was still a physical task of cutting pieces of film together by hand.

But camcorders were plug and play, put the cassette into the camcorder, you could record for an hour or more. After that? Just pop the cassette it into the VCR, or just hook up the camcorder to the VCR, and you're good to go. Editing was done on decks. It was all pressing buttons; it was the ultimate in user friendliness.

So by the mid-eighties, we had an active fandom, based on clubs and conventions, people getting together and being creative with their common interest, a network of tape collectors and traders. Once camcorders were on the market, sooner or later, someone was going to bring one to a fan club, and once there.... Fan films were going to be a thing. The late eighties saw a proliferation of fan films and film makers

The most prominent, and by far the most prolific, of these groups would end up being called 'The Federation' composed of Mark Christenson, Patrick Reardon, Chris Brainerd, Pat Engle, Rob Warnock, Steve Schiller, Kathy Warnock, Jennifer Adams and their friends. Hailing from Illinois, the Federation began as a splinter group from another Doctor Who club called the UNIT Irregulars. They soon fissioned off into a prolific costume and performance troop that went on to make a series of videos through the eighties, before breaking up and eventually reforming in the nineties.

The Federation's forte were crossovers - Doctor Who would cross with *All Creatures Great and Small, It's a Wonderful Life, Monty Python and the Holy Grail* and anything else that seemed fun and funny. A regular at conventions, the Federation were not only fans of media, but very aware of backstage gossip and production. Their skits were as often about the actors and producers as about the Doctors and companions. They were notable for blurring the lines between the show and its production. For example, John Nathan-Turner would appear regularly as a character, initially a hero, eventually the villain.

Also in Illinois, Rusty Ramsay and Jeff Smith did their own spoof, the *Two Doctors and the Anti-Matter Menace.*

In North Carolina and Connecticut, two groups of fans, led by Peter Fagan, worked together as the Beeblebrox Company (BBC). Theirs was a more straightforward series of adventures, featuring a young man, Laurence Klein, as the fourth Doctor.

Over in England, Chris Cook and Barbara O'Quinn took a break from fanzines to produce a pair of animated shorts.

Meanwhile Ad-Lib Productions, founded by Ian Taylor, Mike Hardman, Stuart Glazebrook, Gordon Lengen and Eric Davies, started out apparently trying to do a serious story, but soon veered into *Monty Python* surrealism, with *Labyrinth of the Blud Devil*s. The Ad-Lib production group inspired or became the trigger for other fan groups and fan projects, notably Pacific-UK, with Kevin Taylor and Planet Video, with Nigel Peever. The three groups showed considerable overlap in their casts and crews, with many of the same people working on each other's projects, but produced wildly different efforts.

Planet Video Productions lead by Nigel Peever, Dave Cullen and others, strove to return to the classic stories. Planet Video would point the way to the next wave of fan films which emerged during the dark period of the show's final years.

Reviews: Mid-Eighties Films

A Brief Overview

1980 - DOCTOR WHO AND THE MALFUNCTIONING TARDIS *(20 minutes, live action, video, U.S.)*

STORY: Due to a short circuit in the Tardis randomizer, Doctor Who (in his fifth incarnation) and his newest assistant, Oswan (also a Time Lord) pop in and out of various dangerous situations.

REVIEW: This is the earliest North American attempt at a live action Doctor Who fan film. It exists only as a reference in a contemporary magazine called Cinemagic, Issue #9, dated 1980. The specifications were ambitious: Live Action, colour, videotape with sound. Sets, props and effects included a Police Box; Tardis console room, lasers, explosions, lizard man make up, and a 20 minute running time.

Unfortunately, according to Steve Roman, it never actually got made – Roman was in high school at the time, and was unable to recruit people to help. So the project was abandoned.

CAST: *Steve Roman (Doctor Who), Osman Arphad (Osman), and 12 extras.*

CREW: *Produced, Directed and Written by Steve Roman.*

&&&

1983/1984 - THE FIVE DOCTORS BOOH *(41 minutes, part 1 - 26 min, part 2 -15 min, Libertyville, Illinois, Multiple Doctors)*

STORY: *"John Nathan-Turner tries to eliminate the first five Doctors so that his 6th Doctor will reign supreme. But is it JNT? Who's really behind the plot to destroy the Doctors?"*

REVIEW: Turns out it's the Master, disguised as JNT. Sorry for spoiling that for you.

A 'Colin Baker' shows up as Doctor Number 6, but without his signature rainbow coat, which gives you an idea how very early this was. Colin Baker's first episodes had yet to air on American television. No one making this knew what the new Doctor would look like yet.

This film started off when someone brought a camcorder to a Doctor Who club called 'UNIT Irregulars' in 1983. By this time, several members had costumes, so they decided to do a sketch, *'The Five Faces of Doctor Booh'*.

The 'UNIT Irregulars' fractured under workload and fan politics. The core group who were most heavily involved in the production, split off from UNIT Irregulars by January 1, 1984, called themselves the Federation, and produced a re-edited version under the current title. Both versions are available on YouTube.

Five Doctors Booh established the Federation's signature of metafictional parody which often went behind the scenes of a

A Pirate's History, Page 156

production for its gags. The first official screening of the final version may have been as late as June 1984. This was the beginning of the prolific Federation dynasty.

So, what have we got? It's basically a bunch of teens in homemade costumes, running around and filming each other doing unpolished skits. Shot on VHS and edited on home VCR decks. Pretty much every aspect of the production looks rough, cheap and sloppy. Fair warning, it's pretty tough going, historical interest only.

CAST: Doctors - Mark Christenson, Patrick Reardon, Chris Brainerd, Pat Engle, Rob Warnock; Companions - Sondra Clein, Steve Schiller, Kathy Warnock, Johnathan Bernick, Ethan Guzman-Barron, Mark Engwall, Jennifer Adams, Eric Prellwitz, Dawn M. White, Scott Hajek; The Miser - Dennis Kytasaari; Disguised Miser - Chris Brainerd; Voice of Ok-9 - Pat Engle; The New (6th) Doctor - Mark Christensen; Valley Companion - Lynn Violante; Time Lads - William White, Bill Merlock.

CREW: *By the Book Broadcasting System (BBBS) in Association with the Federation. Executive producer - Chris Brainerd; Producer - Rob Warnock; Directed by Chris Brainerd; Written by Chris Brainerd and Rob Warnock; Videographed by Jennifer Adams; Video and Sount Edit - Chris Brainerd and Rob Warnock; Makeup design - Pat Engle; Star Graphics - Dennis Kytasaari; Special thanks to: Tim Kasper, The Video King, Mrs Christensen, Jay Standish, Mrs Brainerd, Roller Park, John Nathan-Turner;*

&&&

1984 – DIAL D FOR DALEK, *(4 minutes, England, Animated, 4th Doctor)*

STORY: The Fourth Doctor appears on Skaro. He tricks the Daleks with an inflatable copy of himself. This works, so he fills Skaro with dozens more, causing the Daleks to shoot wildly, crashing into each other and eventually blowing themselves up from frustration. Shortly after, the Wizard of Space and Time runs through, knocking the Doctor over. The Doctor holds up a sign asking 'Who do you think taught him about time?'

REVIEW: It's a cute loony toons inspired short, about three or four minutes, which doesn't wear out its welcome.

Shot on Super 8 format, I believe. The one area where Super 8 held an advantage over camcorders was its ability to go frame by frame, which meant that if you were doing cartoon or stop motion animation, this was still a viable format.

The title was inspired by Alfred Hitchcock's *Dial M For Murder* from 1954.

Meanwhile, *The Wizard of Speed and Time* was a 1979 short film by special effects artist Mike Jitlow, which had become a cult item at conventions. Jitlow eventually made a full length version of his short in 1989.

CREW: *Produced and Directed by Christopher Cook. Story - Barbara O'Quinn; Animators - Christopher Cook, Alex Lucyshyn, Dena Porter, Barbara O'Quinn, Lori Avirett, Cindy Ketterling. Background Artist - Dena Porter & Sonya Arundel*

&&&

1984 – DARK ALLIANCE *(34 minutes, North Carolina/Connecticut, 4th Doctor)*

STORY: The Master and a villainess named Princess Felina, enlists an alliance of Cybermen, Daleks and Vardans in a quest to conquer the Galactic Federation. The Doctor has his own problems, having accidentally turned Sarah Jane Smith into a twelve year old girl. His effort to find a cure for her leads him to wander straight into the conspiracy. Along the way, the Doctor locks himself out of the Tardis, and there's a Monty Python gag.

REVIEW: Premiering at Contrast Sci Fi Convention, November 16-18, 1984, *Dark Alliance* was a production of the Beeblebrox Company (BBC), named after the character from Hitchhiker's Guide to the Galaxy. Beeblebrox began June 16, 1984, when Peter Fagan brought a camcorder and a portable VCR to a small Doctor Who event at the North Carolina State University Campus. Charles Wood, who played the Master became the mayor of Lizard Lick, North Carolina. Colleen Parker (aka C.M. Cartier) wrote for the local paper, the Zebulon Record.

Dark Alliance came out within a few months of *Wrath of Eukor* and honestly suffers for the comparison. It's clearly shot on video, with amateur actors and crew and patently homemade sets and costumes.

There are plenty of things to mock. The cast are non-actors and it shows; there are points where they struggle visibly with unfamiliar words. Laurence Klein as the Doctor is particularly grating. Important scenes take place in what's clearly a wood panelled basement or garage. The door to the Master's Tardis is a checkered bedsheet. The costumes of the Federation involve motorcycle helmets, safety vests and cardigan sweaters. The Cybermen are odd looking and impossibly cute. As for the Dalek...you just have to see the Dalek.

It's clearly made by fans, and for fans.

But for all of its flaws there is a sincerity to its naïveté that makes it worth watching. This might not be professional, but there's a lot of dedication and affection that went into it, and that gives the video a certain honest charm. For the people involved, it was a labour of love, and that counts for a lot.

A Pirate's History, Page 159

Whatever you might think of the finished product, I want to emphasize that cast and crew worked hard on this. They treated it as a real production, with crew roles, shot lists, scenes out of sequence, and formal editing and sound mix.

The crew built a Police Box shell and Tardis interior, with the walls and their round things, a full sized console, and at least two adorable Cyberman costumes. The production was organized, with scenes being shot out of order, there were ambitious special effects, at least a handful of different locations, indoors and out.

Charles Wood recalls the actors and crew repeatedly putting in fifteen hour days, one after the other. A lot of effort went into the production. These things are hard to do, and there is a lot of genuine effort that needs to be respected.

Dark Alliance premiered to a receptive fan audience, and it was successful enough that the Beeblebrox Company went on to do their epic, a full length adventure, *Theta G*, 1987, 102 minutes, once again starring Laurence Klein as the Fourth Doctor, with scarf and curly wig. From there, they made a series of short films, mostly in the 1980s and early 90s. In 2003, Fagan collaborated with fan Doctors, Rupert Booth and Johnathan Blum to make a Doctor Who short called When Doctors Collide.

CAST: *The Doctor - Laurence Klein; Sarah Jane Smith - Jenny Cartier; Mature Sarah - Karen Courtney; The Master - Charles Wood; Princess Felina - C.M. Cartier; Morris - Greg Long; Cyberleader - David Kalat; Lady-in-Waiting - Debby Owen; Federation President - Erin Hoagland; Peladon Ambassador - Julianne Weaver; Cyberman - David Seay; Federation Traitor - Susan Pennington; Two-Headed Beast - Bill Blizzard & Bruce Smith*

CREW: Writer - C.M. Cartier and Peter Fagan; Director - Peter Fagan; Producer - C.M. Cartier; Lighting/Sound - Susan Carl; Camera/Boom/FX Multiple; Make up - Carl Susanburg; Wigs - Lisa Gorman; Titles - L.K & Atari 400; Locations - Sue Carl's Garage, NCSU Boardroom,

&&&

1984 – ALL DOCTORS GREAT AND SMALL, *(28 Minutes, The Federation, Libertyville Illinois, Multiple Doctors).*

STORY: "A time dissolve has forced the characters on Doctor Who to assume roles in All Creatures Great and Small. But what nefarious creature has control of the video switcher—and both programs? "

REVIEW: The Federation came back again, this time with a rather clever meta-joke: *All Creatures Great and Small* was an early 80s British television series about a country veterinarian, based on a series of semi-biographical books by James Herriot. It had a minor cult following of its own. John Nathan-Turner had been a producer on the series before moving to Doctor Who. In addition, Peter Davison, first came to attention on the series as a supporting character named Tristan. This was where Davison had gotten to know Nathan-Turner, before taking on the role of the Doctor.

Noted by the Federation people for a fifteen consecutive hour shoot under grueling conditions. It featured the same crew of young people, but this time, they, and particularly Jennifer Adams, Chris Brainerd, Rob Warnock and others had upped their game considerably from The Five Doctors Booh.

Unlike their previous effort, this is watchable, with composed shots, a coherent through line, and an actual effort at performances. Perhaps it was because the whole thing carefully mimics the look and style of *All Creatures*. Indeed, they may have chosen to remake a specific episode, which would have given them a visual road map of shots, sequence and story, to learn from.

In terms of telling a complete narrative story with a structure and an arc resolution, it's actually better than the subsequent productions, Save WHO or Reign of Turner, both of which simply operate as frameworks filled with skits.

This show also has a special place in history because it was specially screened at a convention for John Nathan-Turner and Colin Baker in February, 1985, literally as the cancellation crisis erupted. Shot and Edited on VHS.

From this point, the Federation went on to have a prolific career. A handful of titles will give you an idea of what they were doing:

**A Doctor's Carol*, 25 Minutes, The Federation, Libertyville, Illinois, Multiple Doctors. "The sixth Doctor must relive Christmas memories of his previous selves."

* ***Doctors on 33***, 21 Minutes, The Federation, Libertyville, Illinois, Multiple Doctors.

* *"MTV, Doctor Who style*, which includes ***"The Time Warp** "*done with a bunch of Doctors and companions."

* *Doctor Who and the Holy Grail.*

* *Flake's Seven* a parody of *Blake's Seven*.

Through the remainder of the 1980s the Federation would produce an astounding twenty comedic fan films, and put on a series of live shows, making them far and away the most prolific and widely known fan film producer of their era.

A Pirate's History, Page 162

&&&

1984/1985 – DOKTOR HOO AND THE BUTTERCUPS OF DOOM *(4 minutes, live action, American)*

STORY: The Doctor and his companion, played by a pair of sibling junior high school students, crawl out of the Tardis, played by an unvarnished cardboard box. They encounter a Dalek, played by an upside down trash can which shoots the Doctor with a reasonably nifty effect. After defeating the Dalek, they retreat back to the Tardis, where he regenerates into a girl, presumably a third sibling, who then tries on a few outfits.

REVIEW: Shot on Super8 without sound, this has the frantic, overblown body language of the early silent. There's not much of a story to tell in four minutes. This is probably typical of the 'fan films' that might have been produced in the Super8 era – short running times, shaky camera, amateurish and enthusiastic. There's a few charming effect that show they went a little extra distance – curtains are opened and closed in stop motion to simulate a door or a viewscreen, a Tardis console is depicted by covering a table with a blanket, putting a 'under repair' sign on it, and having a flowerpot rise and fall rhythmically, there's a ray gun beam, a regeneration scene, and even a credits sequence. Verdict: Short but engaging.

&&&

1985 - THE HUES OF DOOM, *(4 minutes, England, Animated, 6th Doctor, 5th Doctor)*

STORY: The 5th Doctor introduces proceedings, munching a celery stick like bugs bunny. The Sixth Doctor materializes on a planet of 'smiley face' aliens. They shoot the Doctor with their ray guns. The Doctor retreats back to the Tardis, where he discovers his coat has been turned charred black and grey. The Doctor changes into a new coat, but it goes gray too. Peri hoses him down with rainbow paint colours, but it doesn't help. He even slams into an actual rainbow. Nothing works. So the Doctor kidnaps John Nathan Turner from a street corner, leaning against a lamppost and steals the colour from his shirt. Turner wakes, as if from a dream, and goes to his closet, to find the Doctor sitting there, grinning at him. .... So no subtext here at all, no sir!

REVIEW: Same crew as *Dial D for Dalek*, and also animated on 8 mm or 16 mm. Oddly, despite the visual similarity, both seem to have had no relationship, beyond inspiration, to the original Doctor Hoo.

Barbara O'Quinn was an English fan known for writing for a contemporary British fanzine named Tardis. She also wrote fan fictions about the 'Doctrix' a female version(s) of the Doctor. This was a little bit racy for its time, with allusions to John Nathan-Turner's sexual orientation.

CREW: Producer & Director - Christopher Cook. Script - Barbara O'Quinn; Animators - Christopher Cook, Dan Kiernan, Alex Lucyshyn, Jerry Collins, Lori Avirett. Background Artists - Jerry Collins & Dena Porter; Script Editor - Dena Porter. Associate Producer - Gerry Cook.

&&&

1985 - LABYRINTH OF THE BLUD DEVILS, *(25 minutes - Ad-Lib Productions, England, 4th Doctor.)*

STORY: The Fourth Doctor comes to earth, out for a bit of sightseeing and cheese shopping. Meanwhile, Auton-like aliens called Zunks begin reanimating human corpses. A zombie rises from the grave and terrorizes a tramp. Before long, the Doctor and the Tramp are prisoners of the Zunks. They barely escape with their lives. Frustrated, the Zunks take off their alien masks and head to the pub for a beer. Things get weird after that....

REVIEW: In 1984 and 1985, a young film maker named Ian Taylor and some of his friends decided to make their own Doctor Who. After a false start or two, they settled on a promising story involving zombies and aliens called Zunks. The zombie terrifies an itinerant tramp played by Gordon Lengen. Meanwhile, a young Doctor, played by Stuart

Glazebrook, modeled loosely on Tom Baker wanders about. For about two thirds of its length, what seems to be a serious story is evolving.

Then in the last third, it feels like the film makers went 'to hell with this' and drift into Monty Python style surrealism. The Zunks take off their mask and go for a beer. The Doctor encounters his earlier companion, Jamie, played by Taylor, and argues with Robin Hood. The fourth wall is broken; characters refer to the script, argue about the plot, and throw gags almost at random. There's a feeling of improvisational riffing, a casual relaxed style of film that engages with goofy humour and a sort of knowing quality. The story vanishes, unremarked, in favour of freewheeling, seemingly off the cuff, humour.

It works. The original story seemed to be developing well, and a lot of the scenes were impressive - the zombie rising from the grave is particularly well done. It's like something out of a Hammer film. A scene between the Doctor and the Tramp in the Zunks' lair is particularly gripping.

But when the change of pace comes, that works too. There's a *Monty Python* sense of anarchy, where anything can happen, and does. The humour is informal and unpredictable, a marked contrast to the more formal 'sketch comedy' style of groups like the Federation. Comedy scenes could lack formal beginnings or ends, or could violate their own logic. It was effective. This approach became the signature for the Ad-Lib Group.

Stuart Glazebrook as the Fourth Doctor and Gordon Lengen as a hobo make an engaging comedy team. They're comfortable with each other and they bounce off each other well. On the strength of that chemistry Ian Taylor had Glazebrook and Lengen back for two loose sequels -

A Pirate's History, Page 166

Labyrinth of the Blud Devils 2 (15 minutes, 1988) a rather free form series of skits, *Labyrinth of the Blud Devils 3: The Butler's Revenge* (43 minutes, 1989) which flirted with a plot of some sort, but refused to commit. The three films can be seen or played as a single feature length unit or various combinations, the anarchic structure allows for that.

Taylor also brought his freeform style to the *Legend of Drog* in 1988, about which I know very little, but which seems to have involved Glazebrook and Lengen, and perhaps a Yeti. In 1991, Taylor's Ad-Lib collaborated with Planet Video, for a short Prequel to the Tom Baker serial, *Robots of Death*, featuring the early life of Taran Capel.

Taylor and company continued to evolve past Doctor Who, making free form, improvisational films off and on through the 90s and beyond.

Taylor, a hard-core Doctor Who fan worked at the Blackpool Doctor Who exhibition in 1985 as a Cyberman. There he met and befriended Nigel Peever, Kevin Taylor, John Field and other fans. The friendship inspired Peever to get a camera and make his own Who projects, starting with *Earthpark*. This was the beginning of Planet Video and Pacific-UK productions.

Through the late 1980s and early 1990s, the three groups shared interlocking memberships, with Ian Taylor and the Ad Lib group doing comedy, and Pacific-UK and Planet Video groups attempting, and sometimes failing, to do more serious fan films. Collectively, they constituted the most active, most prolific, most diverse and ambitious, and most accomplished fan film group in England in the 1980s.

CAST: Stuart Glazebrook - *The Fourth Doctor; Gordon Lengen - Hobo; Ian Taylor - Jaime; Keith Molyneux, Mike Hardman, Eugene Prunty, Eric William Davies, Gareth Preston.*

CREW: Ian Taylor - Director; Photography - Mike Hardman; Ian Taylor & Eric Davies - Script; Stuart Glazebrook and Gordon Lengen - Additional Dialogue.

&&&

1985 - THE TWO DOCTORS AND THE ANTI-MATTER MENACE, *(20 minutes, Illinois, 3rd and 4th Doctors)*

STORY: The Fourth and Third Doctors, assisted by Romana and K9, team up to stop Davros and his Daleks from releasing Omega back into our Universe. After some plot, the whole thing ends up in a Benny Hill style chase scene.

REVIEW: What can you say when Omega's mask is a piece of cardboard tied on with string? Or when the world's sickest looking Dalek shows up? Or when the White Guardian's appearance on a view-screen is achieved by having the actor stand behind a sheet of cardboard with a hole cut in it? We aren't talking cinematic realism here.

Despite this you can tell that Ramsay and Smith went all out. They've built a Tardis console in their basement with liberal amounts of duct tape, and it still looks pretty good. The K9 reproduction is more than adequate. If the cheese factor is high, it's also entirely unapologetic and free-spirited. An engaging bit of low budget insanity, it's worth watching just for silliness.

Jeff Smith would go on to produce a documentary about the Doctor Who fan film Time and Again, called *Order Out of Chaos*, and would be involved in the production of the *Doctor Who 2009 / Fire and Ice* series, slated as one of the writers for the aborted upcoming episodes, including the lost *Guardian of the Solar System*, and eventually producing his own fan edit of *Fire and Ice*.

CAST: *The Fourth Doctor/Omega/Voice of K9, Voice of Daleks - Jeff Smith; The Third Doctor/Davros - Rusty Ramsay; Romana - Stephanie Ramsay; The White Guardian - Chris Skinner*

CREW: *Writer & Director, Sets & Props, - Jeff Smith; Producer, Gaffer, Camera - Rusty Ramsey; Editor - Rusty Ramsay & Jeff Smith; Jeff's Scarf - Lillie Martin. New Digital effects, Rusty Ramsay.*

&&&

1985 - SAVE WHO! THE TWENTY TWO YEARS OF DOCTOR WHO, *(53 minutes, The Federation, Libertyville, Illinois.)*

STORY: After the disastrous end of season 22, Colin Baker joins a PBS telethon to raise the money for the next season of Doctor Who. This was the Federation's first great epic, breaking the fourth wall, spoofing the show, its production and the culture and marketplace around it.

REVIEW: This was one of the Federation's most ambitious productions. Made in direct response to the cancellation/ hiatus, this 53 minute epic comedy features 18 actors in over 50 roles. The production, mostly high school and college students, makes no attempt at professionalism - they know they're kids in costumes and wigs, we know they're kids in costumes, they just go with it, the iconic Tardis walls are reproduced with paper plates, image and sound compositions are often muddy as hell.

Rather than trying to tell a straight story badly, they opt for parody and satire with looser technical standards, and focus on moving the production quickly, Save Who! presents as half

A Pirate's History, Page 169

telethon, half documentary, spoofing scenes and characters through the shows history.

It's heavily influenced by *Monty Python, Mad Magazine* and by the American-made *Kentucky Fried Movie*, at times directly copying *Python* skits, but references and influences include everything from *Wizard of Oz*, to *Blake's 7*, to the *Two Ronnies*. The Federation evolved a very distinct style from that of its anarchic counterpart, Ad-Lib Productions, over in England, less Python/Anarchic, more formal and skit based.

The format of a telethon was a direct response to PBS fundraising drives from the period, which would solicit donations directly and which heavily emphasized Doctor Who.

On display was an encyclopedic knowledge of the series history, both in front of and behind the scenes, sharp timing and a terrific sense of fun. It would be overshadowed by the Federation's subsequent masterpiece/great white whale, *The Reign of Turner.*

CAST: *Colon/Poly/Master - Steve Schiller; Pery/Sara/Nysser/ Ramada1/ Zoey/US Fan - Jennifer Adams; Anncr/Turbough/War Lord/Frankin - Philip Kelley; Hartell/Time Lord/Hairy/Hurtdall - Mark Christensen; Ben - Jim Luttgens; Trofton/Susan/Avon/Dodo - Patrick Reardon; Peewee/Barbara/Tewance/J H-Turner - Chris Brainerd; Brigadier/M. Grate/Cyberman - Charles Morley; Tommy - Pat Engle; A. Ailey/Basil; - Dennis Kytasaari; Adict/Ian/Steven/Bendon/Digam - Eric Prellwitz; Tagun/Ramada2/Ranis - Sue Warnock; Peter/Victorya/G.Downey/UK Fan - Rob Warnock; Jamie - John Wirth; Tewance - Tim Kasper; Jo/Servalan - Kathy Warnock; E. Hufman - Will LaDuke; Cowboy/Dalek - Pat Engle*

CREW: The Federation - A Doctor Who Cooperative; Written, Directed and Produced by Rob Warnock, Jennifer Adams, Chris Brainerd; Executive Producer - 'Jack Daniels'; Producer - Chris Brainerd; Cinematographer - Jennifer Adams. Special Thanks - Libertyville High School, Remco Rentals, The Brainerd Studios, Taco Bell, Northwestern Film Board, Colombia College, John Nathan-Turner,

&&&

1986/1988 – THE TWO COMPANIONS *(39/120 minutes, Mini-UNIT Minstrels aka MUM, Minneapolis/St. Paul)*

REVIEW: Fair warning – I haven't seen any of the MUM productions since the 90s, my memory is hazy. My information comes from online sources. Inspired directly by the Federation's *SAVE WHO*, the Mini-UNIT Minstrels became a prolific fan film producer. Obtaining a script written by two British Fans, Chris Clarke and Rob Strudwick, a riff on *The Two Doctors*, the group secured the cooperation of the local cable provider's public access video facilities. The production was a multi-Doctor affair, involving the 2nd, 4th, 5th and 6th Doctors, as well as companions Jamie, Peri, Nyssa and Sarah Jane. Real life persons Michael Grade, Mary Whitehouse, John Nathan-Turner and Eric Saward would be portrayed as well, with Saward being played by a puppet.

The Two Companions ended with the 6th Doctor consigned to regeneration. This lead in 1987 to a sequel production - *The Wrath of Mikey* (after Michael Grade), written by David Weides, and the introduction of the 3rd Doctor into the crew, the 6th Doctor imprisoned by the BBC. This lead to another sequel, *The Fallout of a Time Lord*, written by Pete DePalma and Christian Erickson, bringing in the 1st Doctor and Susan, as the 6th Doctor is put on trial again, with all the earlier Doctors and companions coming to his rescue. In 1988, all three productions were kluged together, to form The Two Companions movie.

The Two Companions and its successors were heavily influenced by the Federation's sensibility and aesthetics. They adopted the metafictional comic style, taking it a step further, merging front of the camera and backstage events to portray the Doctor's struggling directly with a villainous Michael Grade, as the near cancellation, the hiatus and the *Trial of a Time Lord* were merged. Their follow ups - *Faulty Tardis, Doctor Who: The Motion Sickness, You Only Live Thirteen Times* continued to merge media and metafiction.

CREW: *Writers - Chris Clarke, Rob Strudwick, David Weides, Pete DePalma and Christian Erickson, and others....*

CAST: *Matt Alexander, Sue Bartholemew, Debby Baouer, Brendan Cainen, Judy Chamberlain, Pete DePalma, Christan Erickson, Blanche Hansen, Keith Heiberg, Tom Keenan, Wallace Larson, Lisa Rollie, Mark Rollie, Brinn Urban, Robert Urban, David Weides, Chris Weiss, Stefanie Meemkin,*

CHAPTER 7: THE FALL OF JOHN NATHAN-TURNER

Starting about 1985, and then accumulating with building intensity among fans, there was a sense of disenchantment with the show. They were loyal, but bitter. Doctor Who just wasn't as good as it used to be. Peter Davison, taking over the role in 1982, was rather subdued in comparison to outsize personalities like Troughton, Pertwee and Baker. But he rode on considerable accumulated goodwill. As the show moved towards crisis, that goodwill began to dissipate.

The truth was that for fans, the show had changed, and they wanted the old show back. The inconclusive crisis with Colin Baker and the cancellation/hiatus left everyone confused and frustrated. It would only get worse. The fan base was cranky, divided, rife with conflicts and tension. As much as they loved Who, the fans just weren't happy with it. A lot of this swirled around John Nathan-Turner who had become a polarising figure.

John Nathan-Turner was the longest serving producer on classic Who, from 1980 to 1989. The first half of his career was dramatically successful. He'd overseen Tom Baker's final year, which had included some extraordinary stories. From there, he'd gone on to pilot the successful Peter Davison era, and was now poised to introduce a brand new Doctor.

In America, Doctor Who had become a cult phenomenon, largely because of Tom Baker. Baker was long gone from the show, and it had been John Nathan-Turner who had stepped into that gap, both taking credit and embracing this new audience wholeheartedly. He hadn't created Tom Baker's Doctor, or most of the Fourth Doctor era, but he had just enough connection to attach himself to it. He worked hard to capitalize on that success, and on his connection to it, and promote Doctor Who in America. Nathan-Turner saw a brand new audience in America, and he embraced that audience wholeheartedly.

Nathan-Turner was loud, proud and in your face. He was the first producer to be a star, a sort of homegrown Lucas or Roddenberry. Before him, the shows production team stayed in the background. But Turner made himself as famous and as central as the Doctor himself. As a celebrity producer, he gave interviews, appeared on television and attended conventions. He made himself accessible to fans and fandom in a way the show had never seen before. For fandom of the first half of the eighties, he was a hero.

But he was a flawed hero. At heart, he was a showman. He was more interested in stunts, in casting and coups, and productions, than he was in actual stories. Truthfully, he had no real grasp or interest in stories, he'd come up through production, not writing or directing. He was also a jealous and insecure man. His tantrums and micromanagement became legendary.

No creative person likes restrictions and no one likes to be told 'bad idea.' But creativity doesn't distinguish good and bad ideas. You need people around to say 'no' and to filter out bad ideas.

As Nathan-Turner's star rose in Doctor Who, as he became the central creative force, he tended to push or alienate many other people who worked on the show. When he came to the show, he deliberately made a clean break of many of the previous writers and directors under Baker and Pertwee. He wanted to cultivate new talent.

He also very clearly wanted to be the 'star' and it was hard to share the limelight with other talent. He proved unpleasantly thin-skinned, blacklisting one of his most gifted writers and directors, Peter Grimwade over an imaginary slight. He fought Saward tooth and nail over Saward's attempt to bring back Robert Holmes. He could be furious and vindictive, during a convention; he publicly spat in actress Nicole Bryant's face.

The *Trial of a Time Lord* and subsequent years were extremely stressful, and stress doesn't bring out the best in people. It didn't for Nathan-Turner. On top of that, a lot of dirty laundry had been aired. At different times, Nathan-Turner had been publicly vilified by Eric Saward, Michael Grade and Jonathan Powell. These interviews, these remarks, those criticisms and attacks were out there in the newspapers to be read by anyone, or transmitted through rumours and gossip. The climate was bitter and nasty.

Ultimately, familiarity breeds contempt. All the foibles, all the shortcomings, the petty vindictiveness, the high handedness, the arbitrary disinterest in stories, all this was overlooked when he was riding high.

Instead, his positive qualities, his thoughtfulness, generosity, enthusiasm and showmanship, his gift for promotion were front row and admired.

But when the show was going downhill, all of these positive qualities were overlooked, and the negative qualities were highlighted, particularly because they were true, and they really had hurt the show badly.

The show had genuinely gone downhill. In hindsight, some might trace this back to the Davison years. But it was flatly apparent with Colin Baker's tenure. Through no fault of his own, Colin Baker's reign as the Doctor had led to a series of crises both inside and outside the show, messy departures and terminations, the failure of *Trial of a Time Lord*, the erratic floundering of Sylvester McCoy's first season, and the awkward tonal shifts, slapdash production values and bombast of his era. John-Nathan Turner's Doctor Who from 1985 onwards was a show in perpetual crisis. The ratings were falling, fans were complaining. There were loyalists of course, both to the show, and Turner's vision. But among dedicated fans, there was a lot of conflict.

Nathan-Turner had been the hero taking the credit for Doctor Who's success for the first half of the 80s. Now he became the face of Doctor Who's rapid decay in just about every way, from production values, to scripts, to performances, to collapsed ratings, from *Trial of a Time Lord* *on*.

And like a marriage gone bad, neither side had any option. Nathan-Turner didn't want to be working on the show, it had offered him a series of disastrous humiliations. But he had nowhere to go, the BBC wasn't offering him anything else, and no one else was hiring, particularly after things went wrong.

And while fandom had turned against him, and fans wanted anyone or anything else, there was no one to replace him, and if he left the BBC would shut it down. They didn't want Nathan-Turner, but there was no one else.

Of course, while Nathan-Turner's flaws and blunders were genuine, that overlooks the machinations of the BBC's senior management who were bent on crippling the show until they could safely cancel it. They were quite happy to hum away unnoticed quietly in the background, as fans savaged him.

Turner had worked hard to make himself the public face of Who, and it was blowing up on him. For many fans, Turner was now the enemy, a tyrannical martinet whose arbitrary decisions and ego-driven blunders were destroying the show.

In America, Turner as the current showrunner, had received the credit and the popularity for work he hadn't done. He'd promoted the Tom Baker era in America, but mostly hadn't been involved with producing it. Now he was blamed for everything wrong with the show, including a lot that was not his fault.

In 1984, Turner was loved by fans to the point that the Federation held a special screening of *All Doctors Great and Small* for him as a tribute. He was welcomed. They were willing. He was happy to watch.

By 1987, he was a controversial and often despised figure. He had become the villain of the *Reign of Turner*, a snarky, funny dissection of his career with Who.

By 1989, limping, battered, much of its audience fading away, the fans divided and angry, the BBC put the show on another hiatus.

It wasn't officially cancelled.

A Pirate's History, Page 177

The BBC management had learned their lesson from the previous fiasco. Instead, Cregeen promised the show would return; it was just being postponed a little longer than usual. It was just taking a little rest, that was all. After four years of being bled in a death of a thousand cuts, it was just on hiatus.

This time, they got away with it. No one really cared, except the fans, and they were so busy fighting with each other and pining for the show the way it used to be that they weren't effective.

Given all this, it's no surprise that after 1984, fans of the show became nostalgic. They found themselves looking back to the show 'when it was good.'

In England, Tom Baker had been off the air for five years. New Doctors had taken his place. Davison had come and gone. Colin Baker had come and gone. Now it was the time of McCoy. But the Colin Baker and Sylvester McCoy eras were troubled. The fans were strongly nostalgic for the good old days.

The BBC had begun releasing the old serials on VHS at a rate of twelve per year, starting around 1983.

By the time McCoy was around, there were a good three or four years of accumulated VHS releases floating around out there of Tom Baker, but also of Jon Pertwee and even Peter Davison. - video reminders of what the show had been and what other Doctors had been like.

Added to that a virtual armada bootlegs copied and traded among fans and collectors, and you had a unique situation. Unlike any previous Doctor, Sylvester McCoy was now competing directly with his previous incarnations.

In America, Tom Baker's fourth Doctor had been airing since 1978. But the real burst of popularity had only come about between 1981 and 1983. For many American viewers, new to the show, he was still the 'current' Doctor. Although the other Doctors had begun to air on television, and show up in fan clubs and conventions Baker remained 'The Doctor' of choice. American fandom was literally born nostalgic.

Across America and England, for fans, their Doctor was going to sport a twenty foot scarf. Even though Tom Baker had ceased to be the Doctor for years, even though there had been two or three Doctors since him, fans still tended to look back to the past. When Tom Baker was not the favourite, then fans looked to Jon Pertwee, or as far back as Patrick Troughton, or as recently as Peter Davison.

But no matter what, it would be a rejection of the 'modern' era of the show, of Colin Baker and Sylvester McCoy.

This didn't mean that Sylvester McCoy and Colin Baker didn't have fans and supporters. Each, was in turn, the bearer of a long legacy, and that got a lot of respect. There are still proponents for the McCoy and Baker eras, and still supporters of John Nathan-Turner. That's fine, and it's genuine.

But ultimately, the show had entered its nostalgic phase, and fans pined for past glories.

Review: The Reign of Turner (1989-1998)

STORY: Colin Baker, (played by Steven Hill) following a furious row with John Nathan-Turner (also played by Steven Hill) retreats to his dressing room, to fume and eat donuts. Once there, he finds a mysterious box of VHS tapes with a cryptic note that they can be of use to him in his battle with Nathan-Turner. The video tapes turn out to be a series of parodies of scenes from the show, dating back to Tom Baker's last season, which is also John Nathan-Turner's first. Mixed in with these, are revealing backstage moments - with the actors, crew and Nathan-Turner. In the first series, we see Tom Baker as an out of control ego, battling Nathan-Turner for control. As Baker leaves, Nathan-Turner goes slowly off the rails. He recruits Peter Davison and proceeds to terrorize the crew, firing everyone but the mild mannered Davison, who is desperate to leave. Finally, Davison manages to get himself fired, and Turner almost whimsically calls in Colin Baker. The sequences proceed from there into the future, into the McCoy era, all the while, Turner's cruelty and dementia reaches dizzying heights.

REVIEW: Between 1984 and 1990, the Federation made a staggering 20 or so fan videos, created a video library, released a video-zine for nine episodes, they attended conventions, participated in costume contests, did skits, put on shows, and piled up an impressive list of local awards. They were an out and out repertory company, and one of the most amazingly prolific fan groups in Who history, up to the modern era.

Their fan videos were rapid affairs, someone had an idea, for instance *Doctor Who in It's a Wonderful Life*, or *Doctor Who and the Holy Grail*, mixing and matching cultural products. They ran with it, shooting was done in a day, editing in a week, and then it was out there. It was almost always crude and cheap, driven by ideas and enthusiasm rather than professional or technical competence. They were unpolished, but they understood that an audience forgave anything if you could make them laugh, and they learned to keep it moving.

Inevitably, if you're doing that kind of volume, you get good at it, you get more sophisticated and ambitious. You find yourself wanting to do something bigger, something more ambitious. Eventually, you go after your great white whale.

The Reign of Turner was simultaneously the Federation's masterpiece and its swan song. It is equal parts sloppy, amateurish, unpolished, and brilliant, ruthless and incisive. Both a love letter to Doctor Who's history and characters, as well as ferocious takedown of the shows cliches, and a vicious dissection of its backstage history. It's also funny as hell to boot.

Let's start at the beginning. Who or what was the Federation?

It was just a group of fans. In this case Mark Christenson, Jennifer Adams, Chris Brainerd, Steve Schiller, Rob Warnock and a handful of others. Steven Hill came along a little later. Back in those days, perhaps any day, film production was not an easy thing. Usually, you needed a group of people to share the work. Most fan films were the work of fan clubs.

What usually happened was that a group of people would come together to watch Doctor Who and talk about the show. Someone would knit a twenty foot scarf, or dress up as a Cyberman or build a police box shell. People would start to come in costumes. Someone might have a camcorder. Members of the group might already be amateur film makers. The idea would come up. That was probably as far as most of it got. Sometimes a club, or a group, would get organized or dedicated enough to actually start and finish one. If they were particularly talented or dedicated, they might do two or three, or even a handful.

That's the Federation. That's also Seattle International. It's Timebase Productions. The Projection Room. Beeblebrox Company. Silverwolf Films. Planet Video, Ad-Lib and Pacific UK. Cheapo Productions. Stone Circle. They were just unincorporated associations, groups of fans, not corporations or production houses. You can look at the credits on a production, and you'll see a lot of people in front of and behind the camera, wearing different hats, taking on different roles, multiple roles. The membership would shift, people would leave, people would join, but there tended to be a core.

Most fan videos, especially most of the early ones, tended to be parodies. It's an immense amount of work to even pull one of these things off. It's not just work, skills, and access to tools; you need a decent little workshop to build a Police Box shell or a Tardis console.

You need to find locations. You need to know how to shoot a film or video, which involved the technical aspects like lenses and focal lengths and colour balances, but also visual composition. You need to know how to light a scene. How to frame a shot. You need to know how to write a script or speak lines. There are entire industries built on doing this, there are full time professions and armies of professionals with decades of experience, all making it look easy, but it's tough. The more professional looking, the harder it is.

A lot of people didn't have these skills, they had to learn it or develop it as they went. For a lot of fan film groups, the easiest path, the path of least resistance, was to spoof or parody. That genre was far more tolerant. No one expected spoofs to be hyper-professional, they just had to be funny. The standard was a variety show sketch, not a full on production. It was an easier target to hit. Most of the early videos, from references from that era, turned out to be spoofs like the *Two Doctors and the Anti-Matter Menace*, or *Labyrinth of the Blud Devils*. In this sense, the Federation was no different.

What distinguishes the Federation from all those other early groups is that the Federation, apart from being extremely well documented, was astonishingly prolific. Generally, their production values were not high; they shot on VHS, edited on the fly, and their acting seldom ventured beyond mugging for the camera. But within that framework, they shot a lot and they did it well.

A turning point for the Federation was *Save WHO*. The Federation had been good at cultural mixing and matching, taking Who and combining it with some other production - *Monty Python, MTV*, the *Man From Uncle*, you name it. But the cancellation crisis offered a whole new opportunity, a new direction, the chance to spoof, not just the show itself, but the backstage, the making of the show, the personalities and the politics behind the show.

Save WHO used that telethon structure as the framework for their story, which allowed them to run a promotional documentary, which in turn was just a series of parodies of classic scenes, as well as behind the scenes skits. It was a sophisticated, almost metafictional approach to storytelling, working both inside and outside the universe of the show itself. A sort of quantum leap in storytelling and comic sophistications.

Which brings us to the *Reign of Turner*, and John Nathan-Turner's dramatic fall from grace. In the early 1980s, the controversial producer been a star, the hero of the show, now in the late eighties, he was a martinet, the floundering, micromanaging bully dragging the show down. Or at least, that's how many fans saw him now.

The whole thing is a series of skits of varying quality. Some of them have not aged well. There's a sketch where Tom Baker and Lalla Ward, who in real life had a tempestuous offscreen romance, propose a parody of *Hart to Hart* a 1980s American detective series. There's another parody of an 80s British comedy series, *The Young Ones*. It may have worked then, but it's hard for a spoof to be effective now, if the material it spoofs has been all but forgotten.

Nevertheless, there are so many skits, covering such a wide assortment and coming in such close succession, that the overall effect works. The sheer volume of sketches and parodies overwhelms. Something didn't work? Wait a moment, and you're on to the next one. The production moves past its duds, either by returning to the framing sequences or just moving to new skits. Its momentum keeps it going.

What holds the production together is Steven Hill, who does a startlingly authentic impression of Colin Baker. Most performers who imitate Doctors don't really go much past wearing the costume. But Hill perfectly captures the look and nuances of Baker.

He also does a quiet, creepily menacing portrait of John Nathan-Turner that, at times, makes you overlook the obviously pasted on beard and wig. Hill's Nathan-Turner is appallingly oily, a smarmy, sleazy manager whose ego and misjudgment slowly overwhelms every other aspect of the show.

Another standout is Jennifer Adams, who plays almost every single female companion and actress, and a few more roles. Her performance is broad and uniform. Basically, she changes wigs and clothes, but she does every role the exact same way. That makes it funny. As for the rest, quality varies all over the place, as is expected from an amateur cast and crew.

The production side of things, on the other hand, is frankly terrible. The Federation, over the years, grew steadily more sophisticated in terms of their storytelling and comic sense, but production values tended to remain pretty crude. Shot composition, lighting, sound mix and even focus tended to be haphazard. Their inspiration was sketch comedy parodies, which tended to mean fast, cheap and dirty.

The only really solid component is Rob Warnock's musical scoring. As fans, there were lots of costumes, but no great shakes in terms of sets and locations. Not surprising, their inspiration was the cheap, quick and dirty sketches of television variety shows. It was a working formula - get it done fast, make your hit, and move on. It didn't have to be pretty. It just had to work, and it did.

Ultimately, the rather half-baked production values basically means that it is, and always will be, by fans and for fans. It's best appreciated in a club or convention setting, in a room full of fans, or at a party, where its constant stream of gags and references will have everyone rolling on the floor. But having said all that, it's genuinely funny for the most part and it moves along well. It's easily the best Doctor Who spoof out there, both in terms of comedy, being true to the show, and the sophistication of its approach.

Behind the scenes, however, the Reign of Turner was almost as much of a nightmare as the real life events it parodied. Production began in 1987, with principal photography through 1988 and 1989. They literally shot right up to the cancellation. The open ended 'skit' based style and loose story format invited lots of overshooting. By the end, they had eighteen hours of raw sketch footage.

Meanwhile, the Federation was falling apart. It was the usual thing. People grow up, they move on, leave town, develop new interests, etc. There were genuine personal conflicts, some of them arising out of the stress of production.

The Federation split into two factions in 1988, and then into three in 1989, with people refusing to talk to or work together, which slowed down work. Through the 1990s, the Federation mostly ceased to exist as either a social/fan group, or as a production center.

By 1991, a bloated two hour and fifteen minute version had been edited together by the Adams/Hill faction and was making the rounds. There was another unsuccessful stab at re-editing in 1993.

This eventually provoked a *Mystery Science Theatre 3000* riff by another faction of the former Federation. This was the first and maybe the only time that a Doctor Who fan film got the MST3K treatment. That said, it was kind of mean spirited in its mocking of former friends.

In 1995-1996, Warnock, Adams and Hill went back to the drawing board and edited a new 80 minute version, which is generally accepted as the definitive, if late, version. It premiered at Visions 96.

Eventually, in the late 1990s and early 2000s, the Federation experienced a renaissance, with the members, notably Warnock, Hill and Adams, coming together again to make a new series of films, *Realitywarp, Traumaturge* and *Shadowcast.* These films moved away from parody, into more serious storytelling, and more serious attempts at competent production values. They are worth looking at. They also did the six minute movie project.

Nevertheless the *Reign of Turner* stands head and shoulders above most other Doctor Who parodies, not just for being funny, but as a snapshot of attitudes and perceptions, a reflection of the fans relationship to and views of the show in its dying days.

CAST *Steven W. Hill - Colin Bayker / The Doctor / John Nathan-Turner / Enlightment / Peter Grimwade / Sharaz-Jack Nicholson / Rula Lemka / Scott Wilson / Georgia Davidson / Glitz / Lord Kiv / Mike / King Yrcamos / A Mostly-Red Kang / A Bunnyman; Jennifer Adams Kelly -Mary Tam, Romana No. 1 / Leila Ward, Romana No. 2 / Sara Sutton / Nyssa / Janet Fielding / Taggen / Sarah Jane Smith / Leola / Sandra Dikkinson / Nichola Bryant / Vyvian / Billy; Robert Warnock - Peter Davison / The Doctor No. 5 / Bonnie Layngford / Mal / Dead Man / Auntie Vanessa / Cyberleader / Gary Up-and-Downey / Wilson Scott / Jamie / Dibber / Sil's Slave / Neil; Jay Harber - Tom Bayker / The Doctor No. 4 / Monarch / The Valeyard / Michael Jayston / Shockeye / A Mostly Red Kang; Mark Khristensen - Eric Sayward / Barry Lets / Count Grandad / Terminus / Cyberleader / Gerald Flood / Matthew Robinson /The Doctor No. 2 / Oscar Belcherby / Govenor / A Bunnyman; Jeff Sparrow - The Master / Tramus / Sylvestre McCoy /The Doctor No. 7 / Grahame Williams / Dalek / Rasmus; Philip*

Kelley - Mark Strikkson / Turlough / Crazier / Rik / Ovaline / A Bunnyman; Eric Prelwitz - Matthew Waterhaus / Adric / Romulus / A Bunnyman; Patrick Reardon - Amelia Rumford; Kathy Meyer - Anita / Delta; Janine Reardon - Vivien Ray; Dennis Kytasaari - Maurice Colborn; Debbie Bauer - Mostly-Red-Kang; Colleen Bailery - Mostly-Red-Kang Leader; Doug Winston - Butch Kang; Sue Kueny - Starchild;

CREW *(Abridged): Jennifer Adams Kelly, Rob Warnock & Steven Hill - Writer / Directors / Cinematography / Editing / Props & Sets / Grips & Lighting / Console Design ; Jennifer Adams Kelly - Producer / Casting / Costume / Make-up / Still photographer / Typist; Rob Warnock - Music; Sound Effects Editor / Titler / Storyboard Artist; Steven W. Hill - Collapsible Police Box designer / titler; Dennis Kytasaari - Editing / Set Builder / Console Design / Grip / Driver ; Jeff Sparrow - Camera Operator / Set Builder / Driver; Christine Warnock - Costume; Philip Kelley - Camera Operator / Key Grip/ Set Builder / Driver; Jay Harber - Set Builder / Driver; Tim Kaspar, Philip, Sue Kenny, Don Malzahn - Set Builders; Eric Prellwitz - Grip;*

Review: The Experiment (1988)

Cybermen on the Moors

STORY: The Fourth Doctor, Harry and Sarah Jane, beam down to the barren Earth of the far future. Humanity abandoned the world a long time ago when the sun became unstable. Now, in preparation for their return; the Doctor has arrived to repair teleportation equipment. Unfortunately, the Cybermen are already there, carrying out diabolical experiments....

REVIEW: So why did the Planet Productions group, also known back then as Video 8 for its video format, choose to remake *The Sontaran Experiment*, a minor Tom Baker serial from twelve years before.

According to Nigel Windsor, writing online for the New Zealand Doctor Who fan club, *'My very first memories of the show were as a child watching 'The Sontaran Experiment' and 'Genesis of the Daleks'... In my late teens I discovered fandom; suddenly, socialising with friends became more important than anything else. I met a fan who had a video camera and was also a professional actor, and I had just finished two years at Film and Television school. So with his acting background and my skills as a cameraman we embarked on remaking 'The Sontaran Experiment' over three weekends on the exposed Lancashire hills, with a few 'minor' script changes! Namely we used*

Cyberman costumes instead of Sontaran costumes because those were the only ones we had, so we ended up calling it 'The Experiment.'"

That *The Sontaran Experiment* was a favourite of Windsor's was only part of the reason. The fan he met was actor Nigel Peever, who seems to be at the center of Planet Productions. Back around 1985, Peever had met Ian Taylor, another fan who had landed the plum job of playing a Cyberman at the Doctor Who Exhibition in Blackpool. Taylor had just made *Labyrinth of the Blud Devils*, his own Doctor Who spoof.

This inspired Nigel Peever, and another fan, Kevin Taylor, to make their own films, and Peever had gone out and gotten a camera. Over the next few years, Nigel Peever, Ian Taylor and Kevin Taylor would be the center of a shifting group of friends and fans who would turn out several films under different production names. Nigel called his films Planet Productions, Kevin Taylor would go by Planet UK, and Ian had Ad-Lib, but casts and crews overlapped massively.

So why remake this story?

There were practical considerations at work: It was the only two episode serial made by Tom Baker, and the first two episode serial since William Hartnell's tenure. The Sontaran Experiment, as a short serial was by far the most easily achievable story, simply in terms of time.

Added to that, *The Sontaran Experiment* was a relatively small production. Shot entirely on location at the hills and cliffs of the empty countryside, it's actually quite photogenic, but easy to travel to. Neither the Police Box nor the Tardis interior appears. There's no requirement for elaborate sets or props, minimal special effects. The cast is relatively small, only a few actors, there's only one or two monsters and they're easily rendered. It really is one of the simplest and most reproducible of the Tom Baker stories, perhaps of the entire classic series.

But why not a new story?

"Experiment and Spectre were my attempts at real Doctor Who. We made Experiment because I wanted to do a classic script, in the same way that people want to play Macbeth etc. It's 'real' Doctor Who. It was made in three days over two weekends; 3rd-10th July 1988," Peever recalled in an online discussion.

That's entirely respectable, especially given that Peever was a professional actor in the English stage tradition.

It may also have been a learning experience. Peever and his friends had made two previous attempts at a Doctor Who film - *Earthpark* and the *Last Days of Rassilon*. Neither of them had managed to be completed. His friend Ian Taylor had tried a serious film with *Blud Devils*, and it went off the rails. Kevin Taylor had struggled. Ambition outran ability or resources.

This was followed shortly after by *A Shade of Death*, a half hour short, with John Field playing the Fourth Doctor and Ian Taylor playing the nemesis Shade. *Shade of Death 2*, about ten minutes, featuring John Field as the sixth and fourth Doctor, and Nigel Peever as the second, was a far more polished and intelligent production. But it felt incomplete, not so much a story on its own, but a chapter in a larger story, or an episode in a serial. *The Invisible Menace*, was also abandoned incomplete, but was released with images of script pages to fill in the missing scenes.

After that, we have a flurry of short films and incomplete works, mostly less than ten minutes. *Gangfight*, a couple of *Unit Shorts*. These were relatively competently done, but again, feel incomplete, like scenes without true beginnings or endings.

What it came down to was that the first few years of existence for Planet and Pacific-UK, with Nigel Peever and Kevin Taylor, produced a half dozen abandoned or incomplete short projects. They were having trouble pulling a real film together, which is entirely understandable. It's a difficult thing to achieve, especially back in those days.

Film or television production is not an easy thing. There's a learning curve and it's steep. Every aspect of production is difficult and complicated and it is easy to get wrong. New film makers, working with original material, are often stuck reinventing the wheel and reinventing it badly as they learn.

But remaking an existing serial, that's learning by reverse engineering. You're not reinventing the wheel, you've got an existing wheel and you learn the craft by building one just like it. You're following the path of people who got things right, rather than just striking out blindly. I can see the appeal.

It also speaks to me of a powerful sense of nostalgia, a rejection of the modern Doctor Who that was airing on television screens in 1987 and 1988, a rejection of the conflict and tensions of the cancellation crisis and subsequent hiatus. They were tired of that. They didn't want *Time and the Rani*. They wanted Doctor Who when it was good. I think that there's a very deliberate statement involved in remaking a serial from Tom Baker's first year.

So how does it stack up?

Technically, it's quite good. Almost everything about it represents a quantum leap in production. The shots are effectively composed, the story moves briskly, the performances are in step.

The locations, with the cliffs, and ravines, the outcrops of naked rock, the rolling desolate grassy hills and moors are visually arresting. The Cybermen costumes are top notch. By the same token, the soldiers are kitted out well. John Field produces an accurate Fourth Doctor costume and manages not to break his collarbone. The script has a few changes from the original, substituting Cybermen, and it works nicely.

But John Field is not Tom Baker. That's the thing. You can't just put on a twenty foot scarf. Tom Baker's a uniquely charismatic presence. The very nature of the role means that Field is simply copying Baker, and suffering in the comparison. That's the difficulty in playing an existing Doctor, it's almost impossible to pull off.

If we can set aside that John Field is not Tom Baker it is an interesting performance. Field, perhaps to his credit, doesn't really try to do an impression, he just says the lines his own way. He's more restrained than Baker's sunny ebullience, perhaps more surly and abrasive. His fourth Doctor is discernibly a darker, harder and grumpier character than Baker's version.

Was this an acting choice, not to try and do a Baker impression, or simply the limits of Field's abilities as an actor? Hard to say. But I'm okay with it. Fair warning, the distinctiveness of Field's performance is going to make or break it for you. If you can go with him, fine. If you can't get Baker out of your mind, it won't work.

Ian Taylor, the mind behind Ad-Lib Productions, plays the role of Harry Sullivan entirely competently. The rest of the cast acquits themselves honourably.

Apart from that, the shift of the villain from a lone Sontaran to a pair of Cybermen changes the tone of the story dramatically. As a villain, the Sontaran is more agile and expressive: He scowls, he glowers and threatens; he reacts with anger and frustration.

The Cybermen, on the other hand, are much more impersonal and clinical. Their masks lack all expression. Their movements are deliberate. It makes the experiment rather more chilling. There's a more menacing and disturbing quality to the Cybermen's deliberations. In being less emotionally engaged, it magnifies the cruelty of what they do. The Sontarans see humans as enemies, the Cybermen simply as subjects or lab rats. The Sontaran makes it sadistic, the Cybermen are simply, chillingly, clinical. It's a scarier enemy for a darker Doctor.

Ultimately, *The Experiment* stands as an alternate version of an existing serial, not even a lost serial. It's well done. I think it's worth it.

CAST: *John Field - Fourth Doctor; Sarah Jane - Heidi Jones; Ian Taylor - Harry; Kevin Taylor, Stuart Glazebrook, Nigel Windsor, Jonathan Horn, Nigel Peever, Michael Taylor, John Friar, Philip Osborne.*

CREW: *Director - Various, Script - Bob Baker and Dave Martin, adapted by Nigel Peever, Camera - Nigel Peever and Eric Davies. Visual Effects - Mike Hardman.*

Review: Spectre From the Past (1989)

Two Doctors and a Menace from Beyond Time and Space

STORY: The story opens in an average modern household. A young man announces that he is going to bed. But as he ascends the stairs, he encounters the apparition of an old man descending. The apparition reaches for him, there is a flash, and he is thrown to the floor unconscious. Before he passes out completely, his eyes glow blue. Meanwhile.... The Second Doctor's Police Box arrives on Earth in the 19th century, drawn by dangerous time travel experiments which threaten the fabric of our very reality.

REVIEW: *Spectre From the Past* is almost perfect. Engaging story, engaging characters, terrific imagery and cinematography, vivid locations, they seldom put a foot wrong.

First up, this is one of the most complicated fan stories I've run across. It's reminiscent of El Cheapo's Trident. On the one side, you've got the Second Doctor in the 19th century, confronting the machinations of a Victorian mad scientist whose experiments threaten to tear the fabric of space and time. On the other track, we have the Fifth Doctor investigating mysterious ghostly phenomena in the modern era and confronting an invasion of other-dimensional entities taking over human bodies. The two plots run side by side through the serial, touching just enough to keep the story moving.

Information is offered up in measured doses so that we never get ahead of the unfolding story. Mysteries are resolved. The stakes increase steadily and the plot evolves smoothly, adhering to its own logic, but at the same time, managing to contain interesting twists. In the end, it resolves in a satisfying way.

Trying to play an existing Doctor is an uphill battle because it's almost impossible to capture the magic of the original. You'll always be a copy. This is one of those rare exceptions. Nigel Peever who plays the Second Doctor actually resembles Patrick Troughton, and he's clearly worked hard to capture the nuances of Troughton's voice and mannerisms. He reproduces Patrick Troughton so thoroughly it's uncanny at times.

David Cullen, playing Peter Davison's Doctor acquits himself reasonably well. He's got darker hair and is a bit more lanky than Davison. But Davison always offered up a fairly controlled performance, and Cullen manages to find that pitch. The Fifth Doctor was always the most restrained and subdued of the Doctors, so he's not that hard to imitate.

The rest of the performances are right on. They've either found real actors for this, or amateurs who were at the upper bars of talent. At least as important, they're a diverse cast. One of the giveaways of a lot of fan films is that the cast tends to cluster together in the same age group, often fairly young. Here you've got a group that runs from young to old and across a handful of physical types. Very much real world; very reminiscent of the show.

The production is very polished. I suspect that it was shot on the old Video 8 consumer format, but if so, it looks good. The image is clean and precise. It's well shot and lit. At times, it feels reminiscent of the old Hammer films. There are images and compositions that are just spectacular. These people knew how to point a camera. If The Experiment had been a learning exercise, they'd learned well.

The locations, both interior and exterior, are well chosen and often gorgeous, adding production value. As a special note, apparently the Police Box that the Troughton Doctor exits was one of the few remaining actual police boxes in England. You can't beat that for authenticity. The props and costumes are good. The CGI effects are a bit dodgy, but hell, it's 1989. Regular B-movies and television were no better, and if anything, this helps it fit in with sense of authenticity to the Davison era.

It's not perfect - the Second Doctor's confrontations with the mad scientist tend to go nowhere and drag repetitively. There's only so many ways you can say 'Listen to me!' and 'No!' The cricket game sequence is outright tedious, possibly because I don't know enough about the game to appreciate the gag.

Despite that, I was always glued to the screen. It managed to be interesting, either visually or in its storytelling, or both, all the way through. Cricket game aside, I was never bored, there was always something going on that made me want to see what happened next. It wasn't big spectacular climactic payoff. But that's okay. It was an engaging story.

A Pirate's History, Page 199

Spectre From the Past is even the right length, being a two part serial, running forty minutes and change. The fifth Doctor is notable for doing a number of two part serials - *The King's Demon, Black Orchid, The Awakening. Spectre* fits the overall style of the Davison era. It is actually better than any of the real two part serials. You could slip a DVD of Spectre into the Davison's oeuvre and the average viewer wouldn't do much more than note that Davison's hair is a bit darker this time out. It was simply a pleasure.

Planet Video went on to hit the iceberg with its next project, *Second Spawn*.

Second Spawn was the most expensive and ambitious production they ever tried, with a cast of about 48 people. Notably, they'd acquired the original Krynoid pod from the BBC and were planning on using it.

That story involved the Seventh Doctor rescuing Adric from his death at the end of *Earthshock*, then ending up in the Third Reich, where he confronts the Nazis, works with a squad of British soldiers out to assassinate Hitler and faces the big threat, a Krynoid invasion.

There's a couple of bold moves there: The death of Adric was one of the biggest shock moments in the series history, and fairly controversial even today. So having the seventh Doctor go back to rescue Adric from his fate has a certain enthusiastic fanboy quality.

On the other hand, the Nazis were just dark. There was a reason that Doctor Who through most of its history almost never went near Nazi Germany. Ultimately, it's just too grim for a family show.

There were a number of locations, a lot of period costumes, a Krynoid-man costume was built to show the intermediate stage, and there was even going to be model work with a full sized Krynoid crushing houses. Of course, all those actors and locations and ambitious shots and effects turned into a scheduling nightmare. Eventually, in August of 1990, the project was abandoned.

You can see the surviving footage of the unfinished *Second Spawn* up on YouTube. There's about twenty minutes of it, edited into something somewhat coherent although clearly incomplete, with some fill in narration. It does give you a sense of what they were doing. This is one of those lost films that you wish had made it.

The Krynoid-man costume prepared for Second Spawn seems to have been recycled for a short film titled *Unit-Revival* - basically ten minutes of guys in soldiers uniforms running around in the woods confronting a monster. There was also a second short, *Unit-Powerplay* based around the Autons.

After the failure of *Second Spawn*, the Planet Video players regrouped and made a fifteen minute short - the *Daleks Invade Stockton*. John Field returned for a brief appearance as the fourth Doctor. Nigel Peever stepped out from behind the scenes to play his own version of the Doctor, and he's not bad at all. It's a reasonably efficient piece of work, despite feeling incomplete. Probably the best of their short films. Notable was the participation of Simon Williams, who would go on to make the *Timestealers* series.

Planet Video's informal swan song came in 1994, with the *Trial of Davros*. This wasn't another film or video, but a stage play. Written by Michael Wisher (the actor who had originally played Davros) and Kevin Taylor and produced by Nigel Peever, the Time Lords put Davros on trial for his crimes, not the least of which is creating the Daleks in the first place.

The trial ends with Davros victorious, the whole exercise having been his ruse to turn the tables on the Time Lords.

The production was remounted in 2005, with the explicit approval of Terry Nation, an expanded script and Terry Molloy (the second actor to play Davros) in the role, with additional filmed sequences featuring Daleks, Draconians and others.

John Field, after playing various roles, including the fourth and sixth Doctor for Planet Productions, would eventually return to take up the mantle of the third Doctor in *Gene Genius* for the Projection Room. More on that later.

Nigel Peever would get involved with Simon Williams Timestealers series about the Master, and in particular, the Three Masters would end up reproducing Planet Video's distinctive '80s video synthesizer' score as well as its fiendishly sharp cinematography and editing. Nigel Peever went on to become a real actor, accumulating a respectable list of credits.

The bottom line for Planet Productions, then comes to two remarkably accomplished and polished full length productions, *The Experiment* and *Spectre From the Past*, a stage play, *The Trial of Davros*, an intriguing partially completed lost production, *Second Spawn*, and a handful of short and incomplete work. That's not bad.

CAST: *Nigel Peever - 2nd Doctor; Gary Cullen - 5th Doctor; Ron Pritchard - Robert; Margaret Noble - Helen; Keith Noble - Professor; Pat Hough - Mrs Duff; Danny Davies - Gamekeeper; John Friar - Creature; Ian Fortt - Richard; Allan Jones - Father Adams; Simon Quayle - Vicar; Kevin Taylor - Maddox; Kathryn Shepherdson - Dr. Harvey; Tomas Shepherdson - Gravechild; Hilton Fitzimmons -*

Chronosite; Stephen Berry - AFM; Gareth Owen, Stephen Farral, Pam Willis, Melanie Jones - Party Guests.

CREW: *Tim Peever - Director; Nigel Peever and Kevin Taylor - Script; Paul Furber - Floor Manager; Nick Stone, Nigel Windsor - Assistant Cameramen; Chris Burroughs - Unit 1 Clapperloader; BBC Records - Sound Effects; Trackline - Music; Make up supplied by Bromileys; Costumes Courtesy of Pantwich Planets; Special thanks to Alsager Cricket Club, Crich Tramway Museum, Vicar of Acton Church, Mr & Mrs J.A. Hough; Mrs J. Barnett; Planet Video, 1989, 43 minutes.*

A Pirate's History, Page 204

CHAPTER 8: 1993 FAILURE TO RELAUNCH

In 1989, the official word from Peter Cregeen and the BBC was that Doctor Who was not technically cancelled. Jonathan Powell was the BBC Comptroller, but they were careful to emphasize it was Cregeen's decision as head of programming. It wasn't a cancellation.

It just wasn't coming back after this season.

The BBC had learned its lesson in 1985. Even with four years of bleeding the show dry, of cutbacks and punitive scheduling, an official cancellation or termination would cause a furor. Doctor Who, regardless of the sad state its current incarnation was respected. It was still a British institution of 26 years duration. The British attach a lot of sentimentality to that kind of thing. Cancel it and there would be newspaper and television coverage, there'd be people talking about it in the streets, it would get raised in parliament. All of the 'pointy headed fans' would go nuts.

Grade and Powell had gone through such a gauntlet of fire back in 1985-86 over the last attempted cancellation that they were gun shy. So the BBC just refused to admit they'd cancelled. They'd get evasive.

"The show's not cancelled, it's just having a little lie down, that's all. "

"Cancelled? No, it's just taken a trip out to a farm where it can play with other cats and dogs and telly shows for a while, maybe it will come back. "

"Cancelled? What? No of course not… Hey, would you look at that? I think the Space Shuttle just exploded! "

The bureaucratic approach was to simply say it was temporarily off the air, and be vague as to exactly when it was coming back.

This wasn't something that the media was inclined to cover heavily. They didn't deal well with that kind of ambiguity, it wasn't sufficiently black and white, and truthfully, they'd covered that back in 1985 and it hadn't turned out so well as far as they were concerned. A big story about a sleazy underhanded attempt to destroy a beloved British institution turned into some vague waffle about scheduling. They weren't going to get caught like that again. A cancellation was one thing. That was controversy and uproar.

The BBC messing about with its schedule? That wasn't something that people were going to get upset about, even if the BBC was pretty vague about the return date.

The hard core fans might not like it, but there wasn't much they could do except wait for the promised return. Doctor Who had once again become Shrodinger's cat. It wasn't alive, but it wasn't dead.

Okay, that's fine for 1990. Indeed, Doctor Who 'sort of' came back that year, for a special appearance in a program called *Search Out Space*. Sylvester McCoy reappeared as the

Doctor, Sophie Aldred was back as Ace, and K9 joined them for an educational quiz show.

Available on YouTube, today this production is almost forgotten, but back then I think this kind of left an impression that the Doctor hadn't really gone away, it was just around the corner. It really might be back soon.

It's even fine for 1991. Cregeen did say it would be a longer than normal wait. But then, 1992 rolls around, and there's nothing but ceaseless rumours of movies in development and private proposals to relaunch the series.

To be fair, there was a sincere attempt or series of attempts to make a Doctor Who feature film. As early as 1986, a group called Daltenreys Ltd., comprising Peter Litten, George Dugdale and John Humphreys, had obtained film rights and were trying to get a movie off the ground. In 1990, producer Felice Arden came on board with Dugdale and Humphreys. In 1992, the French film production company, Lumiere joined forces with Daltenreys. In 1993, Lumiere invited Leonard Nimoy to become involved with the project. For whatever reason, the Daltenreys project could never get the deal closed or secure the funding. The license expired in 1994. Daltenreys eventually ended up suing the BBC.

The story of the endless attempts to bring Doctor Who to life as a major motion picture during this era is chronicled by Jean-Marc and Randy Lofficier in their excellent book, *'The Nth Doctor.'* Go out and get it.

Meanwhile in England, there were endless reports of various private enterprises or consortiums trying to buy the rights to Doctor Who floated. At one point, Terry Nation, the creator of the Daleks, and Gerry Davis, co-creator of the Cybermen, joined forces in an attempt to obtain the rights to the series.

Verity Lambert apparently looked into it. Director Graeme Harper and writer Adrian Riglesforth made a pitch There were all sorts of abortive attempts, some clearly farcical, some apparently serious.

But although the BBC was, in this Thatcher dominated era, nominally in favour of privatizing, somehow Doctor Who never ended up on the block. Or perhaps it was simply that most of the companies that seemed to bid may have been either competitors or shoestring affairs.

At one point in the 1990s, it appeared that Amblin Entertainment, Steven Spielberg's company, driven by one of its producers, Philip Segal, entered discussions for a possible American Doctor Who series. Ultimately this went nowhere. But it's likely that the prospect of landing Amblin Entertainment may have motivated the BBC to give the short end of the stick to everyone else. Why bother with all these little proposals when you're trying to hook the ultimate big fish.

So, even if the show was off the air, the rumour mill and backstage machinations were constant. It gave weight to the notion that the show could come back in some form, in any form, at any moment.

But 1993 was a special year.

1993 was the 30th Anniversary. If the series was going to be revived, this was going to be it. There was a lot of anticipation. Everyone was excited, there was a palpable sense that the show was returning. There was talk, there were celebrations, nostalgia, there was all sorts of anticipation. There was going to be a major revival – *Lost in the Dark Dimensions,* a full length project which would unite all five surviving Doctors, including Tom Baker. And from there? Who knows? This was going to be it!

Then it fizzled. We got something of a thirtieth anniversary. There were John Pertwee's two radio plays, *Ghosts of N-Space* and *Paradise of Death*, even a documentary, *Thirty Years in the Tardis*.

John Nathan-Turner was brought back to unite Doctors, Companions, villains and monsters in a pair of seven minute long 3D segments called *Dimensions in Time*. Sentimentality aside, it was appallingly bad. But at least it brought all surviving Doctors back and earned ratings of almost fourteen million, briefly cracking the top ten most watched shows. Surely that proved there was an audience? Justified the return of the show?

The big, eagerly awaited epic – *Lost in the Dark Dimensions* had fallen apart, and despite amazing ratings for *Dimensions in Time*, it wasn't going to lead to a new series. 1993 was the big moment, and then nothing. It's hard to carry the torch after that.

The BBC maintained its discreet ambiguity. The rumors churned - Amblin, Daltenreys, Terry Nation, but nothing was ever solid, it was all smoke and mirrors. There were no announcements. It wasn't going to come back. The big anticipation fell flat, a couple of radio plays, some documentaries, some merchandise and a *"Children in Need Special"* runaround – those were poor consolation prizes. The big anniversary fizzled and was replaced by the big disappointment.

So really, in the years building up, and especially in the years following, I can sort of see enthusiastic groups of fans going 'well this sucks, we're going to make our own.' Back in 1993 it had seemed like the show was going to come back, or at least have a big anniversary production. When then failed to materialize… that was almost like a permission to do it yourself.

Existing groups, Ad-Lib, Planet Video, Beeblebrox and the Federation, all beginning in the 1980s continued to produce video into the 1990s and sometimes beyond.

There were new fan productions between 1990 and 1993. One of the most significant was Randy J. Leblanc's *Professor What* series, set in an alternate universe from Doctor Who. Let's be frank, this was Doctor Who with the serial numbers painted over rather than filed off. The Professor was a Timelord from Gallifrey, who travelled in a diamond insignia cabinet and fought Computrons (Cybermen) and Zaxxons (Daleks), in a series of serial adventures, with each serial running half an hour to an hour total. Initially amateurish but enthusiastic in just about every aspect of production value, the series became more polished as it went along. It never quite shook its amateur roots, but each subsequent production became more competent and more ambitious. The series was, on the whole, watchable. *The Professor What* series is amazing for running from 1990 to 2009, an astonishing nineteen years, thirteen serials and four actors playing the Professor over that time. This is a testament to a single driving personality, Leblanc, who stuck with it across a remarkable span of time.

But 1993, and the failure of the anniversary was a watershed year. That was when Marq English premiered *Resurrection of Evil,* and Florida's Guardians of Gallifrey club released *The New Order.* Timebase Productions lead by Rupert Booth, Paul Ferry, Philip T. Robinson, Lisa Gledhoe, as well as Chris Hoyle and his Projection Room, both started up in 1993.

Over the next few years, the Unnamed Doctor Who Club of Newfoundland started making films. Stone Circle launched a second female Doctor a year or so later with *Rutan and the Alliance*. Thames Valles Time Lords made *the Persephone Complex* and *Still Life*. Jonathan Blum dressed up as the 7th Doctor for *Time Rift*. Simon Williams began to create his stories about the Master. *Time and Again* went into production in 1997. *The Millennium Trap* saw life.

The eighties had produced a bare handful of productions, mostly spoofs. But spoofs were almost always tributes to live shows, comic love letters. What was the point of spoofing a dead show?

The nineties were an explosion. Fans were actually making a serious effort to revive the show. Not all of it was good. As with everything, there's quite a lot that was bad. Sometimes this was simply inferior equipment - shooting on an old VHS camera didn't give you the best image quality. Sometimes this was the limitation of talent or experience; often it amounted to kids with cameras. But there was a surprising amount of ambition and accomplishment. A lot of it turned out to be watchable. The best was on par with the BBC.

This was also the era of the semi-official productions, when fans learned to tease permission, or skirt the BBC's copyright, or even to slice off pieces of it. Technically, this had begun in 1987 with Jon Levene appearing as his Doctor Who character in a half hour short called *Wartime*, for Reeltime Productions.

Really though, it started with Colin Baker playing the Doctor in all but name in 1991's *The Stranger*, for Bill and Ben's Video (BBV). There would be more *Stranger* stories, and new productions like *Shakedown* and *Downtime*. The Sontarans, the Yeti, and even the Autons returned as villains. Sarah Jane, the Brigadier, and the third Doctor's first companion, Liz Shaw, all came back for their own, all new adventures. Nick Scovell appeared on stage with *Planet of Fire*, and he and Rob Thrush began a series of licensed Doctor Who plays.

Look at it in sociological terms. Fans, fandom, these are individuals and groups, a community, organized around a particular cultural product, consuming it, discussing it, interacting with it. What happens when that cultural product expires? When there's nothing more, no more production? What does the community do when its reason for coming together goes away?

Well, we've seen this with *Star Trek* and *Star Wars*, even with the Bronte Sisters novels and the Sherlock Holmes stories. When the cultural product goes away, the fans start creating their own, in one way or another. They become their own producers, and their own audience. Fans create, not just for themselves, but for other fans.

Film or video production is difficult and time consuming; it's a huge personal investment for a lot of people, particularly if you are doing it for free. Normally, people don't work hard and spend a lot of time and money if they don't have to. So they have to be highly motivated. Which, I suppose, is what being a hard core fan amounts to.

But if they were making film or video production, there had to be an audience, there had to be someone out there to show it to, someone that wanted to see it. If you were shut out from conventional distribution channels, which fan films were, you needed a very close knit, very motivated community to distribute the production to. Michael Grade might disparage the 'pointy headed fans' but they were exactly that sort of community.

So you had a constituency that was motivated to make
Doctor Who, a constituency that was motivated to watch
Doctor Who. If the BBC wasn't going to provide, they'd
create their own.

There were other factors at work. Unlike *Sherlock Holmes* or
the Bronte sisters, Doctor Who was a television medium, as
Star Trek had been before it. But unlike *Star Trek* in the 60s
and 70s, it was easy to record and copy episodes. The Doctor
Who community evolved a network of VHS collectors and
traders that by the 1990s were sophisticated, highly organized
and widespread, which was plugged into the network of clubs
and conventions. So you had distribution and audience ready
made. In a sense, the cancellation of the show coincided with
the emergence of technology and social networks that would
allow fans to perpetuate the show.

Consumer video cameras had come out in the 1980s, through
the 90s, they had become steadily cheaper and more
accessible. The quality had gone up. There were more and
more accessories, tripods, lenses, sound recording and tape
editing systems. The pool of people with access to these
systems had grown dramatically, and with time, opportunities
to learn and develop, the diversity and overall levels of skill,
the availability of skills had grown.

This was only part of the story of course. Even within the
BBC, the show never quite went away. Every now and then,
there'd be a rumble, like a sleepy engine turning over.
Dimensions in Time, in 1993. The Paul McGann movie in 1996,
the *Curse of Fatal Death* in 1999, the *Scream of the Shalka* in
2003.

The series had found a new life in books with Virgin's New
Adventures. Virgin publishing had acquired Target books,
which had made good money publishing novelisations of the

serials, usually by the writers. When the series ended and there were no more serials to novelize, Virgin asked for rights to publish brand new novels, and the BBC granted it, from 1991 to 1997. These books would have a major influence on shaping the rebooted television series in 2005.

Audio was a much easier format than video, and there was a proliferation of fan made audio adventures, which culminated with Big Finish Productions obtaining a license from the BBC to do their own audio productions with the 1980s Doctors.

Fan videos were only a small part of a much larger story going on around this time. But it's an overlooked part, and it's the part that comes closest to genuinely reproducing the form and format of the classic series, so it's worth taking the time out to explore it here.

Review: Resurrection of Evil (1993)

Demon in Waiting

STORY: The Doctor and his companion arrive at a deserted English village. As they explore, they encounter a paramilitary of paramilitary thugs, a fleeing journalist, an insane British baron, and a scheme to reanimate the destroyer of worlds....

REVIEW: At seventy-three minutes, this is a charming, if slightly padded Doctor Who film. Seriously, there are all these slow scenes of the Doctor and his companion wandering around that don't really add to the story. Oh, and a bit too much solarisation in the video effects, particularly at the end.

All right, this is absolutely the worst thing that I have to say about *Resurrection of Evil*. The reality of any film or television production, and especially for a fan production, is that there are a million things that you need to get right, a million decisions that need to be made. Unauthorized productions like this are often short on resources, on time, on money, on people. It's almost impossible to get it all right. Invariably, with a million decisions, something somewhere has to go wrong.

All I really have are a couple of small quibbles. That's not bad.

So let's talk about what goes right with this production -
which is just about everything.

To start with, we have the Doctor himself, played by Mark
Bennett. Okay, he looks a little bit like a very young Rowan
Atkinson in a blue leisure suit. I really wasn't sure about him
at first, he seemed like he was trying too hard.

But then, oddly enough, he puts on a hat, and suddenly, he
sells it. He's gets this retro 60s vibe, like you could spot him
walking along in the background of a James Bond or Carry
On movie. Suddenly, he's confident, jaunty, brilliant and
charming, with just a faint echo of the poise of a Tom Baker,
or a more extroverted Davison, or a laid back Pertwee.
Whatever the Doctor has going on, this guy has captured it,
and having captured it, it helps to carry him across a lot of
territory. This Doctor has a lot to do, even in terms of simple
exposition, and at different points, particularly towards the
end, he has to show different sides of his character.

Bennett is one of the earliest of the 'New Doctors', or 'Nth
Doctors' apart from Leo Adams, who was forgotten, and
Barbara Benedetti, who was influential. Up until the early
1990s, most fan Doctors tended to be imitations of the
classics. Simply imitating an existing Doctor? Only Nigel
Peever, Ben Pocock and Steven Hill managed to pull that off
completely. Other actors like John Field or John Walker had
varying levels of success.

But a new Doctor? This would become more popular in the
absence of the show, with people like Rupert Booth, Andrew
Sarlo and others creating new characters who still managed to
express the essence of the Doctor. I'm not sure if fans at the
time got into it, but I think it's clearly the better choice.

Bennett is a charming casting choice, and having him be his own Doctor works. But I also put a lot of credit towards the script and direction. If it drags a bit with a lot of shots of the Doctor just wandering around the streets, the trade-off there is that we had a Director with the patience and willingness to develop the character and story cinematically.

There's a wonderful scene where the Doctor and his friends are being pushed along by the villain's henchmen. Everyone is pretty stressed out and nasty. But Bennett's Doctor just saunters along and then casually sits down and relaxes on a bench. A more frantic or business oriented director wouldn't have taken out the time to shoot a moment like that, he wouldn't have had the patience for it. But that kind of shot is what makes it all work.

Or there's a scene where the leading man shoots a thug who was going to kill them. The Doctor remonstrates the leading man for unnecessary violence, and turns away in a huff. But the minute the Doctor's back is turned, the companion kisses him. That's some really nice byplay, it shows off character for each of them, gives them each a nice moment, and there's a wonderful sense of timing to it all. A hastier director just wouldn't take the time to develop his moments.

The rest of the cast is generally terrific - the bad guy, the Baron, played by Andrew Cottingham, is charmingly villainous in a menacing Hugh Grant sort of way. He's handsome, charming, intelligent, wears a comfortable looking sweater and you just want to like him, apart from the fact that he's also cheerfully, insanely murderous.

The Doctor's companion, played by Liz Cahill, has moments when she gets to express an identity and perspective, when she steps out of the Doctor's shadow. She doesn't actually do much, in terms of advancing the plot, but she's allowed

A Pirate's History, Page 217

enough dialogue to come across as a real personality. The leading man, played by Nik Lusser, is a little thin in the role, but he's okay. His job seems to be to run a lot, look stoic and fill in plot.

The thugs, led by Steve Trasler, look convincingly thuggish - they don't look like kids we so often see in these films. By its nature, fan films tend to be made by groups of friends and associates, so the cast tends to all look the same age, often young. These guys don't look like fans, they look like average, regular people who beat other people up for a living.

The performances are natural and unforced, there's no sense of people struggling with the roles or self-consciously 'acting.' Everyone gets a moment or two where they can shine a bit. You have no sense that the characters are ciphers. Rather, watching them all, you get the feeling that each one feels like the hero in their own story, even the thugs. Some performances are better than others, but there's not a bad performance.

As with the really good fan films, the production locations are extraordinary. Once again, we have some terrific locations, very well shot. There are some sequences of the Doctor wandering along a woodland path that are beautiful. There's effective use of imposing buildings - castles, churches, brick edifices, that add a lot to the feel.

But it doesn't end there. The villain's laboratory looks sufficiently tech-ish and improvised in the right ways. It feels authentic, in a sort of 'Evil Baron has retrofitted a section of his castle into a high tech lab,' sort of way. When you go back and look at it, the camera is quite tight. Marq English knows exactly how to point the camera so that it doesn't take in too much and dispel the illusion. Not everyone gets that.

A Pirate's History, Page 218

The thugs have a military looking jeep to drive around. It's only in a few scenes, but it helps to sell them as an almost paramilitary bunch of toughs. Little details like that are easy to get wrong - you don't have the right kind of car, or you're skating a bit on something. But it adds up. Locations, props, characters, it all continuously builds into the story Marq English is telling.

Past that, there's a good Police Box shell, a very well done Tardis console and console room. I notice they went a little cheap. If you look closely at the console room's walls you'll see that they simulated the roundels by gluing paper plates to the walls. But you have to look closely, and even then, it's only apparent in a couple of shots.

There's also a monster - a nicely realized, longhorn type of demon thingy. He doesn't do much but order people around and wait to be resurrected. But hey, I'm a sucker for an actual monster.

This creature, the big bad, is the heart of the story. He's been dead or dormant a long time, and he's slowly resurrecting. The villain is helping him. The Doctor and leading man are drawn into it in their own ways. It's actually a fairly simple story, and it's telegraphed very early on.

This isn't M. Night Shyamalan stuff, there's no shocking twists, no event that turns the story on its head and makes us reappraise everything we've seen, as we'll see with Trident. But then again, it's not badly handled at all. The story is allowed to develop in an organic way, and as it develops, it fills in with good performances, nice interplay and it builds its tension so carefully and quietly, you don't even realize when you've started to grip the arms of your chair.

A Pirate's History, Page 219

Bottom line, it's an entirely engaging production. For the most part, its flaws and glitches, and they are there: A tree too small to hide behind, a stairwell that doesn't match the architecture of the rest of the building, etc.; are quiet unassuming ones. They're not laugh out loud goofs, like shaking a gun to simulate firing, or foleying in an obnoxiously loud birdsong. Rather, Resurrection's flaws are mostly easy to overlook and don't really disrupt.

Shot in 91 and 92, finally completed in 1993, my impression was that this project may have turned into a bit of a white whale. If you look in the credits, you'll see a terrifying number of locations, eleven in all. Each location shoot is an undertaking - you have to get the cast out there, you have to get the camera and lighting people, the crew, the makeup, you need to arrange vehicles to schlepp those people and that equipment, you need to make sure you've got electrical outlets to run your lights and camera, that the weather is right. It's such an effort you generally only get one location on a particular day, and you can end up shooting several days at a location, hoping for the right conditions. Each location is a project in itself and they have eleven locations.

On top of that, there's a lot of very ambitious stuff here: The monster costume, various effects, the Police Box and Tardis console and set, the composition and lighting of shots, and even the actors doing various bits of play. When people are learning as they go, it means that they're taking a lot of time and putting a lot of work into it. As I've said repeatedly in other reviews, making any kind of film, even a bad one, is an incredible amount of work. Making a good or great one can be exponentially difficult. In the case of these films, it's a huge amount of time and work to go into a production that is fundamentally handicapped in the audience it can reach.

Which may be the reason that English/Bennett/Taylor etc. seem to have only made the one major Who production in the 1990s. That's kind of a shame, because Marq English had a very good handle on his material and on what makes the Doctor. He comes across as a confident Director. Bennett's Doctor was engaging. Despite a few wobbles, he was a thorough Doctor, and I'd have liked to see where he would have taken the character as he gained experience. Still, it was three years of their lives, and if they didn't want to jump back into the meat grinder, I can't blame them.

As it is, there's really only the one English/Bennett (et al) collaboration, and like Spectre From the Past, I think it might have gotten overlooked in the general fizzle of 1993, and the wave of polished unauthorized and semi-authorized productions.

Eleven years later, in 2004, Marq English would return to collaborate with Mark Bennett, Rupert Booth and Adam Manning, for a new project: *Timequake: Reversing the Polarity*. No relation to the Vonnegut novel of the same name. This *Timequake* was a 'mock documentary' about the rise, the fall and the fan following of a television series about an alien time traveler with the ability to regenerate into new bodies. Basically, it's Doctor Who with the serial numbers filed off. Footage from the *Resurrection of Evil, Regenesis, Phase 4* and other fan films are recycled to depict the old Timequake series.

Timequake: Reversing the Polarity is perceptive and funny, acknowledging flaws, mocking ego and foibles, even invoking an American remake that gets it all wrong, and yet thoroughly gentle. Bennett, Booth and Manning appear in clips from their roles in Timequake, as well as their aged later selves. It's well worth searching for.

No surprise, after *Resurrection of Evil*, Marq English went on to be a film maker, racking up an impressive series of IMDB credits.

CAST: *The Doctor - Mark Bennett; Elizabeth King - Liz Cahill; Adam Taylor - Nik Lusser; Farendon - Andrew Cottingham; Mailer - Steve Trasler; Dr. Jones - Lucie McDonnell; Roberts - Paul Taylor; Philips - Kevin Littlefield; Metcalfe - Ritchie Taylor; Security Guards - Lee James, Tony DeGrasse, Noel Daniels, Rob Martins, Mark Stillman; Sullivan - Marq English; the next Doctor - George Murphy.*

CREW: *Writer and Director - Marq English; Cameras - Marq English, Mark Bennett, Kevin Littlefield; Post-Production - Marq English, Kevin Littlefield, Ritchie Taylor; Music and Additional Sound - Ritchie Taylor; Special Visual Effects - Rob Martins and Marq English; Special Alien Make-Up Effects - Stillframe FX; Special Video Effects and Titles - Kevin Littlefield; Lighting Supplier - Barry Croft; Lighting Effects - Lee James, Technical Advice - Mark Stillman; Special Thanks to Tooshka Productions, DeGrasse Productions, Ann Villette; Filmed on Location at Westerham, Kent / Shirley Hills, Shirley / Beddington Park, Wallington / Kingston Park, Wimbledon / Nonsuch Park, Cheam / The Mews Studio, Sutton / Blenheim Gardens, Wallington / Woodmansterne, Surrey / Lloyd Park, Croydon / Royal Marsden Hospital, Sutton / and Broadgreen Studios, Croydon. Enigma Films, 74 minutes,*

Reviews: Vaulkherd, Rutan and the Alliance (1996-1997)

The Next Woman Doctor Goes to Mondas

STORY: Amera, a fellow Time Lord, accompanies the Doctor on a ghostly adventure in *Vaulkherd*. In *Rutan*, as a result of a temporal accident, the Doctor fuses with Amera's body, and she hunts time criminals. In the *Alliance*, the Doctor crosses into an alternate universe where Earth and Mondas have formed an evil alliance, led by the Lord President who has his own dark secret.

REVIEW: Between 1996 and 1998 Stone Circle/ Armageddon Productions produced three fan films, chronicling the adventures of the second female Doctor, played by Sharon Crookes. Each film represented a leap in ambition and ability, culminating in the *Alliance*.

The first film, *Vaulkherd*, 14 minutes, 1996, was a sort of ghost story. Andre Prines played an original Doctor and Sharon Crookes appeared as the Amera, a neophyte female time lord. It's a relatively modest little effort.

Rutan appears to be more or less a direct sequel to *Vaulkherd*. The story opens with the Tardis being struck by 'strange radiation' which kills the two time travellers, but somehow causes the Doctor's life force to reanimate and possess

Amera's body, giving the Doctor a female form and twelve new regenerations, all of which seems unnecessarily complicated.

Anyway, as the story goes, the new Doctor finds herself tracking some strange emissions. She discovers a trio of time criminals hiding out in the 20th century. Unfortunately, in their passage through time, they've dragged along three other hapless humans and a Rutan from across time. The Doctor set out to foil the rebels, save at least some of the time castaways, and is briefly forced to ally with the body-stealing Rutan.

The script is interesting, but the direction slow and the staging is clumsy. The performances are middling. But it tells its story coherently, although it doesn't quite resolve, and there's not really enough time to develop all its ideas properly. Nevertheless, there's a decent homemade console, multiple interior and exterior locations, period costumes and interesting use of CGI effects and a Police Box shell. The best parts are the castaways dragged through time, including the Rutan. There's something engaging about their incongruous archaic costumes and fish out of water haplessness. Crookes is kind of underwhelming as the Doctor, not terrible by any means, but not spectacular.

Stone Circle Productions came back for another sequel in 1998, with *The Alliance*, a sequel to *Rutan*, and a much more ambitious three part story which attempted to replicate the serial format of the classic series.

When I say sequels here, I'm saying this in the loosest sense. There's no foreshadowing in *Vaulkherd* to *Rutan*, for example. There are no carry overs, except the characters of the Doctor and Amera. The transition is handled through a prologue, and there's no direct reference in *Rutan* to the events of

Vaulkherd. Equally, there are no plot threads or allusions linking *Rutan* and *The Alliance*. The only connecting thread is the Sharon Crookes' Doctor, which means its continuity is about on a par with regular Doctor Who, I guess,

Anyway, in *The Alliance*, the Doctor, played by Sharon Crooke once again, crosses dimensions into an alternate universe and winds up on the planet Mondas. Mondas is familiar to us from Hartnell's The Tenth Planet, as the wandering homeworld of the Cybermen.

In The Tenth Planet, Mondas is Earth's evil twin. Literally. The shots of Mondas are of Earth's globe, upside down. According to *The Tenth Planet*, Mondas was once Earth's companion, orbiting on the opposite side of the sun. Somehow, Mondas had been flung out into space on a long wandering orbit, the inhabitants had been forced to transform themselves into Cybermen to survive, and now they were back looking for trouble. From that, you'd expect this to be a Cyberman story. No Cybermen here though.

This alternate universe Mondas was never flung into space, rather, it ended up in a stable orbit with Earth in place of the moon. The people never became Cybermen.

Interestingly, once upon a time, Earth really did share its orbit with another planet, now called Thea. The two planets orbited at Trojan points, 60 degrees apart. Unfortunately, the orbits weren't quite stable. Thea eventually caught up to Earth and crashed into it. Thea's molten core merged with Earth's, and the moon eventually congealed out of the giant ball of dust and debris. Or at least, that's the current theory.

This Mondas, in a stable double planet orbit, partners with Earth as the center of a brutal human space empire, which crosses into other dimensions and devastates weaker worlds.

A Pirate's History, Page 225

There are some impressive scenes of the Alliance's war fleets crossing dimensional barriers to wreak havoc on other versions of Earth, which gives the story a sense of scope and vastness. All is not entirely well with the Alliance, however. It turns out they have enemies, the Trions, who are grinding them down. The Alliance has managed to throw up a defensive force field around the solar system, and are making do by looting alternate realities. The Doctor's dimension is next on the list.

The Doctor is unwillingly drawn into the politics and machinations of Mondas and the Alliance as she slowly works her way into the heart of the mystery. There's plenty of intrigue and plotting going on, mixed with a healthy dollop of space opera heavily influenced by Star Trek.

This was the second major project to feature a female Doctor. Crookes definitely improved as an actress since *Rutan,* and is immeasurably better than she was in *Vaulkherd,* where, to be fair, she wasn't given much to do. This time out, Sharon Crookes is entirely competent in the role of the Doctor. She never commands the screen the way Benedetti did or the way that Baker or Tennant did. She says her lines and hits her marks, and never loses control of her performance. Her style is reminiscent of Peter Davison's Doctor.

Crookes' Doctor establishes herself in an early scene where she and the Prime Minister have a casual conversation. The Prime Minister is flanked by an army of pointing guns. The Doctor never flinches. Neither one of them acknowledges that the Tardis has been forced down. It's a subtle but tense conversation and it shows off Crookes' Doctor as a force to be reckoned with.

Crookes' Doctor never loses her cool, remaining friendly, casual and unafraid no matter how many guns are pointed at her at a particular moment. Her best quality is her unflappable, pleasant calm. Her finest moments as the Doctor come at the beginning when she lands on Mondas; and at the end when she confronts the President.

Unfortunately, the Doctor's companion, Warren Hurst, played by Josh Fielden is kind of a weak link. He brings the same sort of pudgy lack of charisma that we saw in Matthew Waterhouse's Adric, but without the acting chops.

John Isles as Prime Minister Silus, schemer in chief, isn't too bad. He's got the 'lean and hungry' aspect of a Cassius. His acting is a bit limited, and the script does him no favours by giving him large, awkward, chunks of dialogue. The role is a bit too much for him. There are times when he's engaging, particularly when he's scheming to use the Doctor to undermine the President.

Kevin Hile as the Lord President is effective. It's a tough role, his character has to run the Alliance, deal with Silus' plots, confront the Doctor and reveal a dark secret. That's fairly demanding, and would challenge a more mature actor.

The cast is large, which is always impressive. There are a lot of extras to fill out the scenes, and sometimes people are a production value all by themselves. But the cast all seems to be mostly the same age cohort - mature teens or young twenty-somethings. They're not really trained actors. No one truly embarrasses themselves, but the performances seldom approach professional caliber. It's mostly high school level performances.

There's a genuine effort to costume the Alliance and its enemies, which works reasonably well despite the limitations of budget. The wardrobe of the Alliance Starfleet officers is very reminiscent of the *Star Trek* movies - red coats, with a bit more gold embroidery and sashes, reminiscent of *Star Trek's* original *Mirror Mirror* episode.

Indeed, the Alliance comes across as the evil version of the Federation from *Star Trek*, effectively conveying fascism. These are not nice people, but they are people rather than caricatures. They have a world view, even if it isn't very nice. They're competent at acting civilized when they need to be.

The script features decently clever ideas and there's some nice bits of dialogue. I liked the fact that the plot had its own wrinkles - The Alliance has its enemies, it's existing in a complex universe with its own history, raiding across dimensions against weaker worlds, while struggling to survive against an alien enemy. The Lord President has his secrets. Behind his back, his second in command, Prime Minister Silas is plotting to usurp him. You have the sense that things were going on in this world before the Doctor showed. The depth of plotting, the multiple secondary stories, the serial structure, are all reminiscent of classic Who.

This is an immensely ambitious production - the scope is huge. That's hard to pull off. But they give it a decent effort. There's a lot of nice touches - a lot of effort went into costuming, into recruiting a large cast. A subtle touch is that the picture of the Lord President is everywhere, not omnipresent, not prominent, but showing up on walls to illustrate his influence and power in this society. There are limits - they didn't have the money to build a detailed starship bridge, but they do an effective job of simulating one with banks of monitors, a desk lamp, wall hangings and carefully framing their shots. As usual for these films, the production manages to find visually impressive locations. Not standout, but effective: A public garden, some country locations, a large frame building.

One thing that stands out in the Alliance is an early and remarkably ambitious use of CGI. Not photorealistic, but arcade video quality. Decent enough for the time and I give them credit for the attempt. The CGI has this sort of low resolution, grainy luminous quality mostly that distinguishes it from real life textures. At times, you can see the video game style, low resolution edges.

The CGI is used for some very interesting and impressive shots - the Earth looming gigantic in the sky of Mondas, is a subtle successful effect. Rather more obviously, we see Mondas ships landing and taking off, integrated in live action scenes, with real landing strips that real people is standing on. It's an ambitious attempt to integrate CGI objects with live scenes. There's a nice effect showing someone beaming in as an occasionally staticky hologram to have a conversation with the Lord President.

Most notably, the Tardis console is a CGI construct, although the background wall seems to be real. In the previous film they built a basic prop console, and kept it dark to hide its lack of detail. This time, they've dispensed with a physical console and just composited it in. This sort of thing would become a trend in the 21st century fan films, where we watch teenage Doctors romping around spectacular CGI backdrops.

This isn't quite a first tier effort, although I might be unduly hard on it because of the image quality. Sadly, as with Rutan, the image quality, uploaded from what seems to be second or third generation VHS makes it a tough watch. The colour balance shifts constantly, the sound is rough, the composition of shots is mundane at best. These technical handicaps make it hard to give it a fair assessment, much more so than Rutan, in part because it's longer, but also because it is much more ambitious. It's possible that a better quality upload would be much more watchable.

But truthfully, there are genuine short comings that make it something of a mixed bag. There are things that make it stand out, and make it worth inclusion in this book - the Female Doctor, the innovative use of CGI, the ambition of the story and cast. As I watched, I had the sense over and over, that they were doing really interesting things, but they weren't doing them brilliantly, just tolerably well. So not first tier, but a quite interesting second tier work. The Stone Circle group would eventually morph into Westlake films, doing productions like Time Distortion, Deconstruction, Auton Diaries and Future Investment.

On the whole, the production seems to fall into that middle ground - not unwatchably amateur, but not substantively professional. It shows ambition and perhaps talent in spots, but no polish. Rather, it's middling, not for a general audience, but something to be enjoyed by fans who love the show deeply, nothing wrong with that. There's more than enough going on for fans of the Classic series to enjoy.

RUTAN CAST: *The Doctor - Sharon Crookes; Edward Higgins - Jason McMillan; Tudor Woman/Rutan - Lisa Hiley; President - Nicola Crookes; General - Lawrence Petford; Scientist/Passer By - Kevin Hiley; Rejected Passer By - Deanna O'Shea; Glen (Hytoxol B. victim) - Garry McMillan; 17th Century Arrival - Mark Worgan; 13th Doctor - Andrew Crines; Dead Body - Deanna Franklin.*

RUTAN CREW: *Stone Circle Productions/Armageddon Productions, 1996. Produced and Directed - Mark Worgan & Kevin*

Hiley; Written by Kevin Hiley; Camera - Mark Worgan; Computer Animation - Kevin Hiley & Mark Worgan

THE ALLIANCE CAST: *The Doctor - Sharon Crookes; Harren Hurst - Josh Fielden; Silus - John Isles; The President - Kevin Hiley; Captain Beaufort - Jonathan Miles; Demack - Lisa Hiley Chief Madoc - Andrew Crines; Admiral Deverne - Nicola Crookes; Barine - Adrian Wright, Spaceport Officer - Matthew Post; Pelin - Gareth Preston; Alliance Personnel - Nick Cossings, Kate Bevis-Melie, John Crookes, Christine Crookes, Liam Reton, Darren Crines, Lea Horley, Peter Tattersill, Jake Tsoi*

THE ALLIANCE CREW: *Stone Circle Productions; Produced and Directed by John Isles; Producers - Andrew Crines, Kevin Hiley; Script - Andrew Crines; Script Editors - John Isles and Kevin Hiley; Creative Consultants - Mark Worgan, Gareth Preston, Lisa Hiley; Production Designer - Kevin Hiley; Sound Recording & Special Sound - JN & KH Productions; Props - Jonathan Slyman Costume Design - Lisa Hiley, Nicola Crookes; Filmed on location in West Yorkshire Special thanks to: Church of Jesus Christ of Latter Day Saints, Barclay's Bank PLC, Chris Bowle*

Review: Regenesis (1993_

The Doctor of the 1990s

STORY: An Extradimensional Entity has invaded the Tardis. Forced to land on Earth and flee his vehicle, the Doctor ended up in a mental institution. Meanwhile, the entity has been making plans to take over the world. The story starts…. Now!

REVIEW: Based in eastern England, Timebase Productions were a uniquely talented, uniquely dedicated group of fans. Led by Rupert Booth and David Ferry, the egalitarian crew consisted of perhaps a dozen people: Philip T. Robinson, Lisa Gledhill, Ian Johnson, Graeme Nattress, Neil Johnson, Deborah Reilley, Christine Potter, Steven Palace and a few others, sharing a multitude of acting and production roles.

Collectively between 1994 and 2002, they produced a staggering twelve, half hour episodes, divided up into five serials, plus an infamous 'lost' serial, spoofs and incomplete works. Their core output is equivalent to an entire season of Doctor Who.

Timebase's work felt exactly like Doctor Who. It was like watching a season of classic Doctor Who that had slipped in from an alternative universe. In terms of overall quality of production, performance, writing, you name it, it was on a level with the classic series. Whatever intangible quality made

Doctor Who, they had it. You could literally slip it in there, and it would fit. It would fit perfectly.

When I watch *Regenesis*, I'm struck by two things. One is the fidelity to the show; this feels so much like BBC Classic Doctor Who it's surreal. They did an amazing job replicating the look, the style of the original series. The other is, my gosh, one good decision after another. These guys almost never put a foot wrong – the whole serial, their whole oeuvre is all about things that seem cunning and well thought out, there's nothing sloppy or casual.

So bear with me, I'm going to talk about a few of those really sharp decisions that get made and what they add up to:

Format – *Regenesis* is a two-part serial, with 25 minutes per part. That's the first thing it has going for it – it's structured just like the classic series. This is something that gets overlooked a lot. But how you structure a story really defines how it feels and flows. That's why a lot of Hollywood movies feel so uniform – standard three act story structure. The old pulp novels had a headlong energy – why? Short chapters and cliff hangers and plot twists at the end of every chapter. Doctor Who? Serial format – 25 minute episodes, subplots, twists, cliff hangers, etc.

Other productions, before and after, would follow that rough half hour serial format - Planet Productions *The Experiment* and *Spectre From the Past*, Stone Circle's *The Alliance* all the way through El Cheapo with *Trident*. It's always effective in helping create the feel of the classic series.

It's not just the mechanics of the structure either. As an audience, we get used to it; we incorporate it into our appreciation and expectations. Growing up, we've unconsciously imbibed a set of rules and expectations in terms of how long things, are the pacing that happens in them – we know and expect the 24 minute television half hour, the 55 minute television hour, the 90 to 120 minute movie length. The thing is, if we watch something that doesn't fit those formats… Something odd, a 15 minute short, or a 70 or 75 minute piece… it doesn't feel right, it's both too long and too short, the pacing is wrong, the 'beats' of the arc happen in the wrong places.

Believe me, it's real. Try it out sometime. A lot of fan film makers miss that. But the point is, that if you are disciplined enough to work in those formats – if you're doing your Doctor Who as a serial consisting of 25 minute episodes… Then that feels right, it feels natural. It feels like authentic Doctor Who, because for the classic series, we've incorporated that 20 to 25 minute time unit into our basic appreciation or expectations.

Doctor Who did a few two-part serials – Hartnell's *Edge of Destruction*, and *Rescue*, Baker's *Sontaran Experiment*, Davison's *King's Demons* and *Black Orchid*. The modern *Sarah Jane Adventures* were all two part serials. It's really quite remarkable how much *Regenesis* and Timebase's other two-parters really have the feel, the rhythm of these sorts of stories down.

A big part is that working in that serial format forces them to use the same kind of pacing and structure. To us as an audience, it feels authentic to Doctor Who. By the way, I'm sure they worked this out themselves, way back then, because every single episode fits this model.

Opening – We start with a subversive cold open – in media res. There's no origin story here, no regeneration, no Tardis. We don't start at the beginning of the story, but rather, the middle.

A Pirate's History, Page 235

The beginning of the story is that the Doctor is futzing around in his Tardis when an alien interdimensional entity invades. He has to land on Earth. Then, while looking for help, he ends up in a mental institution. That's linear story telling for you. It's okay. It's obvious. It's just there's other ways to do that.

So instead, what they do is they start off in the mental institution. They start half way through the story. That's interesting – provocative. How does he end up there? What happened? That's what we're asking. From that point on, the story is moving in two directions at once – backwards, explaining what happened, and forwards showing how it gets sorted out. That's some nice sleight of hand.

The other counterintuitive thing they do is say, with a voice of considerable authority – this is all tosh! There's no Gallifrey, there's no Tardis, no Time Lords, nothing. It both asserts and refutes the familiar Doctor Who universe simultaneously. That creates a dramatic tension that intrigues: 'What's going on here?' That's where we first see Rupert Booth's character – clearly a mental patient, pleasantly going along with the ride. There's no twenty foot scarf, no attitude. But somehow, he knows a little too much about the Doctor... as if he was the Doctor.

Then there's the brilliant casting of an older, professorial man in these opening scenes. In a lot of fan films, the cast is unfortunately young. Sometimes it's like pre-teen world. That sort of thing, the narrow and often young age range makes it very hard often-times to take it seriously. So here, right at the start, they're bringing out an older actor who, by his presence, gives a lot of gravity and credibility to the scene. It makes it feel professional, it sets the tone right at the start, and we

A Pirate's History, Page 236

won't really notice that every other character from that point on is twenty-something.

That counts. I've written previously about how hard it can be to recover, if your first step is a wrong one. But the converse is true, if your first move is brilliant, then it sets the tone. It makes it easier to ignore weaker spots further on. Now, imagine if the psychologist had been too young to shave…

This is virtuoso storytelling, done by smart people who know what they're doing, who know how to create tension, to set a tone.

The Great Escape – The next set piece shows the Doctor character escaping from the mental institution, barefoot in institution drabs no less! He does this by ingeniously collecting a whole bunch of odds and ends, just meaningless bric a brac, and then cunningly using it to subvert the institution's security systems. There's a fascinating, Rube Goldberg ingeniousness to it.

And not a word of dialogue! It's all silent, and it lays out the character beautifully. Whoever this guy is, he's crazy smart. But more than that, he's a cunning improviser, a planner, he's clever and adaptable. He stays out of the way, there's no confrontations, no fights, he's nonviolent. Without a word of dialogue, we learn a lot about who this guy is who seems to know all about Gallifrey. When, later on, he finally tells someone he's the Doctor… we buy it, because he's shown us the qualities of the Doctor.

See what I mean? These are smart people, and they're making very smart, very well thought out decisions. They know how to work visual elements as well as dialogue, and they know how to make a story work.

A Pirate's History, Page 237

The Companion – Every Doctor needs a companion. At the very least, the Doctor needs someone to ask questions and to explain things to, so he doesn't look like an idiot talking to himself all the time. The Doctor needs someone to care about, to look out for, and occasionally to do things that he can't or won't.

This time around, it's Leslie, played by Christine Potter. She gets involved when an escaped mental patient stops her car, and somehow, talks her into not only giving him a ride, but getting his clothes for him from a railway station.

Okay, this could have gone so horribly wrong – it could have become just a ridiculously implausible cipher of a character. Personally, if an escaped mental patient steps in front of my car, I'm hitting the gas pedal. I'm sorry, that's just how I am.

But Christine Potter sells it. Leslie comes across as a believable, even engaging, character. We buy that she's someone that would help the Doctor out, out of fundamental decency, and out of enjoyment because this man in her car who needs her help to get his clothes is a small adventure and she's entertained, and also someone that the Doctor would develop a fondness for.

The thing with Leslie is that she's smart and sweet and has no real sense of her own mortality or vulnerability. She's glib; she's got a sort of hipster detachment that she uses to protect herself. Basically, she's gone through life, and she's never encountered a situation that she couldn't get out of with a friendly smile and a smart remark. She's a person, whose automatic default is not 'that's dangerous' but 'that's interesting.' When she is in a dangerous situation, there's some part of her that doesn't quite believe it. Leslie is pitch perfect – here's an ordinary girl, a complete smart ass, glib and sarcastic – and in short order she meets a man who turns out to be an alien, and then encounters a genuine alien monster – when she's not actually in danger, you can tell she's tickled pink by the whole thing.

As Leslie sees it, the Doctor is interesting, he's entertaining, and that's why she goes out of her way for him, why she trusts him. That's why we believe it. So we get a very deftly drawn, very likeable, very pretty character. One who can rescue a stranger who turns out to be the Doctor, or listen patiently and sympathetically while a villain rambles on about a dog he had as a child, or toss off a funny and cutting remark without being hurtful.

I kind of get the impression at points, that as an actress, Potter may have been somewhat limited. Not a professional. But that's okay. A good actor is versatile and can work within any character in any script. But if you can't have that, then the best bet is to recognize what the actor can do, and write for that. They've done that here.

She's not the best companion ever. Booth and Potter don't have physical and verbal chemistry, the back and forth, that we saw between Barbara Benedetti and Randy Rogel in the female Doctor stories, or between Tom Baker and Liz Sladen in the old series, or David Tennant and Catherine Tate from the new series. But she's engaging.

About the Monster: Years ago I played a lizard man for a short film. It was hot, stuffy, the mask allowed visibility only through a couple of small pinholes, so I was literally blind. You don't move much, and you don't move fast when you're in a suit like that. Too easy to fall over, or trip, and when you're grabbing, you can't really see what you're attacking. So mostly, you get all looming and lumbering.

A Pirate's History, Page 239

That's why so many old movie monsters moved so slowly and carefully – the costumes are difficult to move in, and difficult to see in, and just difficult to wear. So the script of It: Terror From Beyond Space might have called for a leopard fast predator, but what it got was a lumbering goon. This is true of Doctor Who, the Myrka and Mandrels are particularly horrible examples, but in fact the Silurians, the Sea Devils, a great many others have this problem. It's still true; I can name a couple of recent monsters in the new series that can barely move. They're basically props that contain an actor. It gets problematic. What you really want is a suit that you can actually see well out of and which can move well.

Which brings us to the Tribus monster, designed and built by Philip T. Robinson? The Tribus monster is conceptually terrific – it's a trans-dimensional being's misguided effort to create a human body. But of course, since it's not used to working in only three dimensions, what it gets is an awful distortion. This is realized brilliantly in an asymmetric monstrosity. The face of the Tribus is smeared, recognizably human, yet distorted and inhuman. There's a large misshapen claw on one hand, the other is out of sight, but the suggestion is that it's shrivelled. The body is covered in nondescript robes, but the lurching gait and posture suggests that it's equally misshapen. In short, a very good concept, very well realized.

Most beautifully, it gives the Tribus one good eyehole. It's a mask that allows the actor full visibility, and when you've worn these things, when you've seen these things, that's so important. Compare that with the Silurian costumes for instance, and you'll see that the Tribus for all its deformity is far more fluid and expressive. So basically: Well thought out, conceptually and practically.

A Pirate's History, Page 240

Even in professional productions, there are a lot of costumes or suits that just don't come off effectively. That go horribly wrong. Even the new Who series has had a flurry of costumes that may look terrific but are immobile, or that looked great on paper but fell off a cliff in implementation. There's a gap between what's on the printed page and what can be achieved in the shop. There are designs and costumes that get handicapped for one reason or another. But here… smart, they thought it through, every step of the process, from imagination, to execution, to actually wearing the thing and moving in it. I keep saying it, smart people making smart decisions.

The Doctor – I'll be blunt. I think Rupert Booth is one of best fan Doctors ever, in terms of really grasping and expressing the essence of the character. Only Barbara Benedetti, Nick Scovell and Nigel Peever are on par, and their available bodies of work are much smaller.

It's hard to play the Doctor. Even professional actors struggle with it – look at Peter Cushing's Doctor in the movies, or Richard E. Grant's Doctor in *Scream of the Shalka*. There's a peculiar mix of brilliance and eccentricity, arrogance and compassion, humour and grandiosity that runs through all the Doctors. For the Doctor, it's go big, or go home.

A lot of fan productions try to re-create their favourite doctor, the actor dressing up in a long scarf or a cricket outfit. That's nice, but mostly, it's just dress up. Even really polished fan productions have trouble picking up on the subtle flavour of eccentricity that makes a Doctor. But Booth gets it. Right out of the starting gate he has it.

The Booth Doctor is not derivative. He creates his own persona – a young/old Doctor. Booth appears to have started playing the Doctor in his mid-twenties, at about the same age as Matt Smith, so definitely a young man. There's interesting overlaps with Matt Smith's portrayal. The Booth Doctor wears a bow tie, says Geronimo at one point and likes hats. It's prescient and entirely coincidental, the result of an intersection of a very young man playing someone deeply old and eccentric.

The Booth Doctor's costume is a tuxedo, just slightly ill fitting, the darkness giving the character gravitas, a certain old fashioned quality, while the slightly off fit conveys a certain eccentricity. Booth doesn't have the booming presence of a Baker (Tom or Colin) or a Pertwee, or Tenant or Smith. He's just not a massive guy. Rather, he uses his relative slenderness to disarm his opponents. By refusing to be a threat, he defuses them. His version of the Doctor seems more like Davison or Troughton, cunning but gentle. Booth's Doctor is almost gaunt, he's got very good facial structure, he has striking eyes and eyebrows, which he uses effectively. His face and voice are very expressive. He's one of those people who can convey their thought processes clearly with a shift of expression.

His character maintains the Doctor's dry wit, steady composure in the face of monsters, quick mood shifts, and fundamental decency. The second episode of the serial begins with Booth's Doctor confronting the monster… and having a civil conversation with it – a classic Doctorism. No shock, no panic, no anger or threats, no fear. Just 'Hello, I see you're a monster. How are you doing?'

He's got a really fine comic touch. Later in the episode, after the alien menace has temporarily been defeated, the Doctor and Leslie take a henchman back to her home. The Doctor begins to work on a machine to flush the extradimensional entity out of his Police Box, while Leslie sympathetically listens to the henchman rambling on about his dog. The Doctor ends up constantly interrupting them as he borrows doodads for his machine. It's sly and funny, just a touch of Marx brothers.

Yet, he's serious when he needs to be. You can see wariness or dejection, or slyness, when the moment calls for it. None of it seems artificial or staged. He plays it as if he's feeling it at the moment, that this is the moment it occurs to him to feel it. Rupert Booth is a very capable actor, and he's got the role down. He's simply The Doctor.

Paul Ferry's *Reservoir Dogs* inspired performance as Voltere doesn't quite come off – it's not a bad performance. It's just that the role demands such a range. Ferry's Voltere is a guy trying to be a badass, and not quite up to it, physically or emotionally. He's a weak man blowing in the wind, trying to be a tough thug while currying favour with his bosses. It's a character that needs to be comic and scary at different moments, a little sad and sympathetic at points, and mercurially dangerous at other points. That would be tough for Steve Buscemi to pull off. It would be a challenge for any actor. Ferry wrote the script, so he knew what he was getting into, he understood the character of Voltere better than anyone, and to his credit there are moments when he gets it - a scene with Christine Potter where he talks about his dog is almost sublime.

Finally, there's the story. Any Doctor Who story is essentially the same - aliens show up to menace everyone, and the Doctor comes along to sort them out. What makes it distinctive is what you do with that story, what swerves. Here there are some wild notions - the Tardis is invaded by a sentient dimension, the Doctor winds up in a mental institution and has to cleverly break out, the sentient

A Pirate's History, Page 243

dimension later decides to make a three dimensional body and mucks it up. These are cool ideas.

Bottom line – It's not perfect, of course. There are some problems with the sound mix here and there, levels are too low, or there's too much ambient sound. The voice of the Tribus is over-processed to the point it's hard to understand. There's some dodgy blocking in a couple of scenes. There are rough spots here and there. Making films is a learning experience and this was the Timebase crew's first effort. Well, first effort that they let out of the lab.

But then again, if you're going to watch fan films, you need to carry a certain amount of forgiveness. Hell, with Doctor Who, both classic and new series, sometimes you have to carry a certain amount of forgiveness, period. *Regenesis* feels like classic Doctor Who. Indeed, it feels like excellent classic Doctor Who. It stands quite well with any of the two-parters of the classic series, and better than several of them.

CAST*: Rupert Booth – The Doctor; Christine Potter – Leslie; Paul Ferry – Voltere; Malcolm Herron – Harry; Peter Booth – Consultant; Graeme Nattress – Bev; Chris Allen – Larry; Neil Johnson – Doctor; Jeff Watson – Security Guard; Philip T. Robinson – Tribus Monster; Tribus Voices – Malcolm Herron, Rupert Booth, Graeme Nattress*

CREW*: Paul Ferry – Writer, costumes; Chris Allen – Production Manager, sound, camera; Graeme Nattress – Incidental music, lighting, sound, camera, visual effects, costumes, assistant editor, special sound, video effects, title sequence; Philip T Robinson – director, lighting, camera, visual effects, transport, designer, title sequence; Rupert Booth – lighting, sound, camera, visual effects, transport, costumes, makeup artist, VT Editor, video effects, producer, title sequence; Peter Nattress – sound, transport; John Pattinson – transport; Peter Booth – catering; Malcolm Herron – catering, title sequence; Gavin Chilvers – title sequence*

A Pirate's History, Page 244

Review: Phase Four (1993-1997)

Attack of the Old School Cybermen

STORY: The Doctor and Leslie go for a little holiday to a small town in the English countryside. Little do they know, the Cybermen have taken over, and soon, they and the entire world will be in danger…

REVIEW: Oh no, the Cybermen are up to their old tricks again! This time, they've isolated a small town as part of a larger infiltration and takeover scheme. The Doctor and Leslie separately stumble onto the plot quite by accident. From there on, the story proceeds as the Doctor slowly works out their plot and plays a cat and mouse game with the Cybermen.

This is Timebase's epic. A four part serial, a hundred minutes in total, done up in the classic style, and done well. It was, by far, Timebase's most ambitious production. Perhaps almost too ambitious. Within the context of Timebase's story arc, this is technically the second adventure, begun in 1994 or 1995. But it came out fourth in 1997 – three years after the first story *Regenesis* 1994, but two years after the two stories that should have followed it *Paradise in Chains*, and *Long Shadows* from 1995.

I almost have a sense that *Phase Four* was such a brutally technical and demanding production that it just about broke the bank. Timebase had two major projects after this, The *Churchtown Incident*, which was abandoned, and *Hidden Faces* that was almost a lost film itself, airing in 1998, but only completed in 2002, a full five years later. These things take a lot of enthusiasm and goodwill to make and the sheer effort of *Phase Four* might have used up most of that.

In a real sense though, Timebase's entire history proceeds from *Phase Four*.

As Philip T. Robinson relates in an online posting: *"It all started when Rupert and I thought it would be cool to make a Cyberman costume so I sculpted the mask and Rupert made the chest unit. At almost the same time, we both set about making a Tardis with the help of many friends."*

There's a little bit of history here. Doctor Who had been off the air since 1989, but in 1992, the show had sort of comeback. *Tomb of the Cybermen*, from 1966, was one of the 'Lost' stories, and by all accounts a classic. In 1991, all four episodes were rediscovered, and in May, 1992, it had been released on VHS becoming an instant best seller, and topping UK sales charts. So it's likely that the project Booth and Robinson were working on was a 'Tomb' Cyberman, which would go on to populate Phase Four.

I think that this was a key part of the evolution of many early fan films. Someone puts together a Tom Baker or a Cyberman costume, or they build a Police Box shell, or a Dalek, and the project is satisfying in and of itself. But then, once it's done... Well, it's just sitting there, and it's just crying out for something to be done with it. So a next step just demands to be taken.

"After that, we started to have meetings with Paul to come up with the first story Regenesis. Rupert had already done his first draft of the Phase Four cyber-adventure. It would take another two drafts (the final one by Paul Ferry himself) for that adventure to be realised," Robinson wrote.

Phase Four seems to have been in the works from the beginning, at least as a script in development. From what I can tell, production seems to have started following *Regenesis,* but there was so much work – so many costumes and props, so many model shots, so many scenes, so many effects shots, that its shooting and post-production simply dragged on and on, and in the meantime, the stories that were to come later were finished and released first.

My advice, if you have the opportunity, is to watch them in the order that I think they were intended, rather than the order of release. The Doctor and his companions are going through an arc over the course of the Timebase adventures, and watching in proper order adds a lot more to the experience.

Philip T. Robinson's effort at a Cyberman costume must have turned out well. They went into mass production and they ended up making at least five of them, plus a cyber-Leader and a cyber-controller, and a couple of modern variants - an incredible nine costumes. That's an astonishing amount of work. The BBC seldom went that far. In comparison, the BBC only built four Daleks and three Ice Warriors for their respective serials. The Davison serial *Earthshock* only commissioned eight Cybermen costumes.

The Cybermen are appropriately menacing, not least because they're omnipresent. These Cybermen are the distinctive Troughton Tomb of the Cybermen version, and the costumes are spot on – these are dead accurate and BBC quality.

A Pirate's History, Page 247

Moreover, they're effective Cybermen, organized, cunning, unstoppable. As the classic series aged, the Cybermen went through a process where they looked tougher and scarier, but turned out to be distressingly easy to defeat. Not so these, Cybermen, they're relentless.

The Cyberman have always needed to be handled carefully. The voices are monotone, costumes are bulky, visibility is limited, so Cybermen tend to move slowly and with a certain amount of caution. It's very easy for them to turn into a joke. At times, the classic series seemed to do that, particularly in Davison and McCoy appearances, where they're dispatched rather easily. In one serial, *Earthshock,* a Cyberman is even killed by a math badge. It all depends on how you handle them.

Daleks are scary because they're always on the edge of freaking out; they're twitchy, inaccessible and vicious. Daleks are very interactive, they exhibit a lot of personality, blinking their lights, swivelling their guns and plungers and eye stalks and whirling about.

Cybermen, in contrast, are passionless and expressionless, their moves are slow and deliberate, they don't interact much, they give nothing away. Their intimidation comes from being relentless. No matter what you do, the Cybermen will get you. Fight, run away, hide, it's all the same to them really. They're unstoppable, or they should be. They don't hesitate, can't be dissuaded, they don't react, or interact, they're just implacable. Even if they're slow, they will eventually run you down

This quality comes across well. *Phase Four's* Cybermen, as they all are, are slow. But these are clearly relentless and unstoppable. The Doctor throws up hurdles. But each time, sooner or later they get through it. They adapt. They adjust.

They just do their thing, and it doesn't matter whether we resist or flee or trick them. They keep on coming. Implacable.

These Cybermen are actually true to their concept. No hard feelings on their part, they've got a situation, they're taking the most logical course of action. The Doctor ultimately defeats them by understanding their situation, and then using its logic against them. When he ruins their plan, there's no shaking of metal fists. It's just – time to move on.

It's actually one of the better Cybermen stories - comparable to anything in the series history without being derivative. I can't think of a similar Cyberman story in the actual series, this is a unique take, and it carefully manages to avoid regurgitating any of the classic Cyberman images, while perhaps creating its own iconic scenes.

This is a serious story, although both the Doctor and Leslie have their witty moments, the Cybermen are never played for laughs. Although the Doctor arguably wins out in the end, he's pushed to distress and desperation. Of the five principle supporting characters (apart from the Cybermen themselves) three of them end up dead.

The Doctor through the serial goes through a character arc, which is handled very well. Midway through the serial, he loses someone, and from that point on, you can tell he's no longer having fun. His demeanor shifts slightly, he's cranky, impatient, there's a sense that he just wants done with it. Props to Rupert Booth for playing the Doctor with depth – his character is alternately questing, thoughtful, sneaky, witty and even dejected.

His performance is utterly fluid. There's a blink and you'll miss it moment when the Doctor is a prisoner of the Cybermen, utterly crushed and dejected, radiating apathy, and manages to reprogram their teleport right under their noses without them noticing. There's a moment when the Doctor examines a victim, pronounces them finished, and then an instant later, tells the victim's spouse that 'she'll be fine' with convincing certainty.

Booth is an amazingly expressive actor, you can tell what the Doctor is thinking, but he can also use it to have the Doctor lie, manipulate and plot effectively. He's got a fey sense of humour and a wonderfully deadpan delivery, there's not a moment when his performance rings hollow.

The battle with the Cybermen is a cat and mouse game, with the Doctor subverting their technology, and the Cybermen fixing it. He's mostly one jump ahead of them, but there's a lot of dramatic tension, because it's only ever one jump, and sometimes it's not one jump ahead at all, and he's not ahead of them.

Along with the main Cyberman story, everyone gets a story arc, and in particular, the Doctor and Leslie get a profoundly moving arc as their relationship develops. It's a serial that works on several levels.

All of the supporting cast turn in strong performances, even quirky at points. With four episodes to spread over, they're allowed to develop as characters and identities. They're physically distinctive in looks – the businessman, the biker, the everyman and his wife, and they inhabit those looks and personas – they don't seem like kids playing dress up. The relative youth of the cast doesn't work against them, because they all so clearly come across as people from various walks of life.

It's a big story, and it feels big. It could have felt small, god knows, it's an easy thing to blow. A handful of Cybermen take over a small town, scenes shot in the woods or someone's living room, it could have looked and felt pretty cramped.

But no, this feels big. The town streets are empty; there are a lot of extras willing to lie around playing dead bodies. Or maybe it's just the usual suspects doing double duty over and over again. But regardless, you get the sense of an entire community taken over, a population laid down and out. There's a sense of scope.

That's magnified by the settings and sets. Timebase consistently, throughout all their stories, had a really good eye for choosing locations that enhance the story. This time the shoot covers a lot of ground – country roads, the woods, a church interior, the Cybermen's space ship, even the Tardis interior, and they're always able to make it interesting. At one point, the Doctor shows up on a country road – boring – except that there's a peculiar little vehicle, a kind of mini-farm tractor and wagon, that drives up to give the Doctor a ride. A scene where two characters fight over a cloaking device takes place in impenetrable woods, mirroring the action.

One extraordinary location is the Cybermen's base on Earth. They've taken over an Anglican church, and while the cast struggle a bit with the pews, the visuals of the church interior are amazing. Churches are built that way, you know, stained glass, vaulted ceilings, the whole nine yards. But to fill it with Cybermen and make it their command center, that's just brilliant. There is a juxtaposition of traditional, religious and mystical with the high tech, sci-fi and utilitarian which is unforgettable.

Beyond that, there are actual sets. *Regenesis,* the first story, simply took advantage of locations. Well selected locations, but whatever they could find. On the whole, a great many

A Pirate's History, Page 251

Doctor Who fan films make use of amazing locations - ruins, roman ampitheatres, university spaces, churches, office buildings, etc.

Sets are harder. They actually have to be built, and that takes time, skill and money. It's hard to do, and hard to do right. Impressively, we get to see Tardis interior with its console and time rotor, and it's amazingly well done. The walls with the 'round things' and the door are authentic to the series. It's all a dead replica of the original Hartnell/Troughton Tardis console and interior. The Tardis console is a particularly amazing prop, it lights up properly, it moves, it's simply extraordinary. The number of man hours and skill that must have gone into building and wiring it must have been staggering.

Timebase's Tardis interior flats and console appeared in only one of their other productions – Hidden Faces. But it's been used in at least one other fan film, Tyranny of the Daleks, and it appeared regularly at conventions before it was accidentally destroyed.

As noted, the Cybermen consisted of at least nine full costumes, including cyber-leader and cyber-controller. Almost everyone in the Timebase cast and crew seems to have had a turn as a Cyberman. When you talk to them, just about all of them vividly remember their time in those costumes. They're used effectively. In most of their scenes there's anywhere from two to five, some of them foreground, others just working away at cyber-things in the background. They show up in so many scenes and so many places it looks and feels like there's an actual army, dozens on dozens roaming around, leaving no place to hide. That's a trick that sometimes the original series didn't carry off successfully. In one composite shot, there are fifteen marching along. It feels like there are a lot of them, that they're everywhere, and they're dangerous.

Backing them up, are an ambitious series of props and effects. The first shot is an establishing view of the Cyberman base-ship in space, and then a close up of an airlock opening and Cybermen pods jetting into the night. That little throwaway miniature works well, and I can only imagine the amount of time and effort that went into setting it up. Other sets include Spartan but effective ship interiors with angled walls and Cyberman logos, used variously as a control room, prison cell, teleport station, conversion center, communications nexus. There are cybermats, a communications array, a conversion station, half-converted Cybermen, weapons, consoles.

It feels epic and real, in part because the Cybermen are so fully realized. The sheer scale and volume of props and sets works really sell the Cybermen and their 'world.' As to the Cybermen themselves, in the end, there's an Easter egg, a big reveal that turns what you thought you knew about the Cybermen on its head.

I don't really want to give too much of the story away. I want you to watch it, hopefully, watch the whole Timebase series, and in proper order. That's about it. I could cite the usual caveats – bits where the sound drops, or Cybermen voices are too muzzy, or a shot that doesn't quite work. But why bother? This is classic Doctor Who.

CAST: Rupert Booth - Doctor, Cyberman, Cyber voices; Christine Potter – Leslie; Marie - Lisa Gledhill; Martin - Steve Palace; Royston - Chris Bevis; Mile, Cyberman - Ian Patterson; Cyber Controller - Barry Vaughn; Philip T. Robinson - Cyberleader; Cybermen – Richard

A Pirate's History, Page 253

Knapper, Graeme Nattress, Arthur Banks, Rupert Booth, Philip Robinson, Shaun Whiteheart, Julian Eales, Kevin Crennell, Kristian Wharton, Steven Palace; Convertees – Ian Patterson, Richard Knapper, Graeme Nattress, Peter Nattress

CREW: *Rupert Booth – Writer, Director, Camera, Lighting, Hardware, Titles, set construction, set builder, props, video effects, special sound, incidental music, dubbing, VT Editor, production manager, designer, model builder; Philip T. Robinson – Producer, Camera, Lighting, Cyber Costumes Sculptor, Make Up, set construction, props, production manager, matte paintings; Richard Knapper – Producer, Camera, Costumes, set assistant, props, production manager, Ian Patterson – Director, Camera, Lighting, Costumes, Credits, Set construction, props, video effects, special sound, incidental music, dubbing, CGI animation, production manager, mechanical design, pyrotechnics; Neil Johnson – Lighting, set assistant; Arthur Banks – Lighting, CGI animation; Paul Ferry – Script Editor, set assistant; Sylvia Brown – assistant, special thanks; Barry Williams – assistant, set assistant, production manager; Claire Williams – assistant; Malcolm Herron – assistant; Peter Nattress – assistant; Lisa Gledhill – Make Up, set assistants; Selina Lock – costume, set assistant; Peter Herron – costume; Gavin Chilvers – titles; Philip Robinson – titles; Brian Moss – set construction, electronics, mechanical design, pyrotechnics; Arthur Banks – set construction; Malcolm Herron – set construction; Scott Goodman – set assistant; David Burke – set assistant; Emma Seager – set assistant; Barry Vaughn – set assistant, electronics; Sara Price – special thanks Scott Talbot – special thanks; Allen Memorial Methodist Church, Copyright, 1997*

Review: Paradise in Chains (1995)

A Mystery in the Void

STORY: After defeating the Cybermen, the Doctor ponders the costs. His contemplation is interrupted when the Police Box malfunctions, taking him to a pocket dimension outside time and space. There, he encounters a ghost, a clown, a minstrel, a raconteur, a disembodied voice and a strange young woman who may be in heaven or hell…

REVIEW: With *Paradise in Chains*, we return to the two parts serial structure they established in *Regenesis*. *Regenesis* and *Phase Four* were both very different stories, like night and day from each other. But *Paradise*, which sees the introduction of another companion, Amaryllis, played by Deborah Reilley, is a complete departure from what we've seen before.

It reminds me most of Tom Baker's *Warrior's Gate*, but it's also of a piece with Hartnell's *Celestial Toymaker*, Troughton's *Mind Robbers*, or McCoy's *Greatest Show in the Galaxy*, or Benedetti's *Broken Doors*. Essentially, this is surrealism, not science fiction, and the Doctor, rather than moving through time and space, is caught between dimensions, exploring a strange realm that is as much mindscape as landscape.

It's highly stylized, the sets are basically almost all non-existent black backgrounds, lending the project a feel of starkness and alienation. There are some scenes where we end up at natural locations, but the transitions are immediate, to show that these locations are as unreal and disconnected as the black backgrounds. The Doctor may turn around and find himself in a wooded glade, but he and the audience knows that he hasn't gone anywhere; the emptiness and the danger lurk just beyond.

The natural locations are all set in a park – there's shots on a bridge overlooking a stream, down a flight of outdoor steps, amid a pile of jagged boulders – all carefully or subtly chosen to reflect the Doctor's inner sentiments, and to contrast with the 'otherplace.' Again, you have to admire how good they are at finding really good locations, visually effective locations that aren't simply places that the story takes place in, but that enhance and reinforce the story.

One clever move was the Tardis interior. We don't see it at all. We know that they were building it for Phase Four. I suspect it simply wasn't ready. But if it was, I applaud the decision not to use it. Normally it would be immensely tempting to shoot with and around it.

But it's not that kind of story, it's a mystery with the Doctor being isolated, and so they've very wisely chosen to leave it out. The Doctor is alienated and in an alien place, it would have been a mistake to put him in a familiar setting.

They work hard at building a sense of strangeness. Structurally, it's more than a little like *Warrior's Gate* in that it apparently starts off as mainstream sci fi – in both, we see a spaceship, we see a spaceship interior, we see a pilot and a prisoner. It's got that early 80s feel we associate with *Blake's 7*.

A Pirate's History, Page 256

Then all of a sudden, the pilot is simply this ghost, wandering around making random cryptic remarks. The other characters are almost all archetypes – a raconteur, a poet, a clown, each of them strangely one dimensional and disconnected. All except for the mysterious woman, Amaryllis, who mistakes the Doctor himself for one of those pesky archetypes, to the Doctor's own annoyance.

Rupert Booth explores the Doctor's personality further in this serial, taking him in new directions. This is one of the pleasures in watching Booth work; he manages to grow the character, to do something different, just about every outing.

This time, his character is cranky, snappish, frustrated over his experiences with the Cybermen. He's still hurting, still recovering. He really could care less about the mystery in front of him, he just doesn't want to be bothered – Amaryllis, the ghost, the archetypes – it's all someone else's problem. But he can't help but being drawn in; he can't help but caring. He can't help needing to solve the mystery.

Leslie, sadly, doesn't have much to do this time around. Christine Potter's character barely appears, but that's of a parcel with the Spartan, almost abstract nature of the production.

What carries the production is the deep sense of mystery. Who or what is the ghost? Where is the disembodied voice? What's up with these strange archetypes? And who the hell is this woman at the center of it all? It's about the Doctor's almost unwilling process of unravelling the mystery of where he is and how this place came to be. Again, there's a stellar performance by Rupert Booth as the Doctor. Deborah Riley as Amaryllis is an effective foil, the mystery at the heart of the matter.

A Pirate's History, Page 257

I really have no criticism of this. A lot of the small technical glitches, the small problems in the sound mix, or an awkward shot, or a laboured scene aren't there or aren't nearly as noticeable. This is probably because eschewing a lot of exterior and location work, they've got a lot more control over their production. The things I might complain about, like a stiffness with some of the archetypes/characters are part and parcel of what's being done – this is an abstracted, surrealist journey so it's a lot easier to get away with things.

Oddly enough, despite the utter simplicity of the concept and the sets, this production proved to be a pain in the ass. Rupert Booth wrote online in 1997, in response to a review, *'Paradise in Chains' was plagued, plagued I tell you, with problems, directors wandering off halfway through to become runners on an ill-fated film (not that this gave me any satisfaction you understand, oh no...), clowns going to the toilet for 45 minutes at a time...sets....it makes me shudder to remember."*

Even the simplest productions can be incredibly difficult. Ultimately, these are all volunteer productions, with people giving up a lot of time and energy to work very hard. There's no money to be paid, no perks and no resources. What's often remarkable are not the headaches, but that it gets accomplished at all.

This is an abstract, metaphysical Doctor Who. Let me put it this way, if you liked *Warrior's Gate* then this will be your favourite as a surreal masterpiece. If *Gate* left you cold, this will go to the bottom of your list as a pretentious mess. Personally, I like a good mystery, it's consistently intriguing, it explores the Doctor's character, and in the end, there's something bittersweet and redemptive to it.

When watching Timebase Productions, I'll strongly recommend watching them in order. The Doctor and his companions are going through a journey together. *Regenesis* has to precede *Phase Four*, and *Paradise in Chains* has to follow. That's not the order they were released in, but it's the order that the overall series follows. You can watch them out of order. But it's just more enjoyable the other way, you get more out of it.

CAST: *Rupert Booth – Doctor; Deborah Riley – Amaryllis; Christine Potter – Leslie; Simon Elworthy – Minstrel; Chelfyn Baxter – Raconteur; Gavin Chilvers – Raconteur; Shaun Borthwick – Raconteur; Jonathan Ralph – Pilot; Kevin Crennell – Jester; Philip T. Robinson – Cybermen; Richard Knapper – Cybermen; Chelfyn Baxter – Void; Cameron Smith - Judge.*

CREW: *Paul Ferry - original concept; Lee Patterson – writer, incidental music, studio sound, costume; Rupert Booth – writer, director, lighting, camera, transport, VT Editor, titles, set construction, designer, producer; Philip T. Robinson – camera, transport, costume, titles, set construction, designer; Lee Foster – incidental music; Renny Borthwick – director, lighting, production manager; Gavin Chilvers – lighting, title; Jeanette Smedley – lighting; Arthur Banks – lighting, studio sound, set construction; Malcolm Herron – location sound, set construction; Deborah Reilley – transport, costume; Simon Elworthy – studio sound, transport, costume; Sarah King – production assistant; Chelfyn Baxter – special sound, lighting; Michael Stevenson – set construction; Ian Patterson - computer graphics; Malcolm Herron - catered for the editor.*

Timebase, 1995

Review: Long Shadows (1995)

Shakespeare meets Cthulhu

STORY: A trip into the past, taking Amaryllis to play scrabble with William Shakespeare, leads to an adventure of cross dressing, conspiracy, ancient sorcerers and a confrontation with unearthly powers....

REVIEW: Once again, Timebase goes off in a completely different direction with this two part serial. I think at this point, we're going to have to face the fact that as far as two part serials went, Timebase was actually doing theirs better than the BBC Doctor Who.

The difference is that when the BBC went with a two-parter, usually they were just trying to bridge a bottleneck, there would be some problem in budget or scheduling, so they grabbed up whatever they could and threw it in there. For Timebase, a two part serial was their chosen format, they really committed to it.

This time the Doctor and Amaryllis go to visit Shakespeare. Point of interest: Shakespeare always beats the Doctor at scrabble, he just makes up words as he goes. It's a nice little throwaway gag, a bit of the quirky wit or humour that really makes Timebase's serials feel so much like the real thing.

Shakespeare soon enough drops out of the story, which is a little sad, as he was a fun character, and it looked as if he was going to be an integral part of the plot. Possibly that was the original plan, it does feel that plot threads were being laid out for him and then abandoned. It may be that the actor dropped out or had to leave and they retuned the script. Shakespeare is played by Ian Patterson, who seems to have been quite busy behind the scenes, so I'm not at all sure of that.

Or possibly, it was intended all along. I could see them being clever enough to pull a trick like that – lead the audience into believing it's going to be one sort of story, and then suddenly shift direction and make it a different story. The Simpsons does that sort of trick regularly, opening a story one way and then veering off in a new direction, so I wouldn't put it past the Timebase crew.

Whatever, we are left with Shakespeare's drinking buddy, and his young protégé, who is actually a girl (obviously) masquerading as a boy (not convincingly).

Back in Shakespeare's day, women were not allowed in the theatre, so all the women's parts were played by pretty young boys. Genderbending was a common feature in a lot of Shakespeare's plays – girls dressing up as boys, boys pretending to be girls pretending to be boys. Sometimes it got hard to keep track. In the *Two Gentlemen of Verona*, for instance, I'm pretty sure someone ended up marrying themselves. In *Long Shadows*, Will has helped a girl pass as a boy for the theatre. In turn, the girl is kind of in love with Will, so she's helping him by writing his plays for him while he's too drunk to notice. It's an interesting conceit.

So anyway, here they are, doing a riff on *Shakespeare in Love*, which looked like where they were going, but then, they pull a swerve. They manage to make it continue to work as a plot point, it seems that some cultists need a double sacrifice, a boy and a girl, and guess who they grab as the boy… even as the focus shifts to Curwen an ancient Old/Young warlock and his efforts to awaken his old Master now reincarnated as a washer-woman, and then raise up Cthulhu or someone who looks a lot like him. Yes, this is The Doctor meets *Lovecraft*, with a bit of gender bending thrown in for good measure.

One of the most interesting things about the production was the largely successful effort to marry Shakespearean and Lovecraftian styles. With Shakespeare, we have not just the archaic diction, but the actions of stagecraft, with characters very clearly disappearing stage left and right, or visibly eavesdropping from the edge of stage, unrequited love, a bit of genderbending, some comedic slap and tickle.

With Lovecraft, we have that escalating sense of menace, that Lovecraftian story convention of assembling apparently random pieces into a story, reincarnation and returns of dark things, ambition, an accumulating doom that boils over in a climactic revelation. Lovecraft fans will spot the references, starting with the Wizard Curwen himself – he's actually the villain from the *Case of Charles Dexter Ward*. The elder sign is seen. Even great Cthulhu makes an appearance. Lovecraftian tropes – the degenerate inbred family/cult, or the alien beings outside our dimension trying to get in, are there.

I like it. These Timebase folk, they are people who think about things, who try and do interesting things. They're not just about telling a straightforward linear story, they like to make it interesting, even a little challenging.

Once again, they found some good locations and used them very well to establish setting and sense of place. There's some wonderful cinematography, a shot of the Doctor and

Amaryllis walking along the horizon at sunset leaps to mind. They do a lot of what seems to be genuine night shooting (rather than day for night) and they make effective use of shadows and darkness. As always, they're very clever at making a little go a long way – a good example is the cult, which, through the magic of shadows, photography and getting every warm body into robes (Rupert Booth is listed as doing double duty as a cultist, back in Phase Four he also played a Cyberman) comes across as formidable.

Amaryllis comes off well. That's tricky. *Paradise in Chains* was really about her, and about the mystery at the center of her. It's one thing to be the focus of the story; it's quite another challenge to be simply a part of the story. But Deborah Riley manages to make the transition with a good performance. In some ways, I like Amaryllis less than Leslie. Leslie's character had a sweetness to her. Amaryllis is more worldly, the relationship with the Doctor is more complex. Her character actually has things to do, she's flirty and fun, she stumbles into some deeper trouble, and she acts effectively – she doesn't just stand there and scream, or simply exist to ask the Doctor questions – it's a real role.

Some of the supporting characters are terrific, the guy who plays Shakespeare, Ian Patterson, steals his scenes. The big hairy dude, Malcolm Herron, who initially plays slap and tickle with Amaryllis is a nice stock Shakespeare type. On the other hand, most of the cultists are basically faceless and menacing, but that's their whole point. Physically, the characters are diverse; they don't look like they're all in the same peer group.

Tom Hibbert, the actor who plays Curwen? Sorry. I think he starts off okay, but he's got two problems to wrestle with. One is that, like Rupert Booth's Doctor, he's playing a very old man, in a very young man's body. Rupert Booth and Matt Smith both manage to carry it off by finding subtle ways, dress, references, mannerisms to express that there's something else looking out. Here, Curwen's sort of defeated by it. The other problem is that he's trying to play someone up to his elbows in meddling with Lovecraftian deities… That's just tough.

Similarly, Lisa Gledhill, who wrote the script and was responsible for costumes, plays the washer-woman who is possessed by or the reincarnation of the old Master has an even tougher time. She essentially has to play two characters, one of which is a supernatural magician. Again, that's a tough job.

Do you know a lot of Lovecraftian necromancers? Any idea how to play one? It's tough. Jeremy Irons, a very good actor, came up against the same problem when he got recruited into *Dungeons and Dragons*. What's the point of reference for an evil wizard? Irons ended up biting off huge chunks of the sets and gargling with them.

On the other hand, who knows, maybe that's how Lovecraftian power-mad wizards, either reincarnated or artificially prolonged of life, end up acting. I've never met one, but I assume it takes a heaping helping of 'barking at the moon' crazy. The point is that Gledhill and Hibbert are both playing characters that are massively off the human norm, very ancient people in very young bodies, who party with the horrifically mind boggling.

I've talked about the persistent minor issues with the sound mix and edit before. They're never bad enough to wreck the enjoyment, but they're definitely noticeable. You either forgive it, or let it sink you. The bottom line is that these were amateurs working with limited equipment and resources, and

A Pirate's History, Page 265

some of this stuff, particularly the sound mix – there's no substitute for experience and high end tools. It's amazing that it's as polished as it is.

One of the weaknesses here are the sets. Look, sets are hard. They cost money, and they take time to build. The tavern setting is barely passable. Curwen's lair is cramped. It doesn't wobble, that's the best I'll say for it. Or maybe I'm being harsh: Medieval rooms tended to be small, cramped and cluttered, doorways were narrow, wall hangings provided insulation. So it may actually be too accurate. It's a sign of how good the production is overall when a relatively modest flaw is the most I can come up with.

In some ways, it's reminiscent of Regenesis, although that was more light hearted. In Long Shadows, they make a real effort to cultivate dread and fear. Both Shakespeare and Lovecraft built their stories to climaxes, to pivotal moments. Lovecraft far more spectacularly. Shakespeare sorted out his characters; Lovecraft pulled a monster out of the woodwork. If you're doing Lovecraft, it's hard to get the payoff right, and they managed it. The ending is spectacular,

It's ironic in a way. If this was a one off, it would be a cult classic: Shakespeare, Doctor Who and Cthulhu all wrapped up! It would be an amazing thing.

But because it's Timebase, because *Long Shadows* is keeping company with *Phase Four* and *Paradise in Chains* and *Regenesis,* and because their range is so consistently strong, it's just *"Oh yeah, Timebase did another one."*

It's the Benedetti syndrome - first outing knocks people on their asses. Second outing should knock people on their asses. But people expect it from you, you raised the bar. It's not as

A Pirate's History, Page 266

singular as it deserves to be, simply because it's part of a series which is so consistently extraordinary.

For what it's worth, this is extraordinary.

CAST: *Rupert Booth – The Doctor, Cultist; Deborah Reilly – Amaryllis; Tom Hibbert – Curwen, Cultist; Selina Lock – Judith; Malcolm Herron – Daniel, Cultist; Lisa Gledhill – Sarah; Ian Patterson – Shakespeare; Maude Richard – Cultist; Richard Knapper – Cultist*

CREW: *Lisa Gledhill – Writer, Lighting, Visual Effects, transport, costume, make up, props, assistant editor, credits; Rupert Booth – Lighting, Camera, Visual Effects, transport, props, VT editor, dubbing, video effects, titles; Philip T. Robinson – Camera, transport, titles, Rachel Chamberlayne – Lighting; Malcolm Herron – Lighting; Tom Hibbert – Lighting; Richard Knapper – Lighting, Camera, props; Selina Lock – Lighting, catering; Ian Patterson – Lighting. Camera, props, H&S, special sound, credits; Deborah Reilly – Lighting, transport, costume, make up; Maude Richard – Lighting; Hazel Gledhill – laundry; Rachel Chamberlayne – H&S; Gavin Chilvers – titles; Shot at Broadgate Farm Co-operative*

A Pirate's History, Page 268

Review: The Hidden Face (1998-2002)

The last great Timebase

STORY: The Doctor and Amaryllis follow a strange psychic signal to Earth, to the pastoral English countryside. Meanwhile, Ian and Angie, a young couple explore the supernatural. But who, or what is the source....

REVIEW: Timebase's final two-parter, and yet another change of direction. This reminded me of Nigel Kneale's *The Stone Diaries,* or possibly of the *Wicker Man.* Pastoral gothic? Whatever. One of the strengths of the Booth Doctor's oeuvre is its range, each story is different, there's no retreading.

This one is perhaps the most modest production. It's set in the English countryside. There's a mysterious barrow, some ruins, a ghost that might not really be a ghost, an unfolding story. To say more really gives the game away. The supporting cast is small, but competent. It's not nearly as ambitious as *Long Shadows,* but not as uneven in performances.

As always, with Timebase, it's beautifully shot. They know how to find effective locations. In this case the location appears to be the ruins of a church or monastery. They also know how to compose a shot – for example, there's a quick

throwaway shot of a person standing among some trees –
normally that's just a boring throwaway, but here they
lowered the camera tilting it upward, so the person is in the
foreground, he's framed by a canopy of branches – it's just a
throwaway, but it works so well. This isn't just keeping the
lens focused, but there's an implicit understanding of how to
frame, how to make shots work.

There's another little visual – Amaryllis and Angie having a
conversation in the field, standard two shot, back and forth.
As this is going on, there's a blurry spot far off in the field
that keeps vanishing and reappearing. It's Pandect, watching
from a distance. We've previously seen a distorted POV shot
for her. It's subtle, it's confident, the characters never notice
and make no illusion. It's just effective.

There's quite a lot of nuance built into the characters. The
cast is tiny, in fact, the smallest cast of any of the Timebase
films. Five people, including the two principles – Booth and
Riley, as the Doctor and Amaryllis.

This leaves just Vineeta Rishi as Angie, a spiritualist, in love,
conflicted, afraid, a little jealous that her boyfriend has a
connection to the mystical she so desperately pines for; and
Steven Palace as Ian, questing, uncertain, haunted. Their
relationship feels very real, it has that imperfect quality of real
life, the fact that no matter how much you love each other, or
well you know each other, you are two separate people with
histories and insecurities and sometimes the gears won't
mesh, there'll be little grinds and stutters and empty spots,
but you get past it.

The final cast member, Zoe Rowden, does double duty as the
nemesis, Pandect, as well as playing Amaryllis (it's
complicated). Again, it's well written. Pandect is a being of
certainties and purpose, there's no ambiguity, no doubt, none

A Pirate's History, Page 270

of that fuzziness we associate with humanity. Who or what Pandect is and what she wants drives the story forward for each of the characters.

We get to learn a bit more about Amaryllis — clues that delightfully open up more questions. The story moves along effectively. The Doctor is whip smart and gently comic. The cliff hanger at the end of the first episode is genuinely scary, with a sense of real peril.

In short, a tight, economical project.

Hidden Faces was almost a lost project. Although the first showings were in 1998, it wasn't officially finished till 2002. That was five years after Timebase's last prior release, *Phase Four*, in 1997. For a while, people wondered if it be released at all. There are signs of change, the credit sequences are simple black and white and much shorter. From the credits, it looks like substantially fewer people were involved, perhaps a sign of the group drifting apart.

Unusual for Timebase, the script is by Kate Orman, an Australian Science Fiction writer and author of Doctor Who novels. Up until this point, all of Timebase's scripts were 'in house' - Paul Ferry, Rupert Both, Neil Johnson, Lisa Gledhill. This is the first, and last, outsider story. There are some reports that Jon Blum, another Who writer, and producer and star of his own fan film, *Time Rift*, was involved in the writing. Blum is a friend of Booth's, and married to Orman, so it's not out of the question. But his name doesn't appear on the credits, and Paul Ferry doesn't recall his name on early drafts, so the story may be apocryphal.

It was the final release of Timebase. There were other projects during Timebase's heyday. One lost production is the *Five Unrelated Persons of Oz*, which seems to have been a hilarious Who/Oz spoof. A *Phase Four* Cyberman played the Tin Man, Rupert Booth played a character who 'wasn't the Doctor.' According to Paul Ferry, it was set in Rupert Booth's '*Protoverse*' video series.

There was an aborted or unfinished project: *The Churchtown Incident*, from around 1997/1998, was intended to be a two or three part serial. This featured a pastoral world being invaded by the Sontarans, or at least one Sontaran, using the natives as Guinea pigs. Rupert Booth is back as the Doctor, dressed up in peasant clothing and notably wearing a hat, and Deborah Reilly returns as Amaryllis. Paul Ferry played the Sontaran, Vonyx.

The story, loosely, is that a Sontaran ship crashes on the world of an isolated religious colony leaving a sole survivor. This is Vonyx, the Guardian of the Sontaran Race Bank. Meanwhile, Amaryllis and the Doctor land but are separated from the Tardis. The Doctor, struck with amnesia, is taken in by the colonists, a sort of Amish group, who debate what to do with him. Amaryllis, in turn, is captured by Vonyx, who realizes that the Doctor may be host to its nemesis, a Rutan. But the Rutan switches bodies, but to whom….

Only about half of the feature was ever shot. But, this footage was used to compile a very impressive-looking trailer which displayed not only a full Sontaran costume and mask, but the interior of a Sontaran spaceship, and some good-looking futuristic weapons. The production design, the images and imagery, from what we see, are BBC quality. It's all spot on, as we've come to expect.

That Sontaran costume and mask, with Rupert Booth inside it, would eventually appear in 2001 in the BBV's *Do You Have a License to Save the Planet*. Philip T. Robinson, Timebase's brilliant props and costume builder, would also show up in the Auton and Cyberon costumes for that production, having built those as well.

As to the *Churchtown Incident* itself, it will never be completed. The best we can hope for is that maybe it might get the *Shada* treatment, where commentary or some sort of bridging sequences are used to fill in the gaps. Philip T. Robinson at one point suggested something along these lines. But Paul Ferry is doubtful that it would ever happen. *"There's simply too much missing,"* he said.

Another lost Timebase film was Zero, from 2003. This was from an attempted revival in 2003, inspired by the 40th anniversary of the show. Three films, Zero, Unearthly Stranger and Gaius were planned. According to Paul Ferry, *Zero,* also called *Episode Zero,* was intended to be a bridging story, between the old Timebase serials, and the new ones. A modest two actor production, it would explain Amaryllis' departure, and introduced a new character, a Time Lord, named Sacheverell, played by Barry Williams, for the Booth Doctor to bounce off of. This one was actually filmed and finished, but only a rough cut was ever completed. So far as I know, no one outside the Timebase group has ever seen it. Unlike the *Churchtown Incident*, whose filming was abandoned, no trailer was ever produced.

The next film to follow was *Unearthly Stranger.* Booth told the Journal, in Newcastle, at the time, *"It is a parody of the very first Doctor Who episode. The doctor is kidnapped by a race of aliens and they look back at his life for amusement."*

Booth's new companion, Ryshela, would be played by 23-year-old coffee shop supervisor, Samantha Henley; Barry Williams would return as Sachaverell; Timebase would feature its first Dalek and Paul Ferry would write. According to Paul Ferry, only a handful of scenes were shot.

The last film in the trilogy, *Gaius,* was to be set on Gallifrey and feature the Doctor confronting a tyrannical, mad Lord President Gaius. According to Paul Ferry, it was a massively ambitious project. But it never got to the point of a completed script.

That kind of thing happens a lot. Every film maker has stories of the projects that never made, the stories that never got past a script, or past an idea.

Timebase had a number of them. *Asylum* by Barry Williams was intended to be one of the first three stories, alongside *Regenesis* and *Phase Four.* It proved too ambitious and fell by the wayside. Neil Johnson wrote *Attack of the Bastard Leech Type People,* also known as *Vergelstunswaffe,* or at least wrote the first episode. Rupert Booth completed a script for *Hell Hath No Fury,* set in a gothic mansion. Booth is also connected to two other titles, *A Thing of Beauty* and *Memories of Tomorrow,* but it's not clear that the ever made it as scripts. Paul Ferry wrote two unmade Booth Doctor scripts, *The Vinyl Sky* and *Juggernaut.* Another lost script is *Katagenesis,* a sequel to *Regenesis.*

The most intriguing of the unmade scripts was the *Hollow Dark,* around 2001-2002. Booth was having second thoughts about playing the Doctor. Paul Ferry was going to step into the role. They planned to shoot in the long abandoned Aldwych subway station. Ferry wrote a script, and Matt Carter, a professional director was interested. It collapsed following the London Subway bombings. It's a shame, it would have been fascinating to see Ferry's take on the Doctor, and it showed every indication of being visually extraordinary.

After the *Unearthly Stranger* project fell apart, there were a couple more scripts written around the Paul Ferry Doctor.

A Pirate's History, Page 274

Spectres, by Ferry and *Moonstone Epoch* by Richard Knapper. Sadly, Paul Ferry's only appearance as the Doctor is in *The Pub With No Doors.*

Paul Ferry in an email mentioned, *"We almost did an audio for the 20th anniversary last year but never got round to it in the end. The script's there, so maybe we will do it sometime; it was called After the Flood and concerned a submarine race round an alternate submerged Paris… with Cybermen."*

In April 2016, perhaps inspired by the fact that the show was going to skip a season this year, the Timebase crew announced a pair of new projects - *Memory Failure* and *Man in the Shadows,* produced by Richard Knapper, and starring Paul Ferry as the next Doctor. There were also, photos of the Ferry Doctor interacting with Sea Devils, and some drone footage. But so far, no sign, and the projects have likely fallen through. You never know though, some of these projects have a very long gestation.

Rupert Booth returned to the role as the Doctor for a couple of shorts, which, though not technically Timebase Productions, are worth mentioning:

When Doctors Collide in 2003, No real background story here. It's a three minute short, featuring the Booth Doctor encountering the Seventh Doctor (played by John Blum, from *Time Rift*), with the two of them bickering and cancelling each other out as an asteroid heads for the hotel where a convention is taking place. It's a bit of fluff. It was shot by another fan film producer, (John Fagan of Dark Alliance, Theta G), and edited by Kate Orman, who had written Hidden Faces, so it seems to represent people from at least three 'fan film' institutions coming together at a convention and deciding to have a bit of fun.

The Pub With No Doors: An eight minute short, from about 2005 – *"When the Twelfth Doctor (Sean Corcoran) meets his untimely demise, he joins his previous selves (Steve Hill, Jonathan Blum, Rupert Booth, Paul Ferry, Vasilios Alleganis) for drinking, merriment, and fistfights, in a pub in his mind called 'The Pub With No Doors.' Will he survive the afterlife?"* or so says the write-up on the DW Fan Film database.

Fans play all the roles, including the first (Andrew Beach), Sixth (Steve Hill) and the Seventh (Jonathan Blum) and Eighth Doctors (Tom Kelly). Both Rupert Booth and Paul Ferry appear as versions of the Doctor, with Booth's Doctor grousing at having had to regenerate into Ferry's. Despite several abortive projects, this was Paul Ferry's only onscreen appearance as the Doctor. Another 'shot at a convention' special, Booth improvises the closing line.

This seems to be the fan film equivalent of *Dimensions in Time*, but far more interesting and much better conceived. I wish they'd used this idea for the professional special.

I suspect Booth may look back on his years as the Doctor with a mixture of fondness and embarrassment, the way we do with so many of our youthful passions. He's working and successful in the arts – he's written a biography of Patrick McGoohan, and he's developing a film project: *Protoverse*.

Timebase's 1990s productions are difficult to find these days. They might only occasionally appear on YouTube or other video sites. For the most part, they are in the hands of collectors, shown or traded occasionally. But in their heyday, the Timebase crew and their works were quite influential. The term that often comes up is 'Well respected.'

Although Timebase completed no more videos, they seem to have inspired a number of other Who productions. The props appeared in, and former members of Timebase participated in subsequent videos.

One significant mention is Adam Manning's ambitious four part serial, *Tyranny of the Daleks*, in which Manning's Doctor is kidnapped by the Daleks from the planet Galentor. The imprisoned Doctor is plugged into the Dalek's matrix a counterpart to the Gallifreyan matrix seen *in The Deadly Assassin* (or for that matter, the Keanu Reeves movie). Trapped in the Dalek cyberspace, he plays a series of virtual reality mind games with them, holding out while Romana and her Thal companions try to organize a rescue. This film borrowed the Timebase Tardis console and flats, a little worse for the wear by that time. The production featured impressive location work, extensive CGI and even ambitious martial arts choreography. Three Timebasers: Paul Ferry, Steve Palace and Neil Johnson participated as actors. Tyranny of the Daleks was polled in the top ten of Doctor Who fan films of the first decade of the 21st century. Adam Manning, the creator and guiding mind, also worked with Rupert Booth and Marq English on *Timequake*.

Timebase's offspring also seems to have included Westlake Films *Deconstruction* a harsh and nihilistic story about Cybermen invading an asteroid base. The Cyberman costumes from *Phase Four* were borrowed, or perhaps bought from Philip T. Robinson. Those costumes may have gotten around. They were quite distinctive. There are a couple of other fan films which look like they might feature Robinson's Cybermen.

Timebase wasn't just Rupert Booth. Booth did play the Doctor brilliantly, and if you look at the credits, he was involved in practically everything else behind the scenes as well. But then, he wasn't the only one, Lisa Gledhill, Paul

Ferry, Richard Knapper, Neil Johnson, Neil Hibbert, Philip T. Robinson, Deborah Riley, everyone did multiple jobs, in front of and behind the camera. It seems almost... collegial.

That was Timebase's secret, why their work was so good. It wasn't just a talented person, or even a few extraordinarily talented persons. They were a team, or perhaps, a better word would be a collective. There wasn't just a guiding mind but a group of people, cooperating, trading tasks, learning and teaching each other as they went. I think a lot of people read the scripts and had the chance to have input, to contribute.

In the words of Philip T. Robinson, again writing online, *"Rupert Booth. He is a brilliant Doctor and an even better writer but if it wasn't for the likes of myself creating all the Masks and costumes (what would it be without the Cybermen, Tribus, Demon and soon to be seen Sontaran) and Paul's creative writing skills, Ian and Arthur's CGI, Lisa's fantastic period costumes, Brian's electronic skills and Malcom's stronger than life performances and just about everyone above helping out with the construction of the sets, I'm afraid you lot probably would never have heard of Rupert Booth."*

One person can't do it all. There's always things that get overlooked, that get missed. No decision maker makes a perfect decision every time. The truth is sometimes, we need to work with other people, particularly in creative works, to fill in the gaps, to get insight, critique, support. Working on these serials over the years must have amounted to a Doctorate program in film making.

So what happened to Timebase? It's simple enough. These productions, any productions, are an immense amount of work. To produce to this level, that required not just talent, but an extraordinary agree of commitment – and not just from one person, from a collective. Timebase's five completed films ran eight years from the first to the last.

People get married, they get divorced, they fall in love and break up, they go to university, they get jobs, they move, and more than anything, they move on.

I did make the effort to track down a few of them. I didn't have any sense from them of hard feelings. They all looked back with fondness. They've had reunions from time to time. One of them is actually working on a book about Timebase Productions, which I'd certainly pay money for.

So here is to the Timebase Gang who did something quite extraordinary.

CAST: *Rupert Booth – Doctor; Deborah Riley – Amaryllis; Zoe Rowden – Amaryllis, Pandect; Steven Palace – Ian Green; Vineeta Rishi – Angie*

CREW: *Kate Orman – Writer; Paul Ferry – Script Editor; Joanne Cave – Music; Richard Knapper – DOP; Rupert Booth – props, director; Neil Johnson – director, producer, Mediarats – post-production; Ian Patterson – 1st Asst. Dir, Copyright 2002, mediarats.com/Timebase*

Review: The Chronotron Effect (1998)
A One Man Show

STORY: The story, in brief, is that the Master's Tardis has malfunctioned, so he's kidnapped an Earth scientist to help him fix it. Which is kind of like kidnapping a squirrel to help you fix your Lamborghini, I'm not sure what the Master was expecting.

The Doctor shows up, has a run in with UNIT, and is on the case. The Doctor's plucky companion tracks down the Master on her own, gets captured. This leads to the Doctor and the Brigadier getting captured as they rescue her. Then the Doctor gets captured.... and escapes... and messes with the Master, and soon the whole universe is in danger!

REVIEW: It used to be that it wasn't all that common for the same group to produce several fan films. For every Federation, or Seattle International or Timebase, there were a lot of groups that managed only one or two.

That's because making a film, even a fan film, was HARD WORK. Film and video is a massive undertaking. Go to a Hollywood blockbuster and watch the credits, and it's usually the population of an entire town going past. Minutes of credits, dozens, hundreds, even thousands of people work on it. Even a modest professional production is a massive amount of work. You've got cameras and cameramen, and on the one side you have a director of photography to make sure it's shot properly, and on the other side a focus puller. The camera has loaders, people whose job it is to make sure that there's film. There's a guy whose job it is to make sure that the lighting is right. There's the boom mike guy, the sound recording guy. There's someone on set to make sure that the continuity between shots and scenes is kept. Hell, there's someone whose job is simply to take the actors from the dressing room to the set. This isn't padding, all of these people, and a whole lot more are needed to make sure that things go smoothly.

Fan films aren't really much different. Making a fan film is still a complicated elaborate exercise, that requires a whole pile of steps, and all kinds of challenges. You don't just grab a camera and point. You need a script, you need to break the script down into a series of shots and shot lists, you need to find locations that look good, but if you're using locations, you need to get to them, and you need to get your actors and your crew to the location all together at the right time, and hope it doesn't rain or doesn't get too crowded, and they all have to know their parts and be ready to go. You better make sure your battery for the camcorder is charged, and that you've got spare batteries and a tripod, and you need to take care of that equipment because if there's an accident and something breaks.... Not good. Or you can build sets, but if you do, well, that costs time and money, and it's got its own challenges. Get all your film in the can, then you have to figure out how to put all those shots together to tell the story that was in the script, and hope that there's not something missing that you'll have to shoot. You have to do a sound track along with the visual edit and hope that they synch up.... All this is the tip of the iceberg.

Now, if you're a professional film maker, then you have money and some opportunity to hire and recruit people. If you're a fan film maker, then it's just you, and your friends, and maybe a lot of hard work and sweat equity going into things. Everyone is doing this for free as volunteers, and it's a lot of work, so that can be hard to maintain. People have lives, they have friends, jobs, they get married, go to school. It's a battle.

So for a lot of groups - they do it once, that's it. Sometimes they do it twice. It's just a massive commitment, and sometimes it's heartbreaking. People have falling out, friendships break up. Sometimes, you try so hard and it's just not good. It can be a wonderful experience and learning opportunity. But it's a lot of work.

It's different nowadays. Technology has moved to the point where a sufficiently obsessed fan can do almost all of it on their own. But it's still a lot of work.

So this leads me into Mike Coombs, the creator of the *Chronotron Effect* and *Dealers of Death*. Coombs was remarkable for 1990s Who films for being almost a one man show, singlehandedly building props and sets, wrangling locations, writing, directing and badgering bemused friends and co-workers to appearing in his films.

"From the age of six I wanted to be The Doctor," Coombs told me, *"I couldn't get into a professional acting school as it was too expensive so abandoned my dream as just that, a dream. Seeing that other fan film made me realise I could, even if it was unofficial, be The Doctor. "*

His first project was the *Chronotron Effect*, a two part serial. The episodes are short, about thirteen and fourteen minutes, so in practical terms, it's about the length of one of the old serial episodes.

"So I set out to make it happen. I wrote to the Chief of British Police and requested a copy of the blueprints for the Police Box. They very

A Pirate's History, Page 283

kindly responded a supplied me with an original (which I still own). So my Tardis was 100% authentic when I built it full scale. I then wrote to the BBC and asked for any blueprints of the console. There were none but Mike Tucker wrote back to me with dimensions from the actual prop and photographs to aid my build. (I still have that letter and photographs too)."

Which was very nice of them. It makes you wonder how often the British Police and BBC got requests like that?

"The console room was set up in my parents living room! The TARDIS console for chronotron was trashed shortly after filming completed as I had nowhere to store it. The whole thing was shot over two weekends."

It's not a bad console at all, the lights work, the central time rotor thing goes up and down. It's quite an impressive build. Look, these things are labours of love done by people with no money to speak of. If you manage to build a good looking Tardis console, then that represents a huge investment of personal time, money, skill and what have you. That deserves to be appreciated.

I find myself wondering how his parents felt, having their living room taken over and converted into the console room of the Tardis.

To start with, the *Chronotron Effect* is in black and white, and that adds a lot to it. You have the sense of something from early Pertwee. Yes, yes, Pertwee was shot in colour. But a lot of us were watching it on black and white sets. Colour televisions didn't really become common until later in the 1970s. Anyway, the B&W gives it a nice retro feel and covers up a multitude of sins. Coomb's borrows a lot of the early 70s sound cues. We get a lot of those synthesizer or organ chords, playing in the right spots. It's well done usually, and it evokes a strong feeling of nostalgia. It doesn't always work, but gosh, when it works, it really works.

In terms of story and script, there are some nice bits. The Doctor is an eccentric, and that comes across nicely. That's a defining feature of the character, but it's often hard to get that right. Things play out in interesting ways. The Doctor shows up on Earth, and rather than walking into UNIT he gets captured by them.

Later, once that is sorted out, he gets around to screwing with the Master, it's not so much that they're enemies as you get the sense that these two have been playing a cosmic game of one-upsmanship for a long time, and that's actually kind of cool. It's got a bit of that weird rivalry that Pertwee/Delgado and later Davison/Ainsley had now and then. It culminates in technobabble, which is a minus, and there's a fair bit of bland dialogue and sequences which drag it down. As an example, there's the 'great escape' which is pretty ho hum. But the proceedings have enough curves and the dialogue and situations have enough wit that you can enjoy it.

The opening segment- basically, space based views of Earth. Has nothing to do with the actual story, it just looks cool. That's a thing, actually, a good opening. First impressions really do set a tone for the audience, I've seen very good films that open up with a stumble out of the starting gate, and that's hard to recover from. You can recover from it, but it's an uphill battle, and there's often a lingering aftertaste. And I've seen stuff that opened really well... and even if the rest of it doesn't reach that level or do those things, somehow, that goodwill carries on. So, here we've got some still shots of Earth floating in space, shots of North America from orbit, all laid over with Doctor Who 70s music, and seguing into titles... and I goddamm love it! Has nothing to do with the

A Pirate's History, Page 285

rest of the story. I still goddam love it. It sets the mood perfectly. It's Doctor Who! It's adventure! It just...works!

Okay, so onwards, what do we have? Mike Coombs plays the Doctor, and he doesn't do a half bad job. He's mature for his age, so his Doctor carries as an adult. He's a little bit too straight looking. He sometimes strikes me as a young James Bond. But he's okay. He's a non-actor, so you're not getting a Benedetti or Booth or Scovell performance here, but he does his thing competently enough, and to be fair, he's probably the best performer in the production. He's helped immensely by a script that has a sense of humour and a real feel for the quirkiness and eccentricity of the Doctor, and that's often a hard thing to get right.

Next up is Natalie Fletcher as the (very young) companion Dani Turner; she brings a plucky enthusiasm to the role. She's visibly the youngest member of the cast, but it's not that off putting. Maybe this is because we're used to the Doctor having junior companions.

David Blakeman plays a serviceable Master - it's not hard to do the Master - just wear a lot of black, try to come across as formal and menacing. Blakeman avoids the excesses of Anthony Ainsley or Roger Delgado in favour of a calm ruthlessness, he's a polite villain, saying please and thank you even as he murders and kidnaps. He's a bit young for the role, but carries it off.

The weak link in the cast is Steven Parry, who plays the Brigadier. That's a tough role, particularly since the Brigadier is such a fixed point in the show. The Doctor changes, the companions change, even the Master goes through a few incarnations, so we're kind of willing to accept variations on these characters, even some strongly different takes. But the Brigadier - he's always played by Nicholas Courtney, and

A Pirate's History, Page 286

played the Nicholas Courtney way. So there's just no wiggle room in the character. It's an uphill battle to do the Brigadier, and Parry fails utterly. For one thing, he's a tall, very skinny kid with a Beatles mop top. He's the one cast member whose youth is really really obvious. And he's probably the weakest actor in the cast - not entirely his fault, but the performance is just weak. It's one of those things you have to go 'Okay, we'll just carry on.

Overall the cast looks pretty young. Sometimes it's not so noticeable, you have people playing policemen or scientists, and perhaps it's lack of attention to them, or that they're not playing known character, it slips by you.

Like many fan films, the sound track is tough going. Especially in the early points, it's too low, you can barely hear the characters, and in some places there's a bit too much echo in some indoor scenes. You can hear the recording hiss. And in some of the outdoor scenes, you have that ambient sound crackle. The camera was a basic VHS-C Panasonic home video camera, with a built in omnidirectional microphone. Some of the background music is just misplaced, or a bit too intrusive. That's a recurring weakness for almost every fan film. The reality is that sound design and recording is finicky as hell, particularly using omnidirectional mikes, which can be really hit and miss. And then you've got to mix it in post, and even if you're decent with your videography, it's a whole different set of skills. Even the best ones have glitch sound.

There's also some nice location and sets. There are a couple of vehicles used, including a military looking jeep, and some very decent interiors and exteriors, that give a sense of expansiveness and place. The Brigadier's office is okay, there's some effective warehouse and hallway shots, some nice exteriors. There's even an 'action' shot where the

Brigadier's car does a spin, accentuating a plot point. The scientists' lab and the room where the Master ties up his prisoners... that's kind of weak. Apparently, complex trans-dimensional tech is done on what seems to be a regular table with office furniture. There's an Ed Wood feel to that.

The cinematography holds up nicely. Coombs does well framing his shots. There are some really nice 'inside the car' scenes, or 'car pulling up' shots. Where he's got visually interesting locations, he pulls back a bit so we can appreciate it, and where the sets like the scientists lab are poor, he's clever enough to foreground the characters and ensure that something is happening that we can pay attention to.

The Chronotron Effect, despite shortcomings, has got a charm, a retro-feel, that makes me smile a lot, and forgive a lot. There are a lot of little things that go right, or at least are engaging and cheerful. Somehow, it takes you all the way back to the Pertwee Era, and the magic of the Doctor, Brig and the Master on an old fashioned adventure. There's something genuine to it, there's sincerity that you can't help but find yourself loving. It's a love letter to a show that we all cherish, and it's an enjoyable watch.

CAST*: The Doctor - Michael Coombs; Dani Turner (companion) - Natalie Fletcher; The Master - David Blakeman; Brigadier Stewart - Steven Parry; Professor Jones - Roy Huke; Security Guard - Michael Coombs; Policeman - Steven Guile; UNIT Soldiers - Thomas Beaton, Thandi Lubimbi, Joe Edwards;*

REW*: Written, Produced and Directed - Michael Coombs; Assistant Directors - Steven Parry, David Blakeman, Roy Huke; Visual Art/Graphics - David Blakeman; Costume - Doreen Coombs; Camera Operators - Michael Coombs, David Blakeman, Steven Parry, Roy Huke, Steven Guile; Video Effects and Editing - Michael Coombs;*

Review: The Dealers of Death (1999)

The Master, the Mandragora and the Daleks

STORY: The Master is back on another one of his schemes. This time, he's hooked up with the energy being from the Tom Baker serial the Masque of Mandragora, and they're trying to obtain some Gallifreyan McGuffin which will give them ultimate power, even as they plan to stab each other in the back. As UNIT tries to figure out what's going on, the Doctor arrives. However, his life becomes complicated when the Daleks arrive...

REVIEW: This production is a bit more modern. It's in colour, so it loses some of the black and white charm of the Chronotron Effect, in favour of a late seventies or eighties feel. There's a bit more of the grit to this one that I associate with the Eric Saward and the better parts of the Andrew Cartmel era, and you have a sense that Coombs is consciously emulating the JNT period.

Once again, we've got the Mike Coombs Doctor back again. David Blakeman returns as the Master. There's a new companion, Karla Melomby playing Carla Davies, and a lot of familiar faces and names from *The Chronotron Effect*. Steve

Parry is back, but not playing the Brigadier, which I can live with.

It's a lot more ambitious. Let's face it; the *Chronotron Effect* was about twenty four minutes, divided into two episodes. There's a limit to what you can pack in there. But here, with the *Dealers of Death*, we've got something which is very much like an 80s serial, four episodes running from 16 to 19 minutes in length. Those are short episodes compared to the 25 minute standard of the classic series, but all together, they're very close to an actual serial run time.

As with the *Chronotron*, it opens well, with an intriguing earth from space shot, this one is actually relevant, when an alien spaceship looms into frame, heading towards earth. There's a shift to a group of thugs chasing a young woman down a street. Then the story switches to the Doctor in the Tardis, heading for an Elvis Presley concert. Basically, three openings, but each intriguing in its own way, and it engages the viewer.

Now, here's the interesting thing, having opened in three ways, it keeps on doing this. The narrative keeps going off in all different directions. Daleks appear in their spaceship and have a conversation. The Doctor stumbles into the fleeing woman, and soon they're both being chased. Elswhere, a man tries to burgle the offices of a chemical plant, and discovers (and dies) at the hands of a mysterious villain, and UNIT HQ deals with a mysterious threat.

Through the first episode, we get the sense that something big is going on, and we get pieces of it, but we don't get the whole picture, and the Doctor is barely getting his feet wet. So what we have here is a fractured story structure, which is quite sophisticated in storytelling terms.

There are some specific things to like in this first episode. I'm not going to deconstruct the whole thing, but I will throw some things out.

The chase scenes are brilliantly shot. Coombs takes his camera out to the warehouse district, and then uses long shots, showing his characters in stark relief, dwarfed by featureless stone walls and grim buildings. It's very noir very effective.

The original brightly lit Tardis console and control room built in his parents living room is long gone of course. Coombs new Tardis console is darker and less imposing, along the style of the McGann console. But it is set in what feels like an immense and much darker control room that gives the story more gravity.

The fight scene is quite well done: The burglar is surprised and dukes it out with the bad guys. Now, on the downside, it's a long shot, static camera, and you can see that they're pulling punches and swinging at empty air. But admitting that; it's still a kinetic and effectively choreographed fight. There's a moment when the burglar is thrown over a table, and he's literally flung across it - that's not faked. An instant later, he comes flying over the same table to resume the fight. Fight scenes are hard to do, and particularly hard to do well, even professional productions can struggle with them. So the fact that they've done it here is impressive.

The interrogation scene between David Blakeman's Master and the burglar after he's captured is also nicely done. Unlike the previous scenes, it's pretty static. No running, no fighting, but it provides effective exposition and builds character and tension. Blakeman's Master manages to convey genteel menace and casual ruthlessness.

Overall, the locations, sets and set dressing are very well done. There's a military jeep. Vehicles move well. Backgrounds and locations support the story and add a lot of visual punch.

Coombs told me, "At the time of recording both films I worked for the British Army in a civilian role and I obtained official permission to use one of the regiments actual land rovers and all the soldiers you see were actual soldiers with plastic replicas of their own weapons. All the exterior and interior scenes were various buildings within the military barracks in Woolwich se London. Apart from a couple near the end which was my parents' home."

This kind of thing just amazes me. England must be like some different planet. Some guy walks into the British Army offices and goes, *I'm shooting a Doctor Who fan film, can I borrow some soldiers and jeeps'* and apparently, the British army goes *'Sure thing!'*

Again, and again, I find myself amazed at the production value these fan films are able to secure, often with locations, and cooperation from public agencies.

Not everything is perfect. There's an exposition scene in a living room between the Doctor and Carla that is just slow. There's a cutaway to the Master where it's very clear that the actor is just sitting there waiting for his cue before he starts speaking. There are occasional glitches or failures, for instance one scene features the Doctor being interrogated at a 'police station,' at what seems to be a card table. I'm pretty sure that's not standard police furniture.

And of course, there's the Daleks and their spacecraft.

"The scenes inside the Dalek ship bridge, "Coombs admits, "was actual footage from Doctor who remembrance of the Daleks. Fortunately the original television footage fitted in perfectly with the locations we used.

I'd originally thought that perhaps Coombs might have done the whole thing himself using Dapool toy Daleks and a miniature set. Who fan films almost always borrow music and sound effects from the series, that's often crucial to capturing the feel. Even borrowing particular titles and video effects is pretty common now; filching actual shots from the series is a bit questionable. Still, these shots are well used within the framework of the story he's telling, and he's gone well out of his way to redub them match them up with actual locations. They enhance the story, but more importantly, they work as an integral part of the story.

And to his credit, Coombs has actually built a Dalek for the production. *"There was only one full size Dalek. I constructed it myself from scratch. The Dalek was trashed shortly after filming; again I had nowhere to store it. However it is still out there somewhere as a lady and man stopped by the house seeing the Dalek outside and my parents confirmed it was trash and they took it. "*

So apparently, total strangers gave the Dalek a good home, it's probably still out there, a valued member of some family.

Episode two, the Doctor hooks up with UNIT finally, and from there he's on the trail of the Master. But the Master is a step ahead and captures the Doctor, on to the next cliff hanger. It's not badly done, and mostly avoids dragging. In particular Blakeman's Master comes off well, managing to be simultaneously courteous and murderous.

Episode three, the Master takes Carla hostage and begins to explain what's going on. The Doctor is sent off in search of the McGuffin, and the Daleks make their move. This is where

A Pirate's History, Page 293

Coombs homemade Dalek comes into play, and the construct is an embarrassingly good match for the filched footage.

The Doctor decides that saving the world from a Dalek invasion is more important than searching for the McGuffin. I can't really argue with that.

Luckily, Carla manages to escape the Master by using with pluck, resourcefulness and some badly choreographed knockout, only to be almost immediately captured by Daleks. UNIT confronts the Daleks. The Doctor gets captured. There's some good stuff here. The locations are good, physically impressive. We see a battle between a UNIT squad and a trio of Daleks, which is Coomb's one Dalek cleverly edited.

Final episode finally explains what's going on and what's at stake. The Master rescues the Doctor from the Daleks, but only so the Doctor helps him with his own emerging problem. The Daleks and eventually get sorted out. The Doctor recovers the McGuffin; the Master is double crossed once again by his own ally, the Mandragora.

No big deal, the Master was planning to double cross the Mandragora. Honestly, you can set your watch by the Master's plans going wrong. He's like Wile E. Coyote.

All this occurs while UNIT, played by more stock footage supplied courtesy of the British Army invades the Master's headquarters. Again, the stock footage is integrated fairly well into the story.

Okay, so what's the overall verdict? The key areas are the script and the performances, and here I have to say: Not bad. These are all non-actors, so you make allowances. But with that allowed for, they're actually fairly good.

Coombs Doctor is a bit stiff and formal, he's definitely got a stick up his butt, but he's also got that genuine quirkiness and conviction, an ability to do and say the unexpected, that we expect from Doctors. Coombs Doctor is always utterly self-possessed to the point of being slightly arrogant with a penchant for dry wit.

David Blakeman on his second turn as the Master also turns in a good performance, when he captures the Doctor and Carla, the first thing he does is offer them tea, it's a nice moment. It's particularly effective because the last interloper the Master had a civil conversation with, he casually shot dead a second later. Coomb's script nicely delineates the character and his peculiar 'frenemy' relationship with the Doctor.

Joanne Fisher does a solid job as the Major, filling in for the Brigadier, and she's convincing in the role, a no-nonsense professional doing her job.

Carla, playing the new companion, Karla Melomby, probably has the weakest performance, but she acquits herself without shame. Everyone hits their marks and gets their lines.

Technically the sound quality is a lot better overall than Chronotron, few if any glitches. I think I attribute that to Coombs buying a boom mike, most of the dialogue being indoors in controlled circumstances, and clearly Coombs has learned a bit about ADR and voice over since the first one.

The direction, credited to David Hukes, is good, with the shots generally being well composed, if a bit static. One handicap is that most of the shots are medium, with just a few long shots. We've got almost no close ups, and the intercutting is pretty simple. The production likes to have his camera sit there and not move. It's not bad, but it does slow the pacing, and it kind of gives things a sameness.

A Pirate's History, Page 295

I award points for a Police Box shell, a Tardis console and a full sized Dalek build. I also award points for the UNIT jeep, and for dressing UNIT soldiers like soldiers with passable weapons. I have to take away points for filching some sequences from Remembrance of the Daleks, but at least they're redubbed and used effectively.

Overall, it's startlingly well-polished, with good locations shot well, good use of space, a complicated story that actually unfolds clearly, with adequate twists and turns. Honestly, some of the classic series didn't do this well. Check it out.

DEALERS OF DEATH - CAST*: The Doctor - Michael Coombs; The Master - David Blakeman; Karla Melomby - Carla Davis; Cpl Rogers - Roy Huke; Major Hart - Joanne Fisher; Voice of the Mandragora - Ted Gribben; Street Gang - Wayne Whitwell, Rob Walker, Steven Parry, John Skelton; Unit Soldiers- Jim Murphy, Danny Pamphlett, John Skelton, Adrian Middleton; Master's Security - Rob Walker, Steven Parry; Guard Commander - Alan Kilpin; Repairman - Steven Guile; Dalek Voices - Michael Coombs.*

DEALERS OF DEATH - CREW*: Written and Produced - Michael Coombs; Directed by Roy Huke; Camera Operators - Roy Huke, Steven Parry, Rob Walker, Steven Guile, David Blakeman; Visual Art/Graphics - David Blakeman; Edited and Visual Effects - Michael Coombs; Thanks to 16th Regiment Royal Artillery Woolwich*

Review: Time and Again (1999)

Crossing into Darkness

STORY: After the death of the Master, the Time Lords send the Doctor to secure his lair. Unfortunately, reports of the Master's death have been exaggerated. When his companion is killed by the Master's henchmen, a vengeful Doctor pursues his enemy to a dark parallel universe, where he finds his greatest challenge...

REVIEW: *"Time and Again. The. Best. Fan Film. Ever. Yes. Ever."* Doctor Who Fan Film Magazine, Issue 3.

"I can't believe I watched the whole thing... I just saw it was 2 hours... THIS WAS THE BEST FAN FILM IVE EVER SEENAND IT WAS MADE IN THE 90s MIND BLOWN and FINALLY THE Classic doctor!" YouTube comment.

There are a lot of reviews on YouTube and elsewhere. Who am I to argue with all this? Is it truly 'The. Best. Fan Film. Ever'? Tough question. There's a lot of competition for that title.

As with any good Doctor Who story, a lot comes down to the portrait of the Doctor, played here by Dennis Kuhn. The Doctor is really the center of Doctor Who - they're the classic archetype of the British eccentric, a singular personality, brilliant, unpredictable, cunning and charismatic. He or she is the defining feature the draw for the story.

Not every fan film gets the Doctor right. Arguably, not every official production gets the Doctor right. It can be hard to pinpoint. After half a century, the role has been embraced by a multitude of actors, each with their own take. Is it even possible to define what or who the Doctor is?

But I think that it is there, there's something fundamentally intrinsic to the Doctor. There's a lot of interpretations, but nevertheless, some actors 'get' the Doctor and play the character. Others... don't. I've watched a great many fan productions, and some of them have been very polished but have left me cold. I can sit there and go 'this is very well done, but that's just not the Doctor.'

So what about the Kuhn Doctor?

I wasn't sure about the performance initially, I had a sense that Kuhn was visibly 'acting', and 'high school acting' rather than really conveying the character. His vocal performance seemed high pitched and a bit fussy.

Kuhn's Doctor seemed tentative and high strung. His character is a cerebral, waspish Doctor, very formal, even somewhat repressed. As we see him at the beginning, he's an intellectual Doctor, perhaps a bit too intellectual, careful with his words and morals. He's a bit like Rupert Booth, without the warmth, or Peter Davison, without the assurance. I think the acting style works for this version of the character, particularly so given his arc. His best early scene is where he's trying to break into the Master's lair while his companion narrates, and he keeps interrupting her monologue. That scene is funny, clever and very Doctorish.

Early on in the story, the Doctor's companion, Sylvie Lydon, played by Leah Keumchichel gets killed, and he goes a bit nuts. Literally, he becomes vengeful and bullheaded. It's here that Kuhn's control and repression of the character comes in because, while his Doctor is unhinged, he's still highly competent, he's still high functioning. He doesn't fall apart, which would be normal for his situation, he just drives ahead, and it's his decisions and actions as he drives ahead that reveal he's going hard off the rails.

I think what we have here, and what makes him interesting, is that he's become the PTSD Doctor. When he encounters the Federation guards, he's not quite able to charm them, he's off his game. When he runs across the rebels, he can barely restrain himself to be civil. As far as he's concerned, they're just an obstacle, and he's not shy about telling them. He's become a bull in the china shop. When he encounters his companion's evil twin, he is visibly unmanned. Only when he encounters the Master does he regain any part of his cunning, but even with his survival instinct kicking in, underneath he remains full of fury. It's a little reminiscent of some of the performances of the Capaldi Doctor, actually.

This is a Doctor where something personally important is going on. It's not business as usual this time, not the adventure of the week. No, Kuhn's Doctor is someone whose life gets turned upside down, who is coping with a trauma, and he becomes unmoored from his moral foundation. It's not the clichéd 'hero loses a loved one and goes on a rampage' although that is there, but rather, tragedy strikes to the heart of who he is, and he loses himself. There are all these events happening around him, but he doesn't truly care, they're just irrelevant to his fury and his loss. I think that may be very compelling for many viewers.

A Pirate's History, Page 299

At its core, this Doctor's story is a dark one of loss and heartbreak, of moral compromise borne out of pain, and personal fury. It's a story where the Doctor is personally invested for a change, not just passing through.

This is actually quite interesting, because like most television, the Doctor always operated on a kind of emotional reset switch. Apart from regenerations, and the new personality of each, the Doctor never changes. That's a television thing; the character has to stay the same. The Doctor loses companions, feels sad for a moment, and then he's the same as always. In the *Twin Dilemma*, the Colin Baker Doctor goes mad, almost murders a companion and is overcome with life changing remorse and contrition, but five minutes later the plot kicks in and he's back to normal. In *Earthshock*, a companion, Adric, dies at the end of the serial and he feels bad for a few minutes. But next adventure he's just fine. Nothing that happens to the Doctor has a lasting impact.

Fan Films wrestled with this. Planet Video Production's unfinished *Second Spawn* in 1990 would have had the seventh Doctor rescuing Adric, and then captured and tortured by the Nazis to the point where he's on the edge of despair.

The BBV's *Stranger* series of videos, beginning in 1991, would show a version of the Colin Baker Doctor retreating into depression, struggling to come to terms with his episode of madness and attempted murder.

Timebase Production's Rupert Booth Doctor would lose a companion, Leslie, half way through a serial in 1997, and it would shape his actions for the rest of the serial. The Doctor working his way through grief and anger would subtly continue through the next two serials. It was about having a human reaction, about a Doctor not in perpetual reset mode, but who actually had to process and come to terms with issues.

Time and Again takes it to the next level. The Doctor loses a companion, almost at the very outset. Suddenly, the story, the whole subtext, becomes the Doctor coping with the grief and rage of losing a loved one, the Doctor coping with mortality and tragedy, and not handling it terribly well.

Fan productions have given us Doctors who were not stuck in perpetual emotional reset. They gave us Doctors who could feel, could grieve and evolve, and who dealt realistically with loss. Perhaps this emotional resonance is one of the reasons *Time and Again* is so popular.

Despite that, *Time and Again* avoids melodrama. Kuhn's Doctor, even in fury and despair, is a bit too repressed, a bit too cerebral to go to pieces. He remains restrained, so he doesn't overplay it, it's there, it's important, but it's not sloppy. It could have been quite bleak, but it's also diluted by the fact that most of the other characters, focused on their subplots and their own lives, just don't care about his trauma. Not even the Master comprehends what the Doctor is going through. The Doctor's world is shattered, but everyone else carries on. There's a reality there, because the world doesn't stop for grief, no matter how awful the loss, life keeps on. That's an interesting touch, and it helps to keep the proceedings from sinking into an emotional abyss while retaining the flavour of an adventure.

Beyond that emotional resonance, what carries the production, for want of a better word, is its energy. Things just keep happening. The running time is an hour and forty five minutes, but it never really flags, because all the way through, you have all these characters, sometimes at cross purposes, sometimes oblivious.

A Pirate's History, Page 301

The whole thing starts, for instance, with a trio of Vardans out to loot the Masters lair, now that he's supposedly dead. Unfortunately for them, he's alive and they soon find themselves unwilling, resentful and occasionally bungling henchmen. They trigger a set of events, in which the Doctor's companion is killed, which has the Doctor chasing them, which takes him to this time bubble, in which an alternate universe Federation has taken over Earth and is forcing everyone to dress modestly or go to the forced labour camps.

The Doctor finds himself running afoul of both the Federation and its minions and of the rebels. He eventually winds up facing the Master, who is crazier than ever and kind of emotionally needy. And he is devastated to encounter the alternate universe counterpart of his dead companion, who works for the Federation, and is suspicious of both the Doctor and the Master.

So basically, it's just one damned thing after another.

Time and Again was inspired by the McGann movie, in the sense that it deals with the fallout from the latest of the Master's apparent deaths. But there's very little in it that reminds me of the perspectives or sensibilities of Paul McGann's outing.

Most viewers compare it to the classic series. What they're picking up on is the proliferation of subplots. Everyone has their own agenda, their own story. Most of them don't even really know or care about the Doctor; they're just trying to get on with their own thing. The Doctor is very clearly the central character, but other characters get to have lives of their own. It helps to balance the story and keep it interesting.

The classic series used a serial format, so it needed a lot of subplots to keep the story moving. Here, they've eschewed anything resembling a serial format, but it's still filled with subplots and that makes it a little more unpredictable. So you've got this 'anything can happen next' vibe. That tends to carry you past the occasional weaknesses or awkwardness in the script. Literally, there's no time to dwell, it just keeps barrelling at all sorts of angles. The story moves, it moves in several directions, and it changes direction unpredictably, so that puts it well above a lot of more linear stories.

The dialogue is a little too windy; people just end up talking a lot, and not in a natural way. Speech has a different rhythm than writing, and you can tell the difference a lot of the time. What the cast members are saying are written words spoken aloud rather than natural speech. It doesn't help when, once in a while, one of the actors has to struggle to pronounce a word.

I think that problem is most pronounced with the Master, played by Paul Christopher. The trouble with being an epic villain is that you have to just wallow in it, you go around saying insane things, and you savour it, you chew the syllables, you spit them, you purr and snarl and just wrap the words around you like a blanket. It's tough to say things like *"This is the penultimate phase of my plan for total domination."* Normal people don't talk like that. The sort of person that does, they have to radiate a certain amount of crazy; they have to get off on saying things like that. I think that the actor struggles with that at points, although to be fair, he has his moments when he's radiating the right kind of crazy dangerousness.

The American locale doesn't allow for the extraordinary locations of so many of the British videos. The Brits just seem to have ruins piled on top of more ruins, piled on mansions, roman amphitheatres, cathedrals, palaces, industrial plant, big brick complexes, museums, military bases all just ready for a local bunch to do their Doctor Who production. Not so much here, there are a couple of impressive exterior locations, notably a giant concrete and steel doorway, and some nice downtown exteriors. Mostly though, we get a lot of interiors, and some early CGI background compositions.

Two things to note - one is that the Tardis interiors, with a few reservations are very well done.

The control room console is rather different than the typical one, but the room seems well dressed, if atypical. There's a strong sense of just how big the place is inside. We see the swimming pool, the memory room, the library, corridors, glimpse floor plans. The place is immense. That's a nice effect and one that the classic series often failed to achieve.

Parts of the Tardis interior, and indeed the Master's lair, are rendered as CGI backgrounds. On the positive side, there's a nice sense of space and expansiveness. On the other hand, you can tell it's a greenscreen or bluescreen background by the silhouettes of the people. There's a kind of lack of definition and flatness to the CGI backgrounds. But that's the problem with CGI; it's a continually moving target. An effect which was jaw dropping one year becomes passe a couple of years later. CGI dates quickly. There's nothing wrong with the CGI here, apart from being noticeable for what it is, and it was undoubtedly impressive for its time.

Visually, I think it's passable, not extraordinary, but passable. It's nicely done, everything is entirely competent, but mostly, apart from giving us a wonderful sense of the how vast the Tardis is, it just serves the purpose.

On the other hand, the musical score by Dennis Kuhn is very effective and hasn't dated at all. Superficially, it's less effective, in a modern age when fan film makers are able to simply rip orchestral scoring directly from the original series. But it's terrific to hear a genuine original score which has been tuned directly to the film.

As is so often the case with ambitious productions like this, it was a struggle to get it done. Shooting took place over a couple of years, so long in fact that Kuhn grew a ponytail and had to conceal it under his collar in some shots.

Despite the tribulations of their first effort, the Mendicant productions group tried to do it again. Unfortunately, they didn't get terribly far. Dennis Kuhn stepped out, and Paul Christopher who had played the Master, stepped into the role of the Doctor. After that it was problems with scheduling, with time, with resources, a trailer was produced, it got maybe half shot, but was ultimately abandoned. Kind of a sore spot. But still, these things are so hard to do at all, that even doing one is an accomplishment, much less one as highly regarded as this.

Jeff Smith, who did the Two Doctors and the Anti-Matter Menace way back when, and has been involved in other productions, including the abortive Fire and Ice series, produced a feature length documentary about the making of Time and Again which is entirely watchable and provides a good window into the making of this production, and of fan films or film making in general.

CAST: *Doctor Who - Dennis Kuhn; The Master - Paul Christopher; Sylvie Lydon - Leah Keumchichel; Tam/Cal - Jay Melchior; Ogril - Jackson Kissling; Reme - Brian Allard; Jenn - Krista Allard; Neva - Brian Brawner; Young Doctor - Jeremiah Lynch; Officer 1 - Victoria Trapp; Officer 2 - Jeremy Nienow; Prisoner - Marco Becerril; Guard 1 - Chip Addickes; Guard 2 - Andy Andrekopolis; Little Girl - Rachel*

Tolstad; Transient 1 - Andy Thorson; Transient 2 - Chad Thorson; Body Double - Chris Pederson.

CREW: Mendicant Productions. A Ryan Thorson film. Produced and Directed by - Ryan Thorson; Writers - Jermy Nienow, Ryan Glasspoole, Jeremiah Lynch, Ryan Thorson, Dennis Kuhn; Original Music - Dennis Kuhn; Director of Photography - Ryan Thorson; Costume Design - Ryan Thorson; Prop Construction - Ryan Thorson; Production Coordinator - Dennis Kuhn; Video Editing - Jeffrey Lass, Ryan Thorson; Assistant Editor - Dennis Kuhn; Script Editor - Dennis Kuhn; Camera Operators - John Combes, Karen Wing, Ryan Thorson, Jeffrey Lass, Mark Leske, Andy Andrekopolis; Boom Mike - Chris Pederson, Laura Achterkirch; Sound Mixing/Editing/Foley/Special Sound - Dennis Kuhn; 3D Modelling and Computer Animations - Dennis Kuhn, Kevin Gregory, Chris Gregory; CG Background Artist - Cory Hanson; Matte Artist - Dennis Kuhn; Property Master - Ryan Thorson; Set Construction - Ryan Thorson, Chad Thorson, Jeremy Nienow, Nicky Roland; Set Decorator - Ryan Thorson; Police Box Construction - Ryan Thorson, Dennis Kuhn, Tim Coryell, Victoria Trapp; Police Box Transportation (Logopolitans) - Ryan Thorson, Dennis Kuhn, Chris Pederson, Paul Christopher, Jackson Kissling, Juan Rosa; Console Construction - Stephen Cleveland, Jeremy Nienow, Ryan Thorson; Casting - Jeremy Nienow, Ryan Thorson; Poster Art - Chad Thorson; Stunt Choreography - Paul Christopher; Stunts - Jackson Kissling; Catering - Major Margo's Meats; Camera Mount - Steadicam JR, JVC AXR 30 Video Camera, Sony Super VHS; Music Sequencer - Cakewalk Audio Pro; Graphics Software - Bryce 3D, Ulead Cool 3D, Truespace, 3D Studio, Photoshop; Edited on Video Toaster 4000. Special Thanks to - Joe Anderson, Dr. Ruthanne Benson, Bluff View Inn, Stacey Blair, Jonathan Blum, City of La Grosse, City of Norwalk, Billy Clow, John Combes, Bill Corbett, Mark Davini, Nancy Gerrard, HME Visions Convention Staff, Ryan K. Johnson, Nick Kapanke, Tim Kieffer, La Crosse Community Theatre, Greg Larkin, Mike

Michelson, Jerry Miller, Jeremy Nienow, Nikki Nies, Anne Paape, Craig Parcells, Lynn Proksch, Rivoli Theatre, The Salvation Army, Sunset Stables, Maj. Larry and Maj. Margo Thorson, Dr. Patricia Turner, Todd Wholhert, Tammy Weyker, Karen Wing, UW-La Cross Telecom Dept., UW-La Crosse Theatre Dept., Viterbo College Theatre Dept., WKBT News Channel 8, WWTC Media Center, British Broadcasting Corporation; Filmed on Location in La Crosse, Wisconsin, Norwalk, Wisconsin, UW-La Crosse WMCM TV Studio, WKBT Newschannel 8 TV Studio, WWTC Media Center.

AFTERWORDS

Where Do We Go From Here?

Confession time. When I started this I only planned on one book. But I researched and watched and wrote and researched some more and wrote some more. I started to notice, the book was getting pretty long. I figured 50,000 to 60,000 words maximum for a book of this sort. I blew way past that....

So then I thought, okay, I'll just write it and edit it down. I'm thinking there's no way I can edit this down without gutting. I kept finding new material, exploring new areas. Doctor Who animations, stage plays, audio stories, there was always something new and amazing to discover that I wanted to share. And whoops, closing in on three volumes.

It got away from me, I admit it. But I found so much wonderful stuff, so many interesting productions, so many stories. I loved it, and I hope to convey that love to you, and to inspire you.

This first volume mainly chronicles the fan films from 1984 to 1999, with a wrinkle or two here and there, covering the dark days of the cancellation crisis and hiatus, then the long winter of the 1990s.

So what comes next?

Another PIRATE's History of Doctor Who

Volume II

Before television, there was theatre, so it's not surprising that Doctor Who would appear on stage. The first Doctor Who play didn't actually have the Doctor, just his enemies – Curse of the Daleks. Jon Pertwee was originally going to star in the next Doctor Who play, Seven Keys to Doomsday, but he backed out, and Trevor Martin would become the fourth Doctor, weeks before Tom Baker. In 1989, both Jon Pertwee and Colin Baker returned to their role in Doctor Who, the Ultimate Adventures… and were recorded by fans.

Elsewhere, fans produced their own stage versions of the Doctor, with and without the BBC's permission. Nick Scovell played the Doctor through BBC approved stage plays, and through several classic fan films.

It was the Wilderness years, sixteen years from 1989 to 2005, when the show was off the air, with only occasional flickers of revival.

During this time, due to peculiarities in copyright, fans found a way to make Doctor Who without the Doctor. Sometimes, as with the Stranger series, a Doctor Who actor like Colin Baker or Sylvester McCoy would play a character identical to the Doctor, having Doctor-ish adventures… just under a different name.

Other times, it turned out that you could license characters like Sarah Jane Smith, or monsters like Sontarans and Autons, directly from the creators, and bypass the BBC, for more Doctor Who adventures, featuring companions and monsters.

We'll explore the productions of the BBV, Reeltime Pictures and Dreamwatch, and their skirting of BBC copyrights in Downtime, Shakedown, the Stranger, Daemons Rising and Do You Have License to Save this Planet?

But the BBC's rules on Copyright had a down side. Over two hundred episodes were destroyed. We'll look at how and why this happened.

And we'll explore how, through the efforts of fans, everything that was lost was either recovered or preserved in some form, and how fans worked to re-create lost and abandoned serials through reconstructions and remakes.

We'll revisit the past with Marco Polo and the Loose Cannons, Masters of Luxor and the Road Not Taken, Yellow Fever and Lost Season, Devious and the Secret of 6B, Lost and Found in the Dark Dimensions.

Along the way, we'll explore The Animated Who, including stop motion, line animation, failed TV series, action figure adventures and many more.

Volume III

A Pirate's History, Page 312

Alongside video, there's an entire universe of Doctor Who audio productions, official and unofficial, going all the way back to Peter Cushing, Jon Pertwee and Tom Baker. We'll chart the failed official attempts to do the Doctor as radio or vinyl adventures.

Parallel to that, we'll explore the emergence of a lively and thriving fan audio adventure movement, the rise of the Audio-Visuals and how they in turn spawned the BBV and Big Finish Audio Adventures.

2000 to 2004 was the end of the Wilderness years and the cusp of the revival of the show by the BBV. At the same time, there was an explosion of creativity, and a series of brilliant new fan films that even tempted official Doctors to come back and revisit their roles in a series of homages and recreations of the classic series.

This would continue with the films of the modern era, with a new series of ambitious fan films inspired by the revival – enthusiastic fans, new technologies, and a new show inspired: Fire and Ice, How to Stop a Timelord, Project Fifty, The Forgotten Doctor and the Ginger Chronicles.

Finally, modern technology has profoundly changed both fan clubs and fan films. Gone are the days of meetings and clubs, Super 8, and bootleg videotapes. There's a new era of Cons, video platforms, computer based editing and sound mixing, CGI and greenscreens and new platforms, that have given fans better tools than ever before and unimagined access to audiences.

We'll also cover Dynamic Works 2012, and a 34 episode "visual novel" a stunning coherent work. The emergence of black Doctors like Spencer Edwards and Dominic G. Martin, and another woman Doctor in Velocity.

It's terrific. Tell your friends. Buy copies and give it to them. Have fun.

ACKNOWLEDGMENTS AND THANKS

This is a book about fan films. In a sense, it's a book about a television show that people enjoyed and were so inspired by that they decided to make their own. It's a book about the people that made these fan films.

Fans can be a persnickety bunch. That comes with the territory I suppose. When I began this project, I could see two major problems. No way was I going to make everyone happy.

First, I was going to get called out for mistakes and omissions. If I got a date wrong, or mentioned that The Dalek Masterplan was 10 episodes rather than twelve, spelled names wrong, locations, years. Someone was going to be coming down my throat for something.

Second, I was going to get grief for all the films I didn't review. The ones I didn't have time or space for, the ones that got overlooked or dismissed or didn't make the cut. There are so many films out there....

In the meantime, I need to acknowledge the people and institutions that have made this book possible. First and foremost are the film makers themselves. Mark Sinclair, Nigel Woodley, Kevin Jon Davies, Ryan K. Johnson, Peter Fagan, Rob Warnock, Jennifer Adams, Nigel Peever, Kevin Taylor, Ian Taylor, Paul Ferry, Rob Thrush, Dennis Kuhn, Nick Scovell, Rupert Booth, Randy Rogel, Barbara Benedetti and on and on. These names, as important as they are, are the tip of the iceberg. I've gone to great lengths to list cast and crews because these films are communal efforts. There are literally hundreds, even thousands of people who have invested time and effort, love and talent in these myriad productions. I wish I could acknowledge and thank each one of you. I can only say: Thank you, your work is appreciated.

Beyond them, the Ian Levines, the Mark Humphries, the Richard Bignells, the multitude, the fans, the culture, the network, the clubs and associations, all of it individual that created the environment where these films could emerge, that volunteered time and energy, that were both inspiration and audience, that preserved and circulated, copied and distributed. Thank you, thank you so much. If not for you, these films would not have come down to us. I would not have been able to see them.

This is primarily a book of reviews. The comments and critiques mostly deal with my views and impressions from watching the films themselves. My opinions, of the films, of the show, of the BBC and politics and culture are my own.

Information about the productions themselves usually comes from online sources, primarily from the film makers themselves. Ryan K. Johnson, the Federation, Ad-Lib Productions have all maintained detailed web sites. Bedlam Productions has a Facebook page and has posted extensively on YouTube. There is actually a web page devoted to the Ultimate Adventure. Online searches have often turned up comments from people involved in production. In some cases I've been lucky enough to have made direct contact with some of the creative people themselves.

Beyond that, I've tried to place these films and their reviews within various contexts - of the history and politics of the show itself, of the culture of fans and fandom, of changing technology. This has involved a lifetime of experience, from learning about and watching super 8 films in my grandparent's basement, to wearing a lizard man suit for a short film, to discovering VHS and Betamax and being part of fan culture and trading networks. There are more sources than can be counted easily.

As for the show itself, Doctor Who, with more than fifty years of history backstage and onscreen, and a cult following entering its third generation is incredibly well documented. There is an infinity of books, magazines, magazine articles, fanzines, professional and amateur publications; there are newspaper articles and quotes, online threads, documentaries which seem to canvas every aspect of every moment of production. Having lived through some of it, having been a fan for going on thirty years, I am immersed.

For the record, most of my quotes are taken from online sources - imdb.com, chat threads and comments, newspaper articles online, etc. Relatively few quotes are from direct personal correspondence. I've attempted to at least acknowledge these sources, but if I've overlooked stuff, then no harm was intended and no infringement or theft contemplated.

For the record, there are particular sources that I want to acknowledge which allowed me some context or insight, or were useful references or compilations. First, Shannon Sullivan's Doctor Who website, incredibly thorough and well researched, was often a 'go to'. Wikipedia, Imdb.com, and numerous personal web sites and chat threads were invaluable. The BBC's own Doctor Who DVD releases were an essential tool, not only for the stories themselves, but for an incredible volume of documentary bonuses and literally hundreds of hours of commentaries which in many cases were startlingly honest.

A few books I specifically want to point out: The Nth Doctor by Jean Marc and Randy Lofficier, published through Virgin Books, 2003. It chronicles the efforts to bring Doctor Who to the Silver Screen beginning in the 1990s, with synopsis of a dozen or more abandoned scripts. I made minimal use of it. But I love it to pieces and you should buy this book.

The Doctor Who Discontinuity Guide, by Paul Cornell, Martin Day and Keith Topping, published in 1995, is an essential and thoroughly charming reference work. Again, just go and buy it. If you already have it, buy another one and give it to a friend. I actually got to meet Paul Cornell once.

Finally, Richard Marson's The Scandalous Life and Times of John Nathan-Turner, published 2013, is, I think, the definitive chronicle of the career of a controversial figure, and the last word as to the politics and maneuvering behind the hiatus. The Johnathan Powell quote is taken directly from this book.

I'm very, very pleased to be able to recommend and plug Downtime, The Lost Years of Doctor Who, by Dylan Rees, published 2017, by Obverse books. It is a marvelous chronicle of the gray-market video and audio. Although we cover some of the same ground, our approaches are quite different. His book is marvelous. If you like mine, please go buy his.

In the meantime, thank you.

More Books from the Author

Have you made it all the way here? Have you actually read all this way

Wow. That's amazing. I'm very flattered. I want to give you a hug or something.

Seriously. Thank you! Thank you so much!

I'm going to assume that if you've made it all this way, you've enjoyed yourself. You've learned some juicy new gossip about old Doctor Who, you've found some insights into technology and how it affects what we do, and maybe you found some of the reviews really entertaining.

I will repeat, almost everything I've written about you can find out there, if you look around hard enough. I strongly recommend you do so. I genuinely believe that these films and these Doctors deserve to be remembered.

And I hope you liked my writing and writing style. Because if you did, then I have some non-Doctor Who books, both fiction and nonfiction, that I think you'd love.

They're available on multiple platforms as eBooks, and in some places as print books or audiobooks. Lots of choices.

Please feel free to visit my website: denvaldron.com.

Or just let me tell you about them right now…

ALTERNATE REALITIES

A Trilogy or Strange New Worlds
The Other books

The Fall of Atlantis includes a geo-historical exploration of a real Atlantis ending in a different kind of tragedy; the Retroverse, a fun the accidental cinematic universe of 50s sci fi films, Ancient Rome plausibly crossing the Atlantic, because of coffee(!!!), and the saga of an Alternate Greenland that was never covered by ice.

The Bear Cavalry, the True (Not!) History of the Icelandic Bears, chronicles a history where travelling Vikings domesticated North American Bears and eventually learn to forge them into the most terrifying medieval fight force ever – with excursions into history, biology and art along the way. Bonus story – the Sharebear Apocalypse, is it really just a hug that feels so good.

AXIS OF ANDES
NEW WORLD WAR
A History of WWII in South America

Berlin, 1937, Adolph Hitler and his cabinet meet with a strange delegation from Ecuador. The delegates from the small South American nation beg for help, fearing an impending invasion from their rival, Peru. What happens at that meeting sets in motion a chain of events that sets the entire continent on fire. By the time it's done, millions are dead, nations are in ruins, and the map of Latin America will be changed beyond recognition.

A Pirate's History, Page 321

HEARTS IN DARKNESS

Three Collections of Horror Stories

Featuring riveting stories about a man's cancer learning to talk to him, the ultimate serial killer; Allison, a paralyzed pregnant woman feeling her fetus taking control of her body, a desperate single mother lured down a dark path; the army enlisting the unkillable men in the masks; Silence about a thief hiding in the home of a killer; a ghost that haunts the people around its victim, and many, many more. Melancholy darkness, chilling horror, dark visions.

A Pirate's History, Page 322

LEXX UNAUTHORIZED

LEXX a show about a giant space bug that blows up planets, the cowardly security guard who is its captain, and the undead assassin, runaway love slave, and robot head who form its crew.

Originally billed as 'Star Trek's Evil Twin,' the cultiest of cult sci fi, LEXX's forte was black humor, startling visuals, big ideas, and a sensibility that had more to do with surrealists like Jodorowsky or Bunuel than mainstream science fiction. And, as unconventional as it was onscreen, the story of how it came to be is even more bizarre.

A Pirate's History, Page 323

A Dark Fantasy
of Murder and Redemption

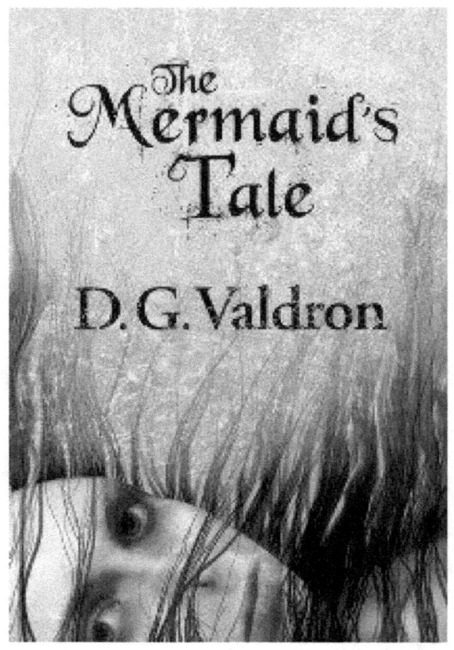

There's a City where all the races come together uneasily.

There's a Civil War gathering, and dark powers assembling.

There's a Mermaid, murdered cruelly, her people distraught.

There's an Orc, lowest and the worst, assigned to solve the murder, before it all comes crashing down.

And there's something else: this world's first serial killer.

Available only as an AudioBook

A Pirate's History, Page 324

Drunk Slutty Elf
and Other Stories
Hilarious Science Fiction and Fantasy

plus the sequel
DRUNK SLUTTY ELF
AND ZOMBIES!!!

Two volumes of savage, satirical, subversive wicked, funny, frantic science fiction and fantasy. Demented ghost hunters, frustrated aliens, horny giants, drunken elves, sneaky ghosts, wayward barbarians and many more.

A Pirate's History, Page 325